W0199443

Working with Images

Cambridge Handbooks for Language Teachers

This is a series of practical guides for teachers of English and other languages. Illustrative examples are usually drawn from the field of English as a foreign or second language, but the ideas and techniques described can equally well be used in the teaching of any language.

Recent titles in this series:

Teaching Adult Second Language Learners
HEATHER MCKAY *and* ABIGAIL TOM

Teaching English Spelling
A practical guide
RUTH SHEMESH *and* SHEILA WALLER

Using Folktales
ERIC TAYLOR

Personalizing Language Learning
GRIFF GRIFFITHS *and* KATHRYN KEOHANE

Teach Business English
A comprehensive introduction to Business English
SYLVIE DONNA

Learner Autonomy
A guide to developing learner responsibility
ÁGOTA SCHARLE *and* ANITA SZABÓ

Planning Lessons and Courses
Designing sequences of work for the language classroom
TESSA WOODWARD

Learner English (Second Edition)
A teacher's guide to interference and other problems
MICHAEL SWAN *and* BERNARD SMITH

Teaching Large Multilevel Classes
NATALIE HESS

Laughing Matters
Humour in the language classroom
PÉTER MEDGYES

Using Authentic Video in the Language Classroom
JANE SHERMAN

Stories
Narrative activities in the language classroom
RUTH WAJNRYB

Language Activities for Teenagers
edited by SETH LINDSTROMBERG

Pronunciation Practice Activities
A resource book for teaching English pronunciation
MARTIN HEWINGS

Five-Minute Activities for Business English
PAUL EMMERSON *and* NICK HAMILTON

Drama Techniques (Third Edition)
A resource book of communication activities for language teachers
ALAN MALEY *and* ALAN DUFF

Games for Language Learning (Third Edition)
ANDREW WRIGHT, DAVID BETTERIDGE *and* MICHAEL BUCKBY

Dialogue Activities
Exploring spoken interaction in the language class
NICK BILBROUGH

Five-Minute Activities for Young Learners
PENNY MCKAY *and* JENNI GUSE

Dictionary Activities
CINDY LEANEY

The Internet and the Language Classroom (Second Edition)
A practical guide for teachers
GAVIN DUDENEY

Working with Images

Ben Goldstein

Consultant and editor: Scott Thornbury

CAMBRIDGE
UNIVERSITY PRESS

CAMBRIDGE UNIVERSITY PRESS
Cambridge, New York, Melbourne, Madrid, Cape Town, Singapore, São Paulo, Delhi

Cambridge University Press
The Edinburgh Building, Cambridge CB2 8RU, UK

www.cambridge.org
Information on this title:
www.cambridge.org/9780521710572

© Cambridge University Press 2008

It is normally necessary for written permission for copying to be obtained *in advance* from a publisher. Certain parts of this book are designed to be copied and distributed in class. The normal requirements are waived here and it is not necessary to write to Cambridge University Press for permission for an individual teacher to make copies for use within his or her own classroom. Only those pages which carry the wording '© Cambridge University Press 2008' may be copied.

The publication and the accompanying CD-ROM are in copyright. Subject to statutory exception, the provisions of relevant collective licensing agreements, and as may be permitted below, no reproduction of any part may take place without the written permission of Cambridge University Press. Notwithstanding the above, material on the CD-ROM may be saved and printed provided it is solely for educational use within the purchasing institution.

First published 2008

Printed in the United Kingdom at the University Press, Cambridge

A catalogue record for this publication is available from the British Library

Library of Congress Cataloging-in-Publication Data

Goldstein, Ben, 1966–
Working with images : a resource book for the language classroom / Ben Goldstein.
p. cm. – (Cambridge handbooks for language teachers)
Includes bibliographical references.
ISBN 978-0-521-71057-2 (pb and cd-rom)
1. Language and languages–Study and teaching–Audio-visual aids. I. Title.
P53.2.G65 2008
418′.0078–dc22
2008037229

ISBN 978-0-521-71057-2 paperback

Cambridge University Press has no responsibility for the persistence or accuracy of URLs for external or third-party Internet websites referred to in this publication, and does not guarantee that any content on such websites is, or will remain, accurate or appropriate.

Contents

Thanks and acknowledgements

The author would like to thank his Flickr™ contacts for allowing their photos to be included and the following friends for their help in providing images: Ellen, Diane, Iñigo, Jordi, Leticia, Nancy, Noah, Rodrigo, Silvia, Xavi, Martha and especially Dani – I couldn't have written this without you.

In addition, I would like to thank Nat for generously providing so many great photographs, and Scott for all his helpful advice, ideas and support throughout the creation of this book.

Special thanks to Dawn Logan of Ashdon House of Children, Margaret Cameron of Coupar Angus Primary School, Alison Richman of Dry Drayton Primary School and to all the children who submitted artwork to be included in this publication.

Also a big thank you to everyone at Cambridge University Press for their hard work on this project, in particular Nóirín, Tracy, Clive and Claire, and my editor Hilary. Many thanks for putting in the time and not panicking at the sight of my art briefs!

To my father's memory.

The authors and publishers acknowledge the following sources of copyright material and are grateful for the permissions granted. While every effort has been made, it has not always been possible to identify the sources of all the material used, or to trace all copyright holders. If any omissions are brought to our notice, we will be happy to include the appropriate acknowledgements on reprinting.

Text

pp. 1–2 and p. 6, quotations from *Reading Images: The Grammar of Visual Design*, p. 15 and p. 183, written by G Kress and T van Leeuwen. Published by Routledge, 1996, p. 8, quotation from *An Introduction to Visual Culture*, written by N Mirzoeff. Published by Routledge, 2000. Reproduced by permission of Taylor & Francis Books, UK; p. 6, quotation from *Practices of Looking: An Introduction to Visual Culture* by M Sturken and L Cartwright. Copyright © Oxford University Press, 2000 and pp. 116–18, idea from 'Picasso Sentences' *Resource Books for Teachers: Grammar* by Scott Thornbury. Copyright © Oxford University Press 2006. Reproduced by permission of Oxford University Press; p. 7 and p. 10, quotations from *The Art of Looking Sideways* by Alan Fletcher. Published by Phaidon Press Limited © 2001 Phaidon Press Limited; p. 8 and p. 180, quotations from *Ways of Seeing* by John Berger. Penguin Books 1972. Copyright © John Berger 1972. Reproduced by permission of Penguin Books Ltd and Penguin Group (USA) Inc; p. 23, ex 1.3, idea from *The Mind's Eye, Teacher's Book* by A Maley, A Duff and

F Grellet. Copyright © 1980, pp. 31–2, extract from *Dialogue Activities* by Nick Bilbrough. Copyright © 2007, p. 33, ex 1.8, idea from *The Mind's Eye, Student's Book* by A Maley, A Duff and F Grellet. Copyright © 1980, pp. 52–4, ex 2.3 and p. 66, variation 3, ideas from *Pictures for Language Learning* by Andrew Wright, Copyright © 1989, p. 109, variation 1, idea from *Stories: Narrative Activities for the Language Classroom* by Ruth Wajnryb. Copyright © 2005, p. 214, idea from 'Identikit' *Drama Techniques* by A Maley and A Duff. Copyright © 2003, pp. 236–8, idea from *Personalizing Language Learning* by Griff Griffiths and Kathy Keohane. Copyright © 2000. Reproduced by permission of Cambridge University Press; p. 72, extract from *Nineteen Eighty-Four*. Copyright © George Orwell, 1949 by Harcourt, Inc and renewed 1977 by Sonia Brownell Orwell. Used by permission of Bill Hamilton as the Literary Executor of the Estate of the late Sonia Brownell Orwell and Secker & Warburg Ltd; p. 101, extract from Bliss Magazine, http://www.mybliss.co.uk. Used by kind permission of Bliss Magazine; p. 107, limerick from *One Hundred and One Best and Only Limericks of Spike Milligan* by Spike Milligan, published by Penguin Books, 1998. Reproduced by kind permission of Spike Milligan Productions Limited; p. 111–12, adapted extract from *Seven, Penguin Readers Level* 4 by Anthony Bruno, Copyright © 1997. Reproduced by permission of Pearson Education Ltd; p. 113–14 ex 3.8, idea based on the activity 'Choose Your Words, Draw Your Picture' (Mixed-level Classes), p.132 ex 4.6 Variation based on the activity 'Jigsaw Pictures'(Mixed-Level Classes) in *Dealing with Difficulties* by Luke Prodromou and Lindsay Clandfield. Used by permission of Delta Publishing; pp. 123–5, ex 4.2, and pp. 137–9, ex 4.9, ideas from *Imagine That!* By J Arnold, H Puchta, and M Rinvolucri. Published by Helbling Languages GmbH, 2007. Reproduced by permission of Helbling Languages GmbH; p. 129, poem *A Martian Sends a Postcard Home* by Craig Raine. Copyright © Craig Raine, 1979. Used by permission of David Godwin Associates; p. 178, adapted text 'Swaziland' from http://www.flagspot/flags/sz.html Reproduced by permission of Flags of the World; p. 205, article 'Swiss Newspaper Falls for Prankster's Fake Gucci Ad' *Associated Press*, 27 February 2007. Reproduced by permission of the YGS Group; p. 216, poem 'Early Sunday Morning' from *Music from Apartment 8: new and selected poems*. Copyright © 2004 by John Stone. Reproduced by permission of Louisiana State University Press; p. 220, poem 'The Hunter in the Snow' by William Carlos Williams, from *Selected Poems of William Carlos Williams*, copyright © 1962 by William Carlos Williams. Reprinted by permission of New Directions Publishing Corp and Carcanet Press Limited.

Photos and images

Pearson Education for p. 3; © 2006 SASI Group (University of Sheffield) and Mark Newman (University of Michigan) http://www.worldmapper.org/ for p. 5; Adbusters for p. 7; Corbis/ The Gallery Collection for p.16 (left); © Photography © The Art Institute Chicago for p. 29; Maria Badaracco for p. 35; Tom Magliery for pp. 36–7;

Getty Images/Time and Life Pictures for p. 42 (top); Ben Goldstein for supplying p. 42 (bottom) and p.81; Nat Rea for p. 61; Geoffrey Ingalls for p. 70 (top); Lee Albrow for p. 70 (bottom); Patrick Thomas for p. 77, p. 155 (bottom) and p. 172; Niro Taub for p. 83; © Munch Museum/ Munch-Ellingsen Group, BONO, Oslo/DACS, London 2008 for p. 124; José María Cuéllar/www.josemariacuellar.com for p. 126; © IOC/Olympic Museum Collections for p. 152; IIT Bombay for p. 155 (middle) and p. 166; Philip-Lorca diCorcia/Adobe for p. 182 (top); Image courtesy of The Advertising Archives for p. 182 (bottom); Eterna SA/KW43 Branddesign, Germany for p. 183 (top); © 2008 MINI, a division of BMW of North America, LLC. All rights reserved. The MINI and BMW trademark, model names and logo are registered trademarks for p. 183 (bottom); Permission of Marcus Kemp/BBDO Atlanta for p. 196; Rex Features/Ilpo Musto for p. 210 (left); Christian Yanchula for p. 210 (right); Corbis/Matthias Kulka/Zefa for p. 211 (left); Corbis/Zena Holloway/Zefa for p. 211 (right); Corbis/Francis Mayer for p. 218; Corbis/The Gallery Collection for p. 222; Copyright © Robert Crumb, 2008 used with permission from the author, as represented by Agence Littéraire Lora Fountain & Associates, Paris, France for pp. 232–3 and p. 234.

Commissioned artwork by
Oxford designers and illustrators, pp. 16 (right), 49, 51, 75, 96, 105, 106, 108, 110, 112, 117, 130, 148, 154, 155 (top and two illustrations middle), 175, 176.

Picture research by Hilary Luckcock and the author, Ben Goldstein.

Introduction

Visual literacy in the language classroom

Images have long played an important role in language teaching. Indeed, for anyone who has been in a language classroom, either as a teacher or a learner, the use of images is taken for granted. It would be hard to imagine a language-teaching context without the presence of flashcards, wallcharts, coursebook images, downloaded photos, time lines, board drawings, learner-produced artwork, and so on. More recently, few teaching contexts have been unaffected by the massive incursion of the visual into domains where written language was once the sole or dominant mode. Indeed, in many walks of life, the screen and the visual stimuli that are projected onto it have all but replaced the page and the written word. Language classrooms are no exception. Interactive whiteboards, CD-ROMs, web pages and blogs are now established ways of engaging this new image-oriented learner.

However, the prominence of images in language teaching does not mean that they necessarily lie at the forefront of what we do. A lot of classroom images are peripheral to the main activity, i.e. the teaching and practising of language. Coursebook images, for example, are often treated simply as decoration – as background to the more important text.

For some critics, this situation has come about because, traditionally at least, text has been prioritised over image in most teaching contexts. (The case of materials for very young learners is an exception.) Günther Kress and Theo van Leeuwen identify a discrepancy between the increasingly important role of images outside school and the lack of attention brought to visual communication within formal instruction:

> *Whereas texts produced for the early years of schooling are richly illustrated, later on visual images give way to a greater and greater proportion of verbal, written text. Newspapers, magazines . . . involve a complex interplay of written text, images and other graphic elements . . . [which] combine together into visual designs, by means of layout. The skill of producing texts of this kind, however important their role in contemporary society, is not taught in*

schools. In terms of this new visual literacy, education produces illiterates.[1]

Kress and van Leeuwen also point out that the concept of visual literacy (a means of analysing images and of uncovering the messages that they convey) is not without its critics. Indeed, there is a feeling that, in education at least, the image is 'taking over' from the 'word' and that, to compensate, we must promote text over image.

In spite of this opposition, the importance of fostering a visual literacy in the language classroom has to be taken seriously. Thanks to digital technology, we live in a world in which images and visual information increasingly dominate our daily lives. Today's youth population, brought up on a digitalised diet of images within real and virtual worlds, are experts at accessing, sharing, transforming and communicating images through a variety of new and ever-changing media. From Second Life® to Flickr™, from Google™ Earth to YouTube™, from PlayStation® to Photoshop®, the visual stimulus comes before text. The aim of this handbook is to reflect that daily reality, granting the image the space it deserves in our classrooms. It is, in a sense, a celebration of the diversity of visual information that exists in our daily lives and an attempt to introduce into the classroom images from a multiplicity of contexts to which previously we had little access in class. It is the intention of this book, in short, to rehabilitate the image and to place it at the centre of our attention.

It is this new accessibility which has, incidentally, made the writing of this book possible. Through the Internet, it has been possible to contact image makers from all over the world and approach them on a personal basis. The vast majority of images in the book were not created or commissioned specifically for the language classroom, nor do they come from an image bank archive. Rather, they were found *out there* in the wider world. In many cases, the image came first and gave birth to the task, a procedure which I feel may become increasingly common in materials writing in the future.

However, the book does not only look forward, but also takes a glance back to exemplify how images have been previously used in language teaching. You will find many well-known task types (e.g. Describe and draw) which are included here not only because they have proved so language-productive, but because they can easily be adapted using the rich visual resources that are now available. In some cases, these have been updated or provided with variations, using a greater variety of images as prompts.

[1] Kress, G. & van Leeuwen, T. *Reading Images: The Grammar of Visual Design*, London, Routledge, 1996, p.15.

In a sense, then, the book serves a double purpose: to reassess the role of the visual image and to introduce new image types into the discussion, encouraging teachers to experiment and to access images for themselves. As such, it is designed to meet the needs of both new and experienced language teachers.

Looking back at images in language learning

Images – as visual aids – have always played an important (if subservient) role in language teaching materials. The Direct Method, for example, depended on the use of wallcharts and flashcards to convey a whole range of grammatical and lexical concepts that might formerly have been conveyed through translation. Some vocabulary structures, such as prepositions, are still presented to learners in this way:

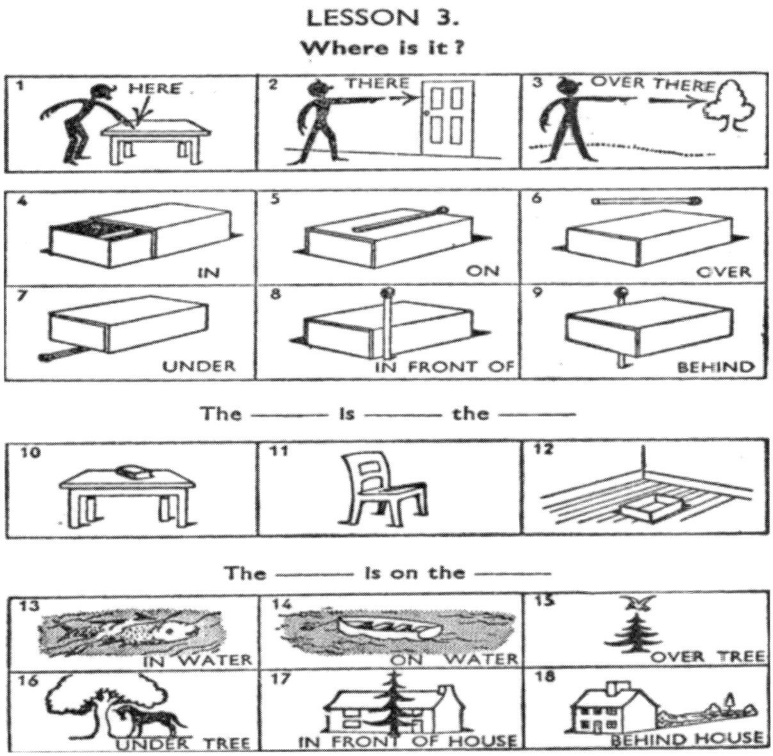

© Palmer, H. E. 1938 New Method Series; *English Practice Books*: Book 1 – Elementary Oral Exercises, London, Longmans, Green and Co, Ltd. p. 10.

The Audio-lingual Method in the mid-twentieth century introduced storyboard-style illustrations (picture stories as well as projected images and film strips) as prompts for the learning and practising of scripted dialogues. As the communicative approach became increasingly popular from the 1970s on, task types such as information-gap activities often relied on visual cues. Moreover, the increasing use of authentic – or semi-authentic – materials, along with their accompanying illustrations, increased the visual content of coursebooks significantly. Test designers also incorporated images into their exams, particularly oral tests. In the same way, video materials specifically designed for the language classroom were introduced, often incorporating role-play situations for students to watch and replicate.

In the present day, a DVD and CD-ROM component is commonly found in language textbooks, and video materials are not only used as an aid to comprehension, but also as a useful tool for developing intercultural awareness and providing interesting and relevant input for learners, as is the case in CLIL (Content and Language Integrated Learning). With the advent of new technologies, interactive multimedia environments in CALL (Computer Assisted Language Learning) programmes incorporate animated and full-motion video as well as still images. Meanwhile, interactive whiteboards and data projectors now allow online and digital images to be displayed in class. Virtual classrooms and web logs (blogs) are other examples in which digital images are now playing a prominent role in language teaching.

With the advent of large-scale ELT publishing, images were used not only as visual reinforcement, but in order to make the finished product more attractive and hence more marketable. However, although texts are largely taken from 'authentic' sources to reflect the real-life language that the books promote, the images are still today largely made up of archive photos. Such images not only lack originality, but more often than not project and promote an affluent and aspirational lifestyle to learners. For this reason, ELT materials, however contemporary they are in topic and outlook, often appear to have a superficial, colour-supplement 'look' to them. Teachers and learners tend not to be presented with images that they would encounter in the real world, but rather a safe, cleaned-up version.

Furthermore, it is still the case that most of these images are used as a *support* to written texts which continue to provide the main focus of our attention in class. For example, on the first page of a beginner's English textbook, you may find a large photo or illustration of two people greeting each other, but students and teachers will tend to focus on the dialogue that appears alongside it, to the extent that the image is under-exploited.

Likewise, an iconic image commonly found in language-teaching materials is the standard map of the world, frequently used to teach the lexical set of continents, countries, cities and nationalities. Its conventions are adopted without question. However, by providing an alternative world map – a cartogram – whose design is based on population density (see below), we will be giving the image *per se* a more dominant role and focusing our learners on the visual component to a much greater extent. The image's vocabulary-teaching potential remains unchanged, but its deeper significance, including its cultural and political impact, is now available for exploration and debate as well. Not only that, but the way that the image was created can also be the subject of discussion. As a result, the task becomes more challenging and engaging for the learner.

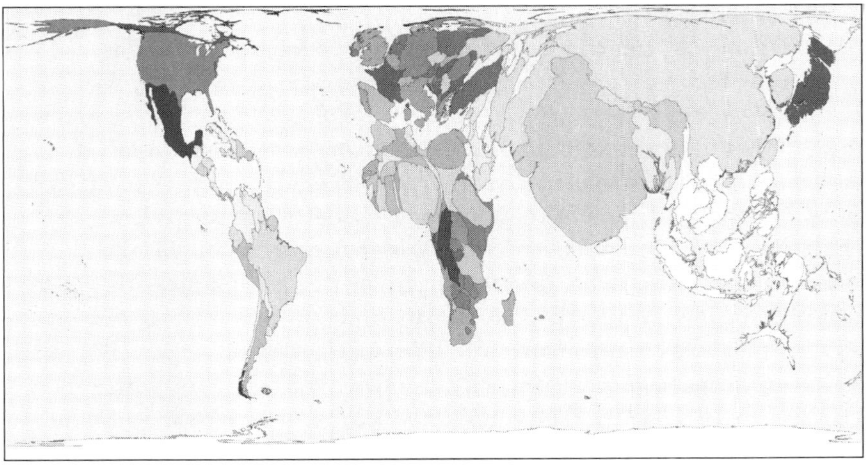

© 2006 SASI Group (University of Sheffield) and Mark Newman (University of Michigan)

See task 2.13. Variation 3. Population density cartogram accessible at http://www.worldmapper.org

Image composition and text

Although I have emphasised the importance of using the visual image, I am certainly not advocating this at the expense of the use of text. Rather, the two should work alongside one another, on an equal footing. One way to explore the relationship between image and text is to look at how both are arranged within an overall composition.

Kress and van Leeuwen have argued that images can be read in a similar way to written texts. In other words, images not only have meaning in themselves, but they accrue added meaning according to the way they are laid out in relation to other elements, both visual and textual, on the page. They argue that a composition can be analysed according to these principles (among others): [2] 1) its information value, 2) its salience and 3) its framing. The first refers to various zones within the overall image: left and right, top and bottom, centre and margins; the second to the placement of elements: the foreground, background, size, focus, tone, etc. and finally by the way certain elements of the image are framed either implicitly or explicitly (through actual frame lines). Such an approach (although a little academic for our purposes) can help when considering multi-modal texts (composite texts which feature different media such as pages in a textbook, or websites).

We can ask students simple questions about composition without resorting to technical terminology or metalanguage: for example, *Why has the image been given that caption and why is it placed at the bottom of the image? Why is the image bigger than the text and why is it on the left and why is the text on the right? Why is that particular text framed separately from the other parts?* Such questions come seriously into play when analysing adverts or journalistic images, for example. An important consideration here is not to take the image and text as separate entities. On the contrary, it is the interaction of the two and how they relate to one another that help communicate the overall message to the viewer. Ultimately, however, the message conveyed will depend on who sees it and where and how we *choose* to see it. This is important because as active viewers we are sometimes reluctant to read images as they may have been designed to be read:

> *Text can ask us to look at an image differently. Words can direct our eyes to particular aspects of the image, indeed they can tell us what to see in a picture . . . [But] It could be said that viewers/consumers of images often choose to read particular meanings into them for emotional and psychological reasons, and ignore those aspects of an image that may work against this response.*[3]

[2] Kress, G. & van Leeuwen, T. *Reading Images: The Grammar of Visual Design*, London, Routledge, 1996, p.183.

[3] Sturken, M. and Cartwright, L. *Practices of Looking: An Introduction to Visual Culture*, Oxford, Oxford University Press, 2000.

The power of image

The adage that 'a picture is worth a thousand words' has never been truer than in today's society. Nowadays, it is often easier and quicker to communicate your message with an image, be that a smiley emoticon in a text message, a digital photo sent from one mobile to another, or a map on a GPS navigation system in your car. Likewise, we recognise one another through an array of visual codes, graffiti tags, logos, tattoos and other symbols. As the graphic designer Alan Fletcher has said:

> *Although words and pictures can signify the same thing, the effect they produce can be quite different. Writing 'stars and stripes' on a piece of cloth is not as effective as illustrating them. The words don't provoke the same emotional charge.*[4]

This can be immediately seen by comparing different versions of the United States national flag, from Jasper Johns's pop-art impression of it to the anti-globalisation organisation Adbusters'[5] 'Corporate Stars and Stripes' (see below). Just try and explain this image fully in words. Not only is it not easy, but any impact is lost when you attempt to do so.

© Adbusters

(See task 5.14.)

[4] Fletcher, A. *The Art of Looking Sideways*, London, Phaidon, 2001, p. 443.

[5] Adbusters is a Canada-based not-for-profit anti-consumerist foundation which runs a magazine of the same name. Their version of the Stars and Stripes flag makes a statement about the corporate powers that they suggest dominate US society today. The flag appears in 6.7 Market leaders as an example of how logos can be placed in a different context to help communicate a political message. Adbusters have parodied adverts from different companies (see 6.8 Subvertising) to make similar points about our consumerist society.

Back in the 1970s, John Berger, speaking within the context of 'high art', saw a new language of images (e.g. art reproductions) as conferring a 'new kind of *power*', within which 'we could begin to define our experiences more precisely in areas where words are inadequate'.[6] He went on to say:

> *The art of the past no longer exists as it once did. Its authority is lost. In its place there is a language of images. What matters now is who uses that language for what purpose.*[7]

Over forty years later, surrounded by downloadable, copyright-free images, Photoshopping and image manipulation have become a form of social critique, and Berger's words could not be more prophetic. Images are ever more powerful and echo in our minds more than a quotation ever could. Think of Dolly the cloned sheep, the World Trade Center in flames, Maradona's 'hand of God': the list is endless. And as technology becomes more advanced and accessible, we have all become journalists, filming or snapping an iconic image before a professional photographer can get to the scene. We have become immune to the power of many images because we realise how easy it is to 'picture' it ourselves (both literally and metaphorically). As Nicholas Mirzoeff has said:

> *Visual culture does not depend on pictures themselves but the modern tendency to picture or visualise experience . . . while such visualising has been common throughout the modern period, it has now become all but compulsory.*[8]

A good example of this is the Google™ Maps software and its extensions which allow us to visualise our own homes in a way that we could never have considered possible only a few years ago. For all the above reasons, the power of presenting an image in class cannot be overestimated. But how do we go about choosing the right one?

Choosing images

As a rule of thumb, if an image has stopped you in your tracks, the chances are it will make your students pause for thought as well. But, of course, your class may 'see' the image differently from you, because they are looking from a different cultural perspective or because they are coming from a different

[6] Berger, J. *Ways of Seeing*, London, Penguin, 1972, p. 33.
[7] Ibid.
[8] Mirzoeff, N. *An Introduction to Visual Culture*, London, Routledge, 2000.

personal angle. It is this open-endedness which makes so many images such a useful resource in language learning. The crucial thing here is to encourage learners not to take images at face value and to look 'beyond the frame' to a world of multiple interpretations, in which there is not necessarily one correct answer. This will lead to interesting speculation and aid intercultural awareness.

It is a good idea, from the outset, to make students aware that visual images do not have fixed, predetermined meanings, but are socially constructed and culturally dependent. Such images evolve due to changing cultural conventions, as well as the particular context in which we find them and their specific purpose at any given time. Consider how the image of the 'bitten apple' has evolved from being known as Adam and Eve's forbidden fruit to the logo for a well-known computer company. But for another viewer who has not come across either of these images, a 'bitten apple' may have other connotations altogether.

Adverts, artworks, music videos, computer games are, as such, interesting and invaluable 'media representations' in their own right, not merely 'innocent' or 'neutral' reflections of a given reality. In this way, such images may carry important political messages and serve as key educational tools, for example to combat prejudice and challenge stereotypical views. It is therefore crucial to select images which can easily be 'read' and explcited on a number of different levels by the students – be that via describing, interpreting or creating tasks. Images which lend themselves to such an open-ended analysis are, for example, stamps and banknotes (showing how certain countries choose to represent themselves), status symbols in advertising, travel brochures offering 'positive' images of countries, fashion icons, to name but a few. To sum up, select images which have both obvious representational meanings and rich associations: the Adbusters flag (see page 7) is a good example of just such an image.

In terms of accessing these images, one of the advantages of using real images from the Internet, etc. (apart from the speed with which they can be found) is that learners may be able to bring their own knowledge and experience to bear on them. In an ideal classroom situation, you might find your students are informing you of things you did not know about a particular image. Tapping that shared knowledge and turning it to advantage in the classroom can come about when interesting, contemporary images are presented. Keep your eye on the news and youth-culture sites such as films on http://www.youtube.com, profiles on http://www.myspace.com or web logs, to get a feel for the kinds of images your students are probably seeing on a daily basis.

Using image-sharing websites like http://www.flickr.com and search engines such as Google™ Images (see below for technical assistance) is the first step to accessing these kinds of real images; simply tap in a key word or 'tag' and you're on your way. It is also a good idea to select images which students can themselves produce and thus personalise. For example, simply looking at a photo of the contents of somebody's bag, the magnets placed on their fridge or the pictures on their wall can say a thousand things to you about a person's character. These images can then be easily created by the learners themselves.

Remember too to train your students in the art of visualising, an extension of which is imaging (a kind of pictorial thinking). Imaging has been defined as 'the ability to conjure up something in the mind's eye, move it around, change it and make judgements'.[9] In fact, this is something that all of us do every day. However, only recently has it been exploited in a language-teaching context. Such imagery work can be used as a first step to connect with students who are used to high dosages of visual exposure, enabling them 'to go inside, extend their attention span and become more centred and clear-thinking'.[10]

Criteria such as familiarity, practicability, impact, openness to multiple interpretation, opportunity for personalisation, etc. should therefore be considered when selecting images for the classroom. Don't forget images are also present around you in class. Consider *realia* (e.g. the example of the bag contents), images in your coursebook (which can also be evaluated in terms of authenticity) and, most importantly, the images in both your own and your students' minds. Indeed, what goes on *'in here'* (in your head) is often more exploitable than images from '*out there*'.[11]

Websites for accessing images

The vast majority of images in this book have been accessed via the Internet through Flickr™ and Google™. For a selection of useful websites for this book visit http://www.cambridge.org/elt/workingwithimages/links.htm

Flickr™

Flickr™ is a popular online photo-sharing service and is totally free. The best way to search for a photo is to insert a **tag** or a key word. When Flickr™

[9] Fletcher, A. *The Art of Looking Sideways*, London, Phaidon, 2001, p. 165.
[10] Arnold, J., Puchta, H. and Rinvolucri, M. *Imagine That!*, Helbling, 2007, p. 10.
[11] A comparison mentioned in Maley, A. and Duff, A. *Drama Techniques*, Cambridge, Cambridge University Press, 2005, p. 116.

users upload a photo onto the site, they tag it with a certain number of identifying words, names, locations, event descriptions, etc. For example, a photo of the carnival in Rio de Janeiro might be tagged 'carnival', 'Rio', 'Brazil', 'costume', 'beach', 'holiday'. Flickr™ allows you to add 75 tags per image. Within Flickr™ there are then countless **groups** which share a common theme. These could be to do with the content of the image, its composition or the way it was taken. For example, for the word 'carnival', you could find groups on the Rio, Notting Hill, Manila or Venice carnivals among nearly one thousand others. You can then search this, either as a slideshow, or photo by photo, in the group **pool**.

You can easily create a group of photos for your class by placing them into different **sets**, tagging each one with the student who took the photo, etc. or using any other identification system you like. You can also add **notes** to photos. **Geotagging** is another special method of identifying photos by their geographical location and is excellent if you have a multilingual class and you want to include your students' photos taken in different countries. Be careful to check the licence arrangements for some photos. Happily, the vast majority of the images in Flickr™ are in the public domain because the photographer intended them to be shared in the first place.

Google™

Go to the Google™ website and simply tap in the key word or tag and then the option **Images** to look for photos and illustrations on the whole of the Internet, or in a particular language or country. If you are doing a Google™ image search with students in class, make sure that the filter is turned on in the Safe Search option. This filters out indecent images. You can also search for images in different size formats. The more specific you are with your image search, the more detailed the results will be.

Picasa

Google™ have their own photo-sharing site, similar in concept to Flickr™. You can access this at http://picasa.google.com/ However, it is best used to locate and organise photos on your computer, as well as editing and adding effects to images.

Flickr™ Toys

Flickr™ Toys at http://bighugelabs.com/flickr/ features a great range of different techniques for manipulating images and placing them in different contexts. You can make a poster, a calendar, a badge, a magazine cover, a cube, a mosaic, a cartoon from any photos just by uploading images and clicking on the 'toy' that you would like to use.

The book's structure

Working with Images is divided into two large sections: **Activity types** and **Image types** which are then split into four and three chapters respectively. The first focuses on what you can do with images (describing, interpreting, creating and visualising them) and the second on some of the types of images that you can use to do this.

There is sometimes an overlap between sections and where that occurs explicitly you will find a cross-reference indicating where you can locate tasks that are related because of either the activity in question or the image-type used.

The book focuses exclusively on still images. The first half looks at generic activities which could work with a number of different images and image types. Although certain images are specified in the CD-ROM, most of the tasks are designed to be versatile and there are website links to help you find other images that could combine well with such a task.

The second half of the book features tasks which are more specifically related to particular images (again found on the accompanying CD-ROM).

In both parts, there are a number of variations and ideas for follow-up tasks. Some of these are quite extensive and feature completely different images. They also give tips for using the activities with mixed-ability groups, different age groups or levels, as well as for adapting the task if you lack the technology.

Before doing a task, it is a good idea to check the CD-ROM in case you consider any of the images inappropriate for your particular teaching context. Images were selected to motivate you and the learner and to provoke debate in class, but some images may prove controversial.

Using the CD-ROM

Although some images can be found in the book itself, the vast majority of the images which are referred to are found on the accompanying CD-ROM. Here you will find around 500 digital images presented on PDF files. These are best projected in the classroom, but, if you do not have the technology to do so, you can also print them and hand them out to your students. As you read through the instructions for the tasks, make sure you look out for the images which relate to each activity. Virtually all tasks include at least one image. However, some others have in excess of 25. Take note that some images will refer to particular Variations or Follow-up activities. Usually, they will be labelled in line with the activity in question. For example, for task 2.15, you will find 15 corresponding images, labelled 2.15A–O. Depending on the nature of the task, some images are repeated, appearing separately and then together on one PDF file. This is the case with task 2.15. Here you will find six separate images of people's bags (2.15C–H), as well as all of them presented together (2.15B). This grants you a certain flexibility when exploiting the images in class.

Images and Cambridge University Press: a continuing tradition …

Whilst researching for this book, I came across a number of other books written on the use of images (or 'pictures' as they were known in the past) in language teaching. Interestingly, many of the most stimulating have also been published by Cambridge University Press over the years.

I am particularly indebted to the following Cambridge University Press titles for providing inspiration:

Earl W. Stevick: *Images and Options in the Language Classroom* (1986): for its contribution to the role of mental imaging in class and its conceptual relationship with language, in particular single words.

Andrew Wright: *Pictures for Language Learning* (1989): for a host of activities that work time and again around 20 years on, whether with digitalised downloadable images or with matchstick men.

Alan Maley, Alan Duff, Françoise Grellet: *The Mind's Eye* (1980): a book that was an inspiration to me when I first started teaching because of its creative ideas and the authenticity and originality of the selected images – such a contrast to the images found in the coursebooks of the time. A quotation from its introduction has echoed in my head throughout the writing of *Working with Images*: 'It is because pictures say nothing in words that so much can be said in words about them.'

A Activity types

1 Describing images

This chapter includes activities in which images assume a relatively traditional role, although they may be open to multiple interpretations. The images used here have a number of different functions: as prompts to language production (e.g. 1.1 Describe and draw) or to enhance and complement text (e.g. 1.7 Speech bubbles).

As a general rule, the fundamental idea of the task is laid out in the initial stages, and Variations are then offered featuring alternative suggestions and image types that could be used. Such ideas are also included to enable teachers and students to introduce their own images within what is a versatile framework. It is important to look carefully at these Variations as they may spark off a connection with a topic or language focus that you are currently covering in class.

Looking at the task types in more detail: in the case of 1.2 Which is it?, students listen to a description and try to make a choice from a selection of similar-looking images. The Variations given here range from images of the pop star Madonna (in all of her different guises), to interior designs for living rooms or virtually identical portraits, to police photos of missing persons and criminal suspects. It is important to bear in mind that although these suggestions are laid out explicitly, they are only intended as examples which would work well with the basic task type. As such, many of the tasks here represent a classic formula which can then be extended or modified according to your needs and particular teaching context.

In other cases, quite different activities are included within the Variations. For example, in 1.3 What can you remember?, an adaptation of the classic 'Kim's game', the Variations represent entirely different tasks based around a central idea. These involve correcting a description, describing half an image, revealing an image, and a visual 'Chinese whispers' game, which involves recounting increasingly more complicated descriptions of an image.

A couple of tasks include exploiting particular websites – Flickr™ and Google™ Images – which will hopefully become familiar to you and your students as you go through this book. 1.9 Flickr™ colours guides you how to search for images on Flickr™ and shows some key examples of the kinds of original images that can be found on this site. These include the wonderfully rich and colourful mosaics ('squircles') created by Tom Magilery and featured in 1.9 Variation 2. These images reflect the originality of many of the artists who upload their work on the Internet. At the same time, they show very clearly how specific software can be used to enhance such ideas (Magilery's mosaics are created by using Flickr™ Toys).

Other areas of interest are also touched on in this chapter: 1.12 Written descriptions looks at issues of register and written style. Language focuses (choice of targeted grammar and lexis) and levels will often vary according to the images chosen for each task. For example, 1.5 Who am I? touches on hypothetical language, while 1.13 What's it for? features the gerund and infinitive.

Note

It is a good idea to show images either using an OHP or as a PowerPoint presentation with a projector or using an IWB (Interactive Whiteboard) if you have one of these, so that they are clearly visible to all.

1.1 Describe and draw

Outline	Students describe images to their partners, who attempt to draw them.
Focus	Fluency practice; listening for specific information; making connections between verbal descriptions and visual stimuli. Basic describing language, prepositions of place, *there is/are*, *on the left*, *in the top right/left-hand corner*, etc.
Level	All (see specific Variations)
Time	30 minutes plus for most Variations
Materials and preparation	CD-ROM image 1.1A Painting by Paul Cézanne – The Card Players; 1.1B Illustration – Matchstick men. Coloured pens or pencils and paper. Collect any types of generic images, such as a set of flags, pictograms (e.g. street signs) or images of furniture, simple landscapes which can be *easily drawn* by all members of a class. You can also use artworks, but make sure that they have clear outlines and/or a focal point and are easy to describe. For example, see *The Card Players* and the basic illustration of it on the following page.

Procedure

1 Seat the students in pairs (or small groups, depending on the class size). Give a set of three or four images to Student A and another, different, set to Student B.
2 Student A selects one of the images and describes it as carefully as he/she can. Student B has to draw what he/she hears as accurately as possible.

Note
Remind students to describe the elements within an image carefully, pausing after each detail. Student A should wait until Student B has finished this part of the drawing before continuing with the description.

3 Student A repeats the description, without pausing, to allow Student B to check. Student B can ask questions where necessary. The idea is that both work in order for the drawing to be as accurate as possible.
4 Student B then shows Student A his/her drawing and they compare it with the original. They discuss any differences between the two images.
5 Give students information on the background/context of each image.
6 Students A and B reverse roles.

Painting by Paul Cézanne – *The Card Players*, © Corbis / The Gallery Collection

Illustration – Matchstick men

Note

For lower-level learners, you may need to pre-teach describing language. This can be done by modelling the task and writing some of the key expressions on the board. For example: *on the left / on the right, in the foreground/ background*. Then ask the whole class to draw an image from your description.

Variation 1: Describe and draw – flags

Note

Make sure you choose specific images according to level. For example, for basic levels, choose flags which are easy to describe and draw, e.g. Switzerland, France, Poland. For advanced levels, you could choose flags which are easily confused, such as the Scandinavian ones, those of Algeria/Pakistan, Costa Rica/Thailand. Avoid selecting flags which include very small detailed images or are difficult to draw. Source: http://www.flags.net

On Wikipedia, you can browse groups of flags according to motifs: for example, those which feature birds of prey, lions, mythological animals; or you can browse by colours, shapes, etc. This makes it easy to choose sets of designs without being an expert in flags.

1 Pre-teach or introduce lexical sets and any other key descriptive language (*There is/are, This flag has*, etc.).

position:	*foreground, background, centre, corner, left, right, middle, third, half*
shape:	*square, circle, rectangle, triangle*
style:	*thin, thick, horizontal, vertical, diagonal*
colour:	*red, blue*, etc. and shades: *light, dark, bright, pale*
motif:	*star, stripe, coats of arms, crescent, diamond*
size:	*small, large, tiny*

2 Describe a simple flag to students. Pause after each colour or detail and give students ample time to draw. When you have finished, monitor students' work and ask the class to guess the country that the flag belongs to.

3 Hand out different images of flags to students in groups or pairs. They can follow the same procedure and do their own Describe and draw tasks.

4 As a follow-up, students can invent their own flags for a made-up country or for their own town.

See 5.14 Flags and insignia for another task on flags.

Variation 2: Describe and draw – Olympic pictograms

Note

The beauty of these images is that they can easily be drawn as matchstick men. Choose pictograms which also feature the equipment that is used, as this will give the students more clues to guess the sport.

1 Student A describes briefly the pictogram of an Olympic sport, e.g. *A figure with legs bent slightly and wearing gloves* (boxing); *A figure swimming with a ball* (waterpolo).
2 Student B has to draw the pictogram and then identify the sport.
3 Students A and B reverse roles.

Source for Olympic pictograms:
http://en.beijing2008.cn/63/32/column212033263.shtml

See 5.4 Olympic pictograms for another task.

Variation 3: Geometric shapes game

1 Pre-teach or revise nouns relating to lines and geometric shapes, such as *line*, *square*, *circle*, *triangle* and *rectangle*, as well as prepositional phrases, such as *on the left*, *on the right*, *above*, *below*, *outside*, *inside*.
2 To practise, 'dictate' to the class a design – that is, describe it so that the learners can draw it correctly. For example, *On the left there is a triangle. Inside the triangle there is a small square and above the square there is a straight line . . .*
3 The class is divided into two teams, and the blackboard is divided in two by a line. Each team has a representative at the board, each with a piece of chalk or a board marker. In advance of the game, you should have prepared a dozen or so different designs incorporating the geometrical shapes, large enough to be seen by all the class, except those drawing.
4 Ensure that the two team representatives at the board cannot see the designs. Select one design and show it to the two teams. Each team attempts to describe the design to its representative at the board, who draws it according to their description. The first team to do this successfully, so that the design is replicated on the board, is the winner of that round. Select another design and the game continues.

Note

Any image can be used for this task, but it is good to use one with clear profiles/outlines and a strong focal point (for example, geometric artworks by Mondrian, Kandinsky and El Lissitzky provide good models).

Acknowledgement: *This variation is based on an idea suggested by Scott Thornbury.*

Variation 4: Picture dictation

1 This task is suitable for lower-level students or young learners and is very similar to the original Describe and draw task. However, this variation is teacher-led and works best when you can produce your own line drawing. Simply dictate an image, detail by detail, monitoring to check that students are keeping up and modifying language accordingly. Make sure that expressions such as *in the middle, There are . . .*, etc. are pre-taught or elicited beforehand. Ensure also that students cannot see each other's work or your original.

2 Once students have finished, they can modify their pictures in pairs, adding details such as colour or other elements. These changes can be dictated by one student to the next.

Variation 5: Whole-class dictation

Show a large picture which has enough blank space in it for more images to be added to it. Students dictate to the teacher what images they want to add and where, until the picture is complete. This game can also be played with groups of three or four students. It can also work with a number of different groups, with each group seeing how they have transformed the original design.

Variation 6: Completing a template

Student A is given a template for an image which he/she has to complete, for example a house with no windows, a face with no eyes. He/she dictates these changes to Student B, who has a copy of the image and has to make the necessary changes.

Note

This task can often be carried out with digital images outside the classroom, especially when designing a profile online, by adding details to a given template. If you have access to computers in class, ask your class to connect to http://skype.klonies.com/ and create their own avatars. They can then compare them and describe to each other how their design was put together, using the vocabulary provided on the website.

Example: *You chose a sad mood, unkempt hair. You're wearing a bandana and red-frame glasses. You chose to stand next to a ski slope . . .*

See also: Second Life® Avatar Templates:
http://secondlife.com/community/templates.php

1.2 Which is it?

Outline	Students listen to descriptions of images that can be easily confused. They select those images which match the descriptions.
Focus	Lexical sets depending on the chosen images, e.g. clothes, physical characteristics, landscapes, furniture.
Level	Pre-intermediate and above
Time	30 minutes
Materials and preparation	Sets of generic images. Collect any type of generic images. It is important for some versions of this activity that the images are very similar. If possible, try to find images from a similar source (e.g. photos of rooms from an interior-design magazine) or of a similar genre. You could also use a selection of different art images (see Variation 3).

Procedure

1 Seat the students in a semi-circle or in such a way that all images will be visible to all. Lay out a selection of images on the board or on the floor, depending on your classroom layout.
2 Ask each student to select an image but not to tell anyone which one they have chosen.
3 Provide an example by selecting an image yourself and describing it. For instance, you could use different photos of models wearing a variety of clothes from a fashion magazine.

Example: *She's wearing a long white T-shirt. She has loose-fit blue jeans . . .*

4 Students listen to your description and identify the image that you have chosen. Choose a volunteer to repeat the same description. How much of your original description can he/she remember?
5 Students do the same task in pairs or small groups.

TIP

Choose images that could easily help you to revise vocabulary which you have recently covered in class. Describe each part of the image gradually, allowing time for students to assimilate the information. Writing out your description beforehand will help.

Variation 1: Themed magazines

1 Seat students in pairs. Hand out a themed magazine to each pair. Choose magazines which have very similar kinds of photos in them. Rooms, buildings and landscapes work particularly well for this task, e.g. travel/architecture magazines, furnishing catalogues.
2 Student A chooses one photo and describes it. Student B listens to his/her description and then attempts to find it, by leafing through the pages of the magazine.
3 Students reverse roles and repeat the task.
4 Students can bring their own magazine photos to the next class and play the same game.

As an alternative, students work in pairs. They write a short description of an image from the magazine on a sticky note. They should make a note of the page number on which the image appears. They attach the description to the front of the magazine and pass it to the next pair, who read the description and then attempt to find the image that matches it. They make a note of the page number and then each pair passes the magazine on again, and the task is repeated. This can continue several times. The pairs then cross-check their answers by reading out the page numbers. This activity can also be done with the class coursebook.

Variation 2: 'New-old-look' portraits

1 This task is like Variation 1 but uses images of celebrities / actors in different roles. Select a number of different photos of a famous person who has changed their *look* many times throughout their career. (Good examples are Madonna, David Beckham, Kylie Minogue, Brad Pitt.) Such photos can be easily accessed online. Choose subtle differences in photos for higher-level students.
   Alternatively, choose photos of the same actors in *different guises*. Students can identify the film roles in each case, if necessary.
2 Students work in pairs. Follow the same procedure as in Variation 1, with students listening to a description and guessing which *look* or *role* has been chosen by their partner.

Example: *In this photo, she has shortish dyed hair and lots of make-up. Her clothes are serious . . .*

3 Students reverse roles and repeat the task.
4 Students bring in photos of themselves at different ages and with different looks. They can play the same game with these images in the next class.

See 2.21 Is that you? for another activity using photos of people taken at different ages.

Variation 3: Art images

This task is like Variation 1 but with images of still lifes, landscapes or portraits. It is suitable for higher-level groups. Select a number of different photos of artwork and get students to work in pairs. Follow the same procedure as in Variation 1, with students listening to a description and guessing which art image has been chosen by their partner.

Note

Because of their religious or symbolic significance, certain icons have been present throughout many different art movements. Some of these have been reworked by contemporary artists (e.g. mother and child, Adam and Eve, monarchs and popes) in interesting ways.

Link: http://www.fictionwise.com/knight/boschfour.html provides a study of two almost identical Adam and Eve paintings by Titian and Rubens.

See 1.8 Minimal differences for more detailed work on such paintings.

Variation 4: Suspects

Put a gallery of portraits on the board. Students select one of the images and imagine they witnessed that person committing a crime. Students describe the person. Others have to guess which one they are describing from the gallery of suspects on the board. Alternatively, Student A describes the picture to Student B (who is facing away from the board), who then turns and chooses the person that has been described.

1.3 What can you remember?

Note	This is a version of the well-known 'Kim's game'.
Outline	Students see an image and reconstruct it from memory.
Focus	Lexical sets depending on images chosen, e.g. clothes, physical characteristics, landscapes. Revision of lexical items for describing images within a frame, e.g. *in the corner*.
Level	All
Time	30 minutes approximately, depending on Variation
Materials and preparation	CD-ROM image 1.3 All the living people. Sets of images based on vocabulary covered in class.

Tip For lower-level groups, make sure that there are not too many elements for students to remember: this can be demotivating. For higher levels, choose images in which there is a lot going on, with many different characters or objects to remember.

Procedure

1 Once you have found a suitable image (e.g. CD-ROM 1.3), show it to the students for a few minutes. (Timing will depend on the image's detail and the students' level.)

2 Hide the image and ask students in groups to recall as much as they can about it, what was in it and where. Alternatively, ask students to recall ten things contained within the image. Monitor the class to find the winning group and ask them to list the ten things in open class.

3 Ask if students can reconstruct the image by remembering the position of each thing from the winning list in the image. Prompt them with questions, e.g. *Was there anything on the floor?*

4 Ask the other groups if there are any parts of the image that the winning group had overlooked. Put language prompts on the board to guide the feedback: *You forgot . . ., You said that . . . but really . . ., You got x right but you didn't mention y.*

5 Reveal the image again in open class. Divide the image into four parts and describe each quarter, eliciting full sentences from different students as feedback.

Two-student version

Each partner is given an image and told to study it. The pairs exchange images. Student A attempts to reconstruct his/her image, which is in Student B's hands. Student B should not correct Student A but give him/her tips, e.g. *Did you say the dog was black?* or prompt Student A's memory when necessary.

Acknowledgement: *The Teacher's Book of* The Mind's Eye *(Maley, A., Duff, A., and Grellet, F., Cambridge University Press, 1980) gave me the idea for this two-student version.*

Variation 1: Correcting a description

1 For lower-level students, it may be difficult to describe a complex image in its entirety. As an alternative, students see the image and then correct a written description, which includes some errors. You can flash up the image again for a few seconds while students are doing the task to help them, but be careful not to show the image for too long.

2 Alternatively, you can describe the image to students but include deliberate mistakes which the students have to correct orally – this is particularly good for sentence stress. Teacher: *The woman is carrying a green umbrella*. Students: *No, she* ***isn't****. She's carrying a* ***red*** *one.*

Variation 2: Describing half an image

1 With more complex images, especially ones which have two clearly differentiated halves, split the image and the class in two. Distribute one half of the image to one of the groups and the other half to the other. Give students time to remember as much of their half as they can.
2 Go round the class monitoring the descriptions, but don't ask the students to read out their descriptions yet.
3 Students hypothesise about the missing half of the picture.
4 Students pair up with someone who has seen the other half of the image. They each 1) dictate what they can remember about their image, 2) describe what they imagine is on the other side.
5 Reveal the image to the whole class, first one half and then the other. Correct any descriptions where necessary. Were their hypotheses right?

Note

Paintings by Old Masters based on classical or religious tales can often work well for this task because of the number of different people on the canvas, and the dramatic content which makes hypothesising easier. Also, any paintings which have the form of a diptych are excellent. Remember not to give the names of the paintings.

Examples: Jacques-Louis David: *The Lictors Bring to Brutus the Bodies of His Sons*
Tintoretto: *The Annunciation*
There are a number of photographic images that could work very well for this task when cut in half vertically, e.g. Alfred Stieglitz, *The Steerage*:
http://www.metmuseum.org/toah/hd/stgp/ho_33.43.419.htm

Variation 3: Revealing an image (lower levels)

TIP

Ideally, you should select an image which has a lot going on in it, so that there is something new to describe each time you reveal a bit more of the image.

1 Find an image and show only a small part of it to the students. (This can be done using an OHP and a blank piece of paper. You can also use

Photoshop® to cut your image into pieces or cover the image by placing sticky notes on top.) Cover that part of the image. Students describe what they can remember in pairs or small groups.
2 Reveal a little more of the image each time, cover it once more and ask students again to recall as much as they can about it. Correct or refine descriptions at each stage.
3 Do this until you have revealed the whole image.
4 Remove the image. Can students recall the whole description, part by part?

Variation 4: Chinese whispers

TIP

Once more it is important to choose an image in which a lot of things are going on and/or there are a lot of characters. Seurat's famous painting *A Sunday on La Grande Jatte* works well:
http://www.artic.edu/artaccess/AA_Impressionist/pages/IMP_7.shtml

1 Seat students in a circle. Pass an image around. Each student describes one detail and then passes it on to the next. The next student has to recall the previous description and add one of his/her own. This continues as the image goes around the room.
2 Repeat with a number of different images and then ask students to report back, refining the descriptions of each. Go through this in some detail, asking students to reformulate their descriptions where possible, e.g. *You said there was a dog sitting in the shade, but it's standing.*
3 Ask students to bring in their own images to class to play another round the next day.

1.4 Points of view

Outline	Describing images from different points of view. Showing that images are open to multiple interpretations, all of which may be valid.
Focus	Fixed expressions: *It reminds me of . . ., It makes me think of . . ., I am reminded of . . .*
Level	Upper intermediate and above
Time	30 minutes
Materials and preparation	Sets of images based on vocabulary covered in class. Many different images could work for this task but, generally speaking, it is a good idea to use historical photos, around which there is a real story to tell. A good source of archive images: http://www.magnumphotos.com

Procedure

1 Seat the students in groups of four. Show the same image to each group. Each student has to write how they feel about the image *from the viewpoint of a different person* – this could be four different professions or four people of different ages.

Note

It is a good idea to make the roles quite differentiated so that it is easier for students to adopt distinct perspectives.

Example:

Group A	Group B
a) an old person	a) a government worker
b) a young child	b) a doctor
c) a middle-aged parent	c) a monarch/president
d) an adolescent	d) a wife/husband

2 Give the students a prompt to get them going, for example:

When I see this image, I think of . . .
This image makes me think of / reminds me of . . .
What strikes me most is . . .

3 Students write a short paragraph with their impressions and then exchange their work with members of another group. The other students have to guess from which point of view they are speaking.

Example: Dorothea Lange's photo, *Migrant mother*:
http://en.wikipedia.org/wiki/Dorothea_Lange
Having to cope with three children like that, I know how she feels = a parent

4 Students report back to the whole class. Make sure that the image is visible to the class at the same time.

5 Explain that the Lange image above is a famous archive photo. Tell the students a little about its history or ask them to research this at home. Notice the photographer's description of how the photo was taken on the Wikipedia site above.

Variation: What's the context?

1 Students imagine that an image can be used as:

– a campaign advert
– the cover of a novel

- the front page of a newspaper
- an illustration in a textbook
- inspiration for the opening of a poem/story.

Students write the caption or the short accompanying text that would appear alongside the image in that new context.

2 Students read out their work and the others have to guess the context.

Example: Dorothea Lange's photo (see link on page 26).
Seventy years on, there is still poverty in California. Help the homeless. This may be the accompanying text for an advertising campaign.

1.5 Who am I?

Outline	Students create a role for a person in an image, describing their character's feelings, and then guess the role created by others.
Focus	Tense overview: uses of the present continuous for present and future; uses of the present perfect and the future and constructions such as *I wish / I regret . . .* Hypothetical language: *You must be . . .*, etc.
Level	Intermediate–Advanced
Time	30 minutes
Materials and preparation	CD-ROM image 1.5 Painting by Edward Hopper – Nighthawks. Sets of images based on vocabulary covered in class. Choose images in which there are a number of characters present, so the students have a wide choice, but not so many as to make it difficult to distinguish one person from another. It is better not to choose images of famous people. The ideal number is between four and ten. It is best if the characters seem to have different roles.

Procedure

1 Show the students an image in which different people are present. Each student individually chooses one of these people and thinks about him/her for a couple of minutes.

2 Write the following questions on the board. It is a good idea to keep to this structure so that students can practise the different tenses. However, you may want to modify them according to your class level.

a) *What's my name? Where am I?*
b) *What is happening / What has just happened (to me)?*
c) *What am I feeling now?*
d) *How do I relate to the other people here?*
e) *What will happen next?*

f) What do I regret or what am I looking forward to?
g) What do I wish most in the world?

Alternatively, ask the class to ask you the questions, changing *I* to *you*, *my* to *your*, etc.

3 Flash up an image as an example and answer the questions verbally for one of the characters. This will provide a model for the students. It is better if students use the first person here, to make the exercise more immediate.

4 Read out this sample of a student's work based on the Edward Hopper painting, *Nighthawks* (CD-ROM 1.5), to give students a model to work on.

I am at a 24-hour café in a big US city. I am waiting for something important to happen. I'm feeling tense and nervous. I am worried that they're looking for us, that they'll hurt us. We're in trouble. We should never have done what we did. We shouldn't have taken the money, but we needed it. We'll just sit here quietly and pretend nothing bad will happen . . . I wish the waiter would stop working, making that noise. Oh, no! . . . It's so late, I can't keep my eyes open. I wish I were somewhere else . . .

Answer: The woman in the red dress at the bar.

Alternatively, for lower-level students, provide a skeleton text with prompts for the students to expand upon:

(A) I am in . . . (B) I am . . . (C) I feel . . . (D) They will . . . (E) I regret . . . (F) I wish . . .

5 Monitor students' writing, paying particular attention to the more difficult constructions, e.g. *I wish, I regret.*

6 Seat students in groups. Each student reads out his/her work. Students guess which person in the image they are talking about. Monitor and select some interesting examples to be read to the rest of the class.

Alternatively, students ask each other questions in order to identify the person.

Variation: Asking questions

For lower-level students. Choose images with lots of people. Students select one of the characters in the image and the others have to guess who they are by asking questions: *Are you standing next to the wall? Are you wearing a white shirt?*, etc. This is good for practising specific structures, such as relative clauses, e.g. *Are you the person who's talking on the phone?*

Painting by Edward Hopper – *Nighthawks*, © Photography © The Art Institute of Chicago

See 7.3 Art poems 1 for another task based on an Edward Hopper painting.

1.6 What's missing?

Outline	Students see how images 'connote' or 'suggest' meaning rather than explicitly 'tell'.
Focus	Interactive speaking, focus on fluency.
Level	Intermediate–Advanced
Time	15 minutes
Materials and preparation	Adverts are a very good source for this task, especially those which don't explicitly show the product that they are advertising, or in which the product is not obvious.

Procedure

1 Show an image which has a vital element missing. In other words, without this element, the image is ambiguous or unclear. A good idea is to choose an advert and remove the brand name, logo or any other information which identifies the product. See Variation 2.

TIP

In class, you can easily cover part of the image (e.g. the brand name) with a sticky note.

2 In groups students describe the image and imagine what's missing. Ask: *What surrounds the image? Where does it come from? Where would you see it?*
3 Individual students/groups report back. Then round up with whole-class discussion.
4 Reveal the missing parts of the image. What do students think of the 'full picture'?
5 Encourage students to bring their own examples to the next class and play the same game.

Variation 1: Comic strip

Remove a vignette from a comic strip, for example the final image. Get students to look at the adapted comic strip and try to think of the missing punchline or the final vignette from the visual clues provided. They can create their own stories and then compare and contrast in groups.

Note

The last image/vignette may not be the element which you wish to remove.

Variation 2: Two sides to an advert

Show students one side of a double-page-spread advert, in which the product is not revealed. Students hypothesise about the missing half. What image will be shown? Get ideas from the class before revealing information about the product.

Note

Many adverts use a left/right axis in this way. The given easily-understood information is presented on the left-hand side, whilst the 'new' information is found on the right (e.g. the product).

See 6.1 Analysing adverts: a basic procedure 1 for similar tasks based on adverts.

1.7 Speech bubbles

Outline	Adding descriptions/comments to images. Empowering students to make images their own.
Focus	Exploring conversations from visual prompts/stimuli. Contextualising a visual image.
Level	Intermediate–Advanced
Time	30 minutes
Materials and preparation	CD-ROM image 1.7 The Twickenham streaker. Comic strips, photos, stills from silent movies. All the images must show people clearly having a conversation. Other people in the image who are not speaking can also be used, through 'thought bubbles'. Speech bubbles and captions can be easily added to any digital image by using Flickr™ Toys. See Introduction page 11 for details.

Procedure

1 Seat students in groups. Hand out a suitable image (e.g. CD-ROM 1.7). Ask students to describe the situation/context.

For lower-level students, break down this description into the following questions. (In fact, you can adapt these questions to almost any image.) This can be done in groups or as a whole class, depending on students' familiarity with such questions.

1 *When was the photo taken? How do you know?*
2 *How many people are there in the image?*
3 *Where are they?*
4 *What are they doing?*
5 *How do they feel?*
6 *What has just happened?*
7 *What is about to happen?*

2 Indicate what a speech or thought bubble is. Ask students to imagine what each person is talking or thinking about.

3 Students work in pairs, adding speech or thought bubbles to the image. Students compare ideas in groups and come up with the best dialogue. They can act these dialogues out if necessary.

Sample speech/thought bubbles for 3 based on *The Twickenham streaker* (CD-ROM 1.7):

	Speech/thought bubbles:
Streaker:	*I left my clothes here!*
Policeman with helmet:	*Did you know that about 10 million people are watching you, right now?*

Man with coat:	*At least this will keep him warm.*
Second policeman holding wrist:	*This is so embarrassing!*
Policeman holding arm (to other policeman):	*Well, the match was pretty boring anyway.*

Variation 1: Redistributing dialogues

1 Each pair of students is given one image. They discuss options for the dialogue and write their best version on a separate piece of paper.

2 Collect the dialogues and pin them around the classroom. Redistribute the images to different students. Their task is to go around the room reading the dialogues and find the one which best fits their picture. When they find the match, they should attach the image to the dialogue.
Alternatively, the images could be posted on the walls, and the students attach the dialogue to the correct image.

3 Students can quiz each other and explain their dialogue if necessary.

Acknowledgement: *The idea for this task came from* Dialogue Activities, *by Bilbrough, N., (Cambridge University Press, 2007).*

Variation 2: Dialogue and genre

Suitable for higher levels. As Variation 1 (all students can have the same image) but ask students to write the dialogue in different genres: tragic, comic, romantic, thriller-style, melodramatic, etc. Students then read out their dialogues and the rest of the class have to guess the genre.

Variation 3: Matching speech bubble and image

Find a series of different images with speech/thought bubbles (one or two per image is enough). Separate the speech/thought bubbles from the images and get students to match them up.

Variation 4: Comic strips / Cartoons

Students complete vignettes in a comic strip and then compare with the original. With individual cartoons, students attempt to match the punchline and the cartoon or all three different items: 1) the image, 2) the first part of the joke, 3) the punchline.

See 7.10 Conversations for a similar activity.

1.8 Minimal differences

Outline Students describe differences between one image and another. Raising awareness about iconic images in art. An alternative to the classic 'Spot the difference' task.
Focus Comparatives and superlatives, language of conjecture.
Level Intermediate–Advanced
Time 30 minutes
Materials and preparation CD-ROM images 1.8A All 5 photos of doors and windows; B–F A window to the sea, House of the Half Moon, Rapunzel's window, Wooden door, Red, yellow and green door. A great source of images for this activity can be found at http://www.flickr.com

Procedure

1 Seat students in groups of three or four. Hand out a different image to each student. Choose very similar images for the highest-level students as they will take longer to tell them apart.

Note
Select landscape shots of the same place taken in different seasons, portraits of the same person at different ages, shots of the same room when tidy and untidy, etc. Another option is to choose a recurring image and show different examples of this, e.g. photos of different hands, windows, clocks, bags, doors.

2 Each student takes it in turn to describe their image without showing this to the other students. The others mentally note down the differences between this image and their own. The students can then ask as many questions as they like until they each get a mental image of all three/four images.
3 Students then show each other their images. They compare the differences between their mental images and the real shots they have before them.
4 Students now imagine the surrounding context for each of these images. For example, with the different photos of doors and windows (see CD-ROM 1.8 A–F), they can answer the following questions:
1) Can anything be seen from the door?
2) What lies behind each one?
3) What is the rest of the building like? How do you know?
4) How old are they?
5) Which of these doors/windows do you like best and why?

Acknowledgement: *The original idea for this task came from* The Mind's Eye, *Maley, A., Duff, A. and Grellet, F., (Cambridge University Press, 1980).*

1.9 Flickr™ colours

Outline Students relate mental images with colour, and describe different images which share the same colour. Students search for images on the Flickr™ website and contextualise them.

Focus Vocabulary: colours and their association. Fluency practice.

Level Elementary–Advanced

Time 30 minutes

Materials and preparation CD-ROM images 1.9 A All the red images, 1.9 B–I Red Path, Arrows and target, Candy, Puma tag, Fire extinguisher, Voodoo doll back, Toy Ferrari, Che Marilyn; 1.9 J–Q Squircle mosaics: Green, blue, yellow, orange, black, white, red, radiance. The key source for this activity is http://www.flickr.com.

Note For example, if you want to search for **groups** with photos featuring the colour red, simply search for 'red' and then press the 'groups' key: http://www.flickr.com/search/groups/?q=red Once you gain access to a certain group, a **pool** of different images pops up. Within each pool you can access more photos according to their other **tags** (e.g. red → flower). It is a good idea to organise these groups by 'most relevant'. For example, one of the best pools for the colour red is: http://www.flickr.com/groups/red-rojo-rouge/. Within this pool the most common tags are red, japan, rojo, flower, light.

Procedure

1 Ask students in groups of three or four to brainstorm a particular colour and the different images that they associate with it. Make sure each group chooses a different colour. Ask students to work individually first and, depending on the level, to imagine up to five, ten or twenty images.

Example: *Red → strawberry, leaves, blood, stop sign, lips, poppy, Santa Claus, Manchester United, bricks.*

Ask the students in each group to create a mental image of each association. For example, *I see a plate of strawberries in orange juice on a hot summer's day . . .*

2 Students then compare answers in their groups. They should compile the top five images which they shared and then assign a spokesperson to report their findings to the rest of the class.

3 Conduct class feedback to find out the most popular images associated with particular colours.

4 Students in their groups access the http://www.flickr.com website and find a particular group based around their colour.

5 Present them with the following questions:
   1) What is the image that was most frequently found in your Flickr™ group?
   2) What other kinds of images can you find there? Were there any surprises? (e.g. The example of a red path.)
   3) Which were the most commonly found tags within the group?
   4) Where did the contributing photographers come from? (Click on the map link to find out.)
   5) Which was your favourite image and why?
   6) Did any of the images coincide with the group's initial mental images?

Variation 1: Website searches

1 Students use Flickr™ to find the top five mental images that they had come up with in their groups. Which were easy/difficult to find? How different are their mental images from the others they discover on Flickr™?

2 Show the examples of red images from Flickr™ on the CD-ROM (1.9A–I). Students describe each image and the mental images that come into their minds as they see them. In what way are these red images more atypical? What connection can they find between the colour red and image 1.9I?

Che Marilyn, © Maria Badaracco

Sample answer: This is a graffiti montage of Marilyn Monroe and Che Guevara. MM: red lipstick; CG: red is the colour of the political left wing.

3 Use a different website such as http://www.bigstockphoto.com and ask students to search for colours and categories. For example, on such sites you can key in 'red' and then categories such as 'architecture' or 'landscape'. Ask them to imagine what kind of images they will find in certain categories and whether their guesses proved correct.
4 For higher-level groups, you can make the search even more specific, e.g. *red > architecture > details and close-ups*.
5 Students use the Flickr™ website to discover **collocations** with red. They can look up expressions with *red – red tape*, *red robin*, etc. and collect images that may help them to remember these expressions.

Variation 2: Squircles

Note

These squircle (square/circle) mosaics (CD-ROM 1.9 J–Q) will look excellent if you can project them through a computer or in a PowerPoint presentation. It is essential that students can see clearly the 36 images in each mosaic. Show the images in colour if possible.

Squircle mosaic – black, © Tom Magliery

Squircle mosaic – white, © Tom Magliery

1 Assign students (individually, in pairs or in small groups, depending on your class size) to a particular colour. You can choose from seven: red, orange, yellow, green, blue, black, white.
2 Students brainstorm objects they associate with this colour, as step 1 in the main task.
3 Students look at their relevant mosaic of 36 different squircles (CD-ROM 1.9J–Q). Ask them to organise the images in any way they like and describe each.

   For example, in the orange squircle you could organise the images in this way:

   Signs
   Food and drink
   Neons and light
   Words/letters
   Wheels
   Household objects.

4 Students can compare with others who have a different colour and they each describe their squircles. There will be a number of different squircles that the students cannot identify. They should try and guess these.

5 The class can check the answers on Tom's Flickr™ website: http://www.flickr.com/photos/mag3737/ Each squircle mosaic has a list of links below it which indicate the object in each case.

1.10 Google™ it

Outline	Students analyse associations between key words and images on the Internet.
Focus	Words with multiple meanings.
Level	Intermediate–Advanced.
Time	30 minutes
Materials and preparation	CD-ROM images 1.10 A–E Apple for the teacher, Adam's apple, NYC The Big Apple, An apple a day . . . , Newton and the apple. Access to a search engine such as Google™, or a photo library such as Flickr™, is necessary for this task, or it can be set for homework.
Note	Make sure that the Google™ Safe Search facility is activated to strict or moderate filtering to avoid students coming across obscene images.

Procedure

1 Establish the notion of a 'tag' or a 'key word'. Explain that if you want to search for an image online, one way to do so is by inserting a key word.

2 Begin by brainstorming a key word and asking students what mental images they associate with this word. As an example, begin with the word 'apple'.

TIP

Ask students to think of a specific visual image, not just an abstract idea.

3 Show students the five images on the CD-ROM (1.10A–E). Ask them what the relationship is between these images and the word 'apple'. Students discuss and report back to the whole class.
Answers: 1.10A: An apple for the teacher. The teacher's pet traditionally brought an apple for the teacher, to curry favour with him/her. 1.10B: This part of the body is known as the Adam's apple. 1.10C: The city of New York is known as the Big Apple. 1.10D: There is a traditional saying which goes: An apple a day keeps the doctor away. 1.10E: Legend claims that Newton witnessed an apple fall off the tree and formulated his theory of gravity.

4 Students then connect to Google™ Images and insert the word 'apple' or 'apples'. Ask students in groups to describe the images as best they can. Were any of the images that appeared similar to their mental pictures?

5 Are students surprised by these images? Allow them to report back their opinions in open class.
6 Students choose five of the different images from the first page and go into the original source page. They should now do the following:
   1) Describe the same image in more detail.
   2) Describe the original website in which the apple image appears.
   3) Report back to the class something they have discovered from that particular website which they didn't know previously.

   If you have access to a computer room, a networked projector or an interactive whiteboard, show the example online.
7 Students comment on the results. (For example, in the case of the apple, there were no images of Adam and Eve, Isaac Newton's apple, an Adam's apple, and very few pictures of apples in general.)
8 Students do their own searches. If you want more control over the activity, ask them to choose from the list below. It is a good idea to choose words with multiple meanings.

Examples: box, lap, rock, state, face, ball, light, bank, tip.

Variation 1: Flickr™ clusters

Instead of Google™ Images, use the http://www.flickr.com website, which features original photographic material only. The resulting images will be more artistic and, of course, non-commercial.

It is a good idea to use the cluster function, which groups similar images together. For example, if you are looking for images of apples key in the following address:

http://www.flickr.com/photos/tags/apple/clusters

Here there are four clusters for the word *Apple*: 1) Mac, iPod®, computer, etc. 2) fruit, red, tree, etc. 3) NYC, Apple store, 4) desktop, tiger, wallpaper. To create different clusters using the website, replace the word 'apple' in the link above with a different word.

Variation 2: Multiple meanings

1 Make 'multiple meanings' the centre of your activity. Allow students to discover these through images and find out different words which collocate with them.

   For example, if we insert the word *tip* into Google™ Images, we get many different meanings of the word.

In Flickr™ we can find the following clusters:

– pencil, flower, plant
– rubbish, dump, trash
– money, bar, dollar.

2 Students can also use image searches to prepare quiz questions for each other, e.g. *What do Isaac Newton, NYC and Adam and Eve all have in common?*

See 5.8 Image history for an activity on apples and other icons.

1.11 Shadowplay

Outline	Students look at images of shadows and describe actions.
Focus	Fluency practice with an emphasis on the present continuous tense and verbs of movement. For Variation: future tenses.
Level	Elementary–Intermediate
Time	15 minutes
Materials and preparation	CD-ROM images 1.11A–H Shadow photos. You can also use images of shadows of objects and ask students to guess what they are. It is easy for students to bring in their own photos of shadows as well.

Procedure

1 Mime a few actions and ask students to describe what you are doing. Ask students if they ever played with shadows as children. What shapes did/can they make with their bodies?

2 Show students the photos of shadows on the CD-ROM (1.11A–H) and ask them in turn to describe them as best they can.

TIPS

Begin with the simple images with actions that are easier to describe. Provide a prompt for the more difficult actions, encouraging students to paraphrase if they don't know the exact words. For example, for photo G, we can say: *He is holding something in his hand*, as well as the more precise *He is holding a remote control* or *He is turning on the television*.

3 Students report their answers back to the rest of the class.

Answers: 1.11A Pointing, 1.11B Tying a shoelace, 1.11C Reading a book, 1.11D Having a drink, 1.11E Waving, 1.11F Putting sunglasses on, 1.11G Using a remote control, 1.11H Raising a thumb.

Variation: Freeze-frame moving images

Find a piece of action involving different characters doing different actions. Use the freeze-frame button to stop the image and ask students what each person is doing at each moment and what will happen next. For higher levels, this can be particularly good for revising specific verbs of movement which are often difficult to translate directly.

1.12 Written descriptions

Outline	Identifying key differences between formal and informal descriptions of different photos. Raising awareness of register.
Focus	Examining the difference between written and spoken texts.
Level	Pre-intermediate – Upper intermediate
Time	45 minutes
Materials and preparation	CD-ROM images 1.12A V-J Day in Times Square; 1.12B Three brothers. You can also choose your own photos: 1) a well-known image that has become iconic, 2) a family snapshot. Two written descriptions, one written in a formal style and the other informal (similar to spoken discourse).
Note	Describing photographic images forms an intrinsic part of many oral exams, hence it is a task which many students will have to do in the classroom.

Procedure

1 Show the class the two photos (CD-ROM 1.12A–B), pointing out that one is a famous image and the other a personal snapshot.

2 Which words/expressions from the pairs do the class think will be used to describe: a) an iconic portrait, b) a snapshot?

alongside	*next to me*
contrast	*difference*
shows	*depicts*
looks like	*seems*
to the left/right (-hand side)	*on my left/right*
composition	*picture.*

V-J Day in Times Square, © Getty Images / Time and Life Pictures

Three brothers

3 Students read the descriptions in Texts A and B and check their answers to question 2.

Answers: Informal language: *next to me, difference, shows, looks like, on my left/right, picture.*

Formal language: *alongside, contrast, depicts, seems, to the left/right (-hand side), composition.*

Text A: An iconic portrait

A sailor kisses a nurse in Times Square, New York, so celebrating the definitive end of World War II. The photo first appeared in *Life* magazine and clearly depicts the relief and happiness that was felt at the end of the war. It seems a spontaneous image but, in fact, the whole thing could have been posed by the photographer. Even the dark clothes of the sailor and the white dress and shoes of his beloved are a deliberate contrast. Alongside the couple we can see the happiness and sense of freedom felt by everyone in the streets. To the left, we can make out another sailor ambling along, seemingly without a care in the world. It is, indeed, a photograph that invites the viewer in. It seems that we could also join them and have a party. It is one of the most celebrated photographic compositions of its generation and it has been widely reproduced.

© Cambridge University Press 2008 PHOTOCOPIABLE

Text B: A family snapshot

My favourite family photo is this one. Look – you can see that's me in the middle, looking very cheeky as always. Next to me are my two brothers, Dan and Josh. My brothers must have been at school because you can see that they're wearing uniform, so I must have been about four years old here. I remember that sofa very well. We always used to have all our photos taken there. It was an effort for the photographer to keep us still, that's for sure. There's a big difference in our expressions, of course – it looks like my brother Josh is being the most serious, whereas Dan (on my right) is obviously finding something very funny. He'd always be laughing at something. I've always loved this picture because I guess it shows how different the three of us were back then.

© Cambridge University Press 2008 PHOTOCOPIABLE

4 Students decide which elements in Text A could be considered examples of a formal style and which features make Text B similar to a spoken text.

Answers:
Text A: Use of the passive voice (*it has been widely reproduced, was felt*) to create a distance between the writer and the image. Inclusion of formal link words (*in fact, indeed*), use of more formal adjectives (*spontaneous, deliberate*).
Text B: Use of first person pronouns, use of modals of supposition (*I must have been*) similar to those used in conversation to show that the speaker is thinking at the same time. Use of fillers (*I guess*), and emphatic expressions (*that's for sure*). Use of *there* to indicate that the speaker is pointing directly at something in the image.

Follow-up

Students find either a family snapshot or a portrait / iconic image, and write a description of it. Remind them to consider the style when they do so. They could use these questions as a guide:

Family snapshot: *When was it taken? Who appears in it? What memories do you have of the moment that the photo was taken? What does it evoke / remind you of now?*

Iconic image: *Why are you attracted to this image? What does it represent/ symbolise for you? Do you know / Can you find out any background/ historical information about it?*

For higher levels: Students can write descriptions in contrasting styles, i.e. write an 'artsy' description of a family photo and a 'chatty' one of an 'art' photo.

1.13 What's it for?

Outline	Describing everyday objects in terms of material and function. Paraphrasing. Survival-situation role play.
Focus	Constructions for describing objects: *It's something you use to . . .*
Level	Elementary–Pre-intermediate (young learners)
Time	40 minutes
Materials and preparation	CD-ROM images 1.13A Illustration – 15 objects; 1.13B Illustration – 12 tools.

Procedure

1 Ask the class (in mother tongue if necessary) what you can do when you want to communicate something and you don't have the exact words to do so accurately (e.g. use body language, paraphrase, circumlocution).

2 Hold up any object and ask the class to describe it in a number of different ways. Elicit/highlight the expressions to describe material, function, etc.

It's made of . . .
It's used for . . .
It's something you use to . . .
It's useful for . . .
You can . . . with it.

3 Print out or display the 15 images from the CD-ROM (1.13A) for the students. Demonstrate a role play in which a person is in a shop but doesn't know the name of the thing that he/she wants to buy. Select one of the 15 objects, for example the lighter, and go through the following script, asking the students to guess the object from the images on display:

I want one of those things, you know, it's made of plastic and it's useful for lighting cigarettes . . .
Oh, you mean one of these . . . (pointing to the lighter)

4 Get students to role play the dialogues for the other objects. Monitor carefully to check students are using the constructions correctly.
5 Once they have described most of the 15 images, the students can choose their own objects to paraphrase.

Variation: Lexical groups

1 Depending on the vocabulary that you wish to highlight, focus on a certain lexical group.
2 Show the grid of tools on the CD-ROM (1.13B), either with a projector or as printed-out copies for students. Model the activity, by reading out a number/letter combination, pointing to the illustration and saying what it is and what it is used for.
3 Students play the same game in pairs.

See 2.15 What's in your bag?

2 Interpreting images

This chapter moves away from the purely descriptive and asks students to think more deeply about the image in front of their eyes. In reality, here they are asked to look beyond the frame and interact with it on a deeper level – in other words, to 'make the image their own'. This very often means working at the level of either serious hypothesis or a more playful kind of guesswork (which tasks 2.3 Connecting people and 2.21 Is that you? encapsulate respectively).

Analysing images in this way follows a model established by John Callow in an article called *Literacy and the Visual*[1] in which three dimensions of viewing are established: the *affective*, the *compositional* and the *critical*. Here, the 'affective' acknowledges the individual's role and his/her personal, sensual reaction to an image. The second, the 'compositional', looks at how different elements and signs create meaning within the image's formal structure. The third, the 'critical' perspective, emphasises the importance of bringing a social critique to the understanding of an image. When students practise contextualising, ranking, sequencing and matching images among many other disciplines, they will, although unconsciously, be interpreting an image from these three different perspectives.

They will also look at the relationship between image and text in tasks such as 2.17 Cartoon captions and with specific image types in a number of other activities: with different kinds of maps and cartograms in 2.13 X marks the spot and with abstract works in 2.14 Abstracts. Students are also trained in a skill which is becoming essential in our digital age, that of 'tagging' or categorising and labelling images with a single word; this is seen in 2.7 Tag it.

There are also a good number of tasks which explore the 'everyday' image, often taken by amateur photographers and artists. This can be seen especially in 2.15 What's in your bag?, which features the contents of people's bags and their face photos. This is also true of 2.21 Is that you?, which looks at snapshots of ordinary people from childhood to the present day, and 2.18 Room with a view, which shows everyday views from people's houses and

[1] Callow, J. *Literacy and the Visual: Broadening Our Vision*, English Teaching: Practice and Critique, May 2005, 4, pp. 6–19.

flats. These 'real-life' images represent the antithesis of the bland, airbrushed shots from the stock libraries and online image archives which predominate in language teaching material as they do in all walks of life – advertising and promotional texts, as well as print media and corporate literature. Allowing access to more personal and less professional images will also encourage students to bring their own images into class and make comparisons.

Students are also introduced in this chapter to the basic vocabulary of image composition. They are asked to analyse images from the point of view of how and where the images were taken in the first place (2.11 How was it taken? and 2.12 Where was it taken?). Likewise, in the age of the digital photo in which software such as Photoshop® reigns supreme, students are asked to consider whether they believe an image to be real or a fake (2.10 Is it real?), and that includes smiles! Following on from that theme, students tackle digitally manipulated images in 2.6 Out of focus and extreme close-ups (macro photos) in 2.14 Abstracts.

There is also an important focus here on learning about the world through image, for example in the analysis of cartograms in 2.13 X marks the spot. Visual poetry has an important part to play in this chapter, particularly in 2.16 Concepts, in which visual representations of the words *happiness* and *silence* are featured. Humour also has an important part to play here, in 2.15 What's in your bag?, 2.17 Cartoon captions and 2.21 Is that you? among others.

2.1 Odd one out

Outline	Categorising images to find the odd one out and justifying decisions. Raising awareness about different national symbols.
Focus	Fluency practice. Lexical area of symbols and emblems.
Level	Intermediate and above
Time	20 minutes
Materials and preparation	CD-ROM images 2.1A Illustration – All national emblems; 2.1B–I National emblems for USA, India, Iran, England, China, France, Eire and South Africa. You can use many types of images for this activity. For this example, I have chosen national symbols or emblems but there are countless other images that would work well (see Variations).

Procedure

1 Seat students in groups. Ask if they can think of any symbols or emblems that are often associated with their country. Do they know the origin of these symbols?

2 Show students the three emblems for the USA (CD-ROM 2.1B) and ask them to try and identify the odd one out, i.e. the symbol that doesn't match the indicated country. Write these words on the board: *the bald eagle, the Liberty Bell, the bulldog*. Write the following as a prompt: *The bulldog is the odd one out as it is a symbol of the UK, not the US* or *The bulldog doesn't fit because . . .* Students can confirm if they identified the correct image.

3 Present the students with the symbols on the CD-ROM (2.1A–I) or photocopy page 49. Ask them to say which is the odd one out in each set.

Key:
USA: bald eagle, Liberty Bell, bulldog
India: elephant, camel, banyan tree
Iran: lion and sun, three crowns, nightingale
England: lion, Britannia, sun
China: dragon, plum blossom, cedar tree
France: rooster, Marianne, red rose
Eire: maple leaf, harp, shamrock
South Africa: springbok antelope, palm tree, protea flower

Answers (in brackets the countries which *are* identified by this symbol):
USA: bulldog (England)
India: camel (Eritrea)
Iran: three crowns (Sweden)
England: sun (Argentina/Uruguay)
China: cedar tree (Lebanon)
France: red rose (England)
Eire: maple leaf (Canada)
South Africa: palm tree (Cuba)

4 Students discuss in groups or pairs and report back their answers to another group.

5 Students report back their answers to the whole class. Explain, or elicit an explanation of, any of the new vocabulary. (Alternatively, supply groups with bilingual dictionaries.) Ask students why they think these particular symbols are representative of a certain country.

Example: *The springbok antelope is a symbol of South Africa because it is commonly found in South Africa. The South African rugby team are known as 'The Springboks'.*

USA

India

Iran

England

China

France

Eire

South Africa

© Cambridge University Press 2008

PHOTOCOPIABLE

Follow-up

Students select a country and do some research on its symbols, emblems, coats of arms, etc. Their aim is to find as much as they can about these different images and report back to the other students in the next class.

Variation: Other images

The Odd one out task also works well with the following images: flags, coats of arms, stamps, banknotes, postcards, still-life paintings, generic advertisements, similar-looking photos, etc.

See Chapter 5 for more tasks featuring symbols.

2.2 Ranking

Outline	Students categorise and rank images in order of quality and effectiveness.
Focus	Specific vocabulary depending on images/genre chosen. Fluency practice: arguing your case.
Level	Intermediate and above
Time	40 minutes
Materials and preparation	CD-ROM images 2.2A Illustrations – Anti-smoking campaigns; 2.2B–F Five children's pictures for anti-smoking campaigns 1–5; 2.2G–O Cake, chocolate, bananas, grapes, vegetables, cheese, bread, meat, tart with cream.
Note	For this activity, I have chosen images for advertising campaigns. But there are many other images that would work equally well with such a task, from categorising the healthiest foods to ranking home interiors. (See Variations.)

Procedure

1 Brainstorm with students different advertising campaigns that have some political/social aim. Suggest the following if students are slow to respond:

drink-driving
AIDS awareness/prevention
anti-smoking
illegal drug use
speeding

2 Choose one of these campaigns (e.g. anti-smoking). Seat students in groups and ask them which images are often used to encourage people to give up smoking.
3 Students discuss and report back in open class.
4 Present students with images CD-ROM 2.2A and ask them to rank them according to the degree of positive effect they would have on the general public in a campaign, from the most to the least effective. They should give reasons for their decisions. Give students the opportunity to complete the thought bubble in the cowboy image with their own ideas, e.g. *It's really more cool not to smoke.*

© Cambridge University Press 2008 PHOTOCOPIABLE

5 Students compare answers in groups. Are they able to reach a consensus as to the best image?
6 How would they use the image in an advertising campaign? Alternatively, what images could they create themselves for an effective campaign?
7 The class finally look at anti-smoking posters designed by children (CD-ROM 2.2B–F). What are the differences between these images and the previous ones? What do the children choose to emphasise? Which is the most effective?

Variation 1: Basic level and young learners

More basic visual images can be ordered by students in similar ways.

For example, rank the photos of foods on the CD-ROM (2.2G–O) from the most to the least healthy, from the tastiest to the least tasty.

Other ideas for ranking tasks could include photos or rooms from interior-design magazines or furniture catalogues, or images of holiday destinations from travel brochures.

Variation 2: Magazine competitions

Many magazines and websites run competitions which rank images in order of quality. You can cut/print these out and students can rank them and then check if their answers match the final verdict, always giving reasons for their decisions. The media is full of other contexts in which readers have to rank and categorise images, especially in the gossip and celebrity media. Search for the 'best' and 'worst' dressed stars on Oscar night, for example.

See 6.5 Campaigning for more activities on advertising campaigns.

2.3 Connecting people

Outline	Students are challenged to find ways to connect different images, or match images with texts, both subjectively and objectively.
Focus	Matching language (*This would suit / be right for . . .*). Specific vocabulary depending on images/genre chosen.
Level	Intermediate and above
Time	30 minutes
Materials and preparation	CD-ROM images 2.3A–J Ten portraits of different kinds of people.

Procedure

1 Organise students into groups. For each group, a set of images is placed face down – these could be anything from film posters, landscapes, types of food, famous album covers, etc. Each student is then given three photos of different people. (There should be a good variety of people types from young to old, conventional to eccentric, etc. See CD-ROM 2.3A–J for examples.) Students take it in turns to pick up an image and decide which person would like this particular thing and why.

Example: (Image: Harry Potter poster) *I think this person would like Harry Potter because he looks like him a bit!*

2 In their groups, students listen to each other's argument. If they are convinced by it, the student can keep the picture. The aim of the game is to make as many connections and collect as many images as possible.
3 Students report back their 'connections' to the whole class. Does the rest of the class agree?

Note

Excellent images for this game are photos of people's bedroom walls and fridges decorated with magnets because they say a lot about the personality of the person concerned. Images can also be used in conjunction with text to create all kinds of connecting tasks/games. You can connect slogans with adverts, quotations with pictures of famous people, definitions with images, etc.

See also 2.15 What's in your bag?

Variation: Connecting movie posters

1 Organise students into groups. Select three movie posters which have something in common. This could be the subject matter, the genre, the colour, design elements, the use of light and shadow, the position of images and text type. But don't give too much away at this stage: let the students seek out the connections. Examples of movie posters can be found at http://www.impawards.com You can search for individual designers' work here. For example, *Apocalypse Now*, *Star Trek V* and *Excalibur* were all designed by the same artist, Bob Peak. A list of artists/designers can be found at: http://www.impawards.com/designers/artists.html
2 Show a selection of posters and ask students to answer the following:

   – *Describe each movie poster, including their different elements and features.*

- *What connections can you make between them?* (Give prompts where necessary here.)
- *Make deductions about the type of film from the images shown. What do you think the film will be like?*
- *Which poster do you like the most? Which is the most persuasive?*
- *Which attracts the most attention? Why?*
- *What role does the text play in the poster?*
- *Do you think they are by the same artist?*

3 The different groups report back their answers.

Follow-up

Students can bring in their own favourite movie images in the form of the DVD covers to original films and do the same tasks. What kinds of posters are most/least popular?

Other images which can be used for this task type include book jackets, CD covers and food and drink wrappers. It is a good idea for you to single out a particular genre so that it is easier for students to make connections.

Acknowledgement: *The initial task has been adapted from 'Gift game', from* Pictures for Language Learning, *Wright, A. (Cambridge University Press, 1989).*

2.4 Spot the difference

Outline	Finding differences between similar images.
Focus	Present continuous tense. Descriptive language (*in the foreground/background, on the left-hand side, in the top right corner*, etc.). *There is / There are*, present continuous, question forms. Specific vocabulary depending on images/genre chosen.
Level	Beginner–Intermediate
Time	10–20 minutes depending on the complexity of the image
Materials and preparation	CD-ROM images 2.4A Bedroom; 2.4B Bedroom with 15 changes. There are thousands of Spot the differences on the Internet. http://www.spotthedifference.com is a good example which includes photos. Students can do the tasks online and describe the differences once they have completed the task.

Note

This classic task is many teachers' first use of the visual image in class. It has a long history, but was particularly favoured by advocates of communicative language teaching as the tasks provide an 'information gap' that is conducive to communicative interaction.

In other contexts, Spot the difference is a real-life game and remains a valid classroom activity as it generates a great amount of controlled language in class. Here, I have presented a number of different Variations on the classic task, as well as different image types which work well with each.

Procedure

1 Find two images which are very similar but in which there are 'hidden' between five and ten small differences (see CD-ROM 2.4A and B as examples).

Note

You can also create these images yourself using Photoshop®.

2 Either:
Ask students in pairs to look at both images and identify the differences. This will take less time and is less strictly communicative. It could be turned into a race: the first pair to identify all the differences correctly are the winners.
Or:
Ask students, working in pairs, to keep their images hidden and to describe them to their partner in detail. They should move slowly from one detail to the next and pause to allow the other to assimilate the information.
Using this option, the students will gradually discover the differences and will need to listen more carefully to each other, and to ask questions.

3 Students report back the differences in open class.
There are 15 elements missing from Image B:

– the body's legs
– books on left-hand table
– clock on chest of drawers
– blue book on right-hand table
– croissant on plate
– right-hand lamp on wall above fireplace
– cushion on bed
– rose on side table
– finial on left bedpost
– door handle on clothes cupboard
– lower right drawer on chest

– photo frame on left-hand bookshelves
– log in fireplace
– leaning book on right-hand bookshelves
– alternate studs on side of chest in foreground.

Variation 1: Questions and answers

1 Distribute four or five similar-looking images around the class so that two or three members of the class have the same image. (Photocopies will do, as long as the differences can be clearly seen.)
2 Instead of simply describing the images and checking for differences, students circulate around the class, asking and answering questions to see if they have the same image.
You could provide question frames on the board to help lower-level students.

Is there a man standing/sitting next to . . . ?
Has he got . . . ?

3 Once students have found the person with the same image that they have, they should sit down with them and describe their image in more detail.
4 Then show all the similar-looking images and compare the differences with the whole class.

Note

Good images for this variation would be similar paintings by the same artist (e.g. similar still lifes by Cézanne, similar portraits by Rembrandt), cartoons with the same characters doing similar things (Peanuts/Tintin), movie posters (see Variation 3).

Variation 2: Doctored images

Sometimes it is more interesting to use authentic material that has not been especially designed for a Spot the difference task. Many original photos are doctored for political or aesthetic purposes (see 2.10 Is it real?). In this case, it is sometimes very hard to spot the difference, but the task is made more motivating because these are real-world images and the change has come about for a specific purpose. Search on the Internet for some real 'before and after' pictures and get your students to spot the differences.

See http://www.cs.dartmouth.edu/farid/research/digitaltampering/ for examples of digital tampering.

Variation 3: Draft versions

Sometimes different versions of the same image are designed before a definitive choice is made. This is often the case with commercial images, adverts, etc. in which various drafts or test samples are made first, or different versions are designed for different markets. Use the examples of posters from the James Bond movie *Casino Royale* at http://www.impawards.com/2006/cc.html or any other movie poster website. Get students to compare the posters and spot the differences.

2.5 Partial pictures

Outline	Students study images to identify the missing parts.
Focus	Vocabulary of objects and their separate parts. Describing what is missing.
Level	Beginner–Intermediate (young learners)
Time	10–20 minutes
Materials and preparation	CD-ROM images 2.5A Illustration – All incomplete images. 2.5B–P Images of objects with missing parts; 2.5Q Illustration – All complete images; 2.5R Illustration – Half bodies. Paper and coloured pens and pencils. These images are easy to create yourself by just cutting out a part of any flashcard that you might have, in order to distort the overall image. Another alternative is to cover parts of an image with a sticky note.

1 Make large copies of the images (CD-ROM 2.5B–P) and show them to the whole class as flashcards, one by one, or show them all the objects at once (CD-ROM 2.5A). The first to identify what is missing from these objects is the winner. Encourage the class to use modal verbs of supposition.

Note

In some cases the missing parts of the images may not be immediately obvious, for example the missing part of the lamp shade. Provide clues where necessary to guide students to the answers. To make this harder and to add an element of suspense, reveal a part of the image little by little. This can be done easily with an OHP, spreading a piece of paper over the main image and gradually removing it to reveal the image.

2 Students report back their answers and explain which images were easy to 'complete'. Give them a prompt.

Example: *That **had to** be a guitar because no other instrument looks like that.*

3 Students then look at the drawings and their complete version and describe what is missing.
4 Students in pairs create their own drawings with coloured pens/pencils. They can rub a part off and ask their partner to guess the object.

Answers: (You can suggest that learners look for a way to paraphrase if they don't know the exact words here. Also recommend that they experiment with different ways of saying the same thing as below.)

The guitar is missing its strings.
The mobile phone doesn't have any keys.
The lamp is missing the rims on its shade.
I can't see the top of the toothpaste.
The kettle needs its lead.
The wing mirror needs some glass.
There's no main switch on the remote control.
There's no plant in the plant pot.
The candle doesn't have a wick.
The binoculars are missing the part that you look through.
The sandwich needs its filling.
The illustrator has forgotten to draw a logo on the cap.
The hammer needs a proper handle.
The stamp is missing its value.
The plug doesn't have one of its contacts.

Variation 1: Half bodies

This Variation can be used to practise negative forms at elementary levels.

Once again, you can use various pictures with certain elements clearly missing (see CD-ROM 2.5R).

Students describe the drawings. Put up the following prompts on the board to help:

X doesn't have . . . / needs . . .
The illustrator hasn't . . . / has forgotten to . . .

I can't see any . . .
There's a . . . missing.

He can't . . . because he doesn't have any . . .

Ideas for basic illustrations: An empty fridge/wallet, a table with three legs, an empty bottle of wine, a hotel room without a bed.

Variation 2: Colouring or improving it

Show an illustration to the students and ask them how they would change it.

Example: *I think this needs a bit of colour. I would make this red. I would remove those chairs. It looks too crowded.*

Variation 3: Erasing the image

Draw a large and relatively complex image on the board, e.g. a room with lots of furniture in place. In pairs students look at the image carefully and describe it to their partner in as much detail as possible. Then erase almost all of the image, just leaving very small traces of it, and test the students' memories, asking them to piece the complete image back together.

2.6 Out of focus

Outline Students manipulate images digitally and attempt to decipher digital images which have been distorted. Exploiting visual clues to interpret an image.

Focus Identifying places from visual and verbal cues. Language of supposition / guessing language: *I guess . . . , I suppose . . . , It must be . . . , It could be . . . , It looks like . . . , It is too . . . to be . . .*

Level Elementary–Intermediate

Time 20 minutes

Materials and preparation CD-ROM images 2.6A–J Ten photos: Acropolis (manipulated), Christ the Redeemer (manipulated), Hong Kong Harbour (manipulated), Statue of Liberty (manipulated), Zocalo Square (manipulated), Acropolis (original) Christ the Redeemer (original), Hong Kong Harbour (original), Statue of Liberty (original), Zocalo Square (original). CD-ROM images 2.6K–O Five fisheye photos: Tunnel, London Zoo; Climbing frame, Hampstead Heath, London; British Museum, London; St Bride's Church, London; St Paul's Cathedral, London. Digital images and a means to distort them using the programme below or similar.

Note One of the best tools for distorting and transforming digital images can be found at Flickr™ Tools: http://www.bighugelabs.com/flickr/
At this site, you can change your images in the following ways:

1) Make captions and speech bubbles for photos
2) Fragment images into different pieces or create customised frames for them
3) Create mosaics with a variety of images
4) Create art cubes, magazine covers, badges from your photos.

Techniques for distorting images can be found in many software programmes. If you right-click on an image in Microsoft® Word, you will find a drop-down menu: click on the command 'Open Picture Toolbar' and then click on effects such as 'Watercolor' or 'Mosaic' and you can play around with the image as much as you like. Make sure you choose images which have relatively clear profiles so it is not too difficult for students to guess. If you don't have access to a computer, the OHP can also be used to this end, i.e. by using the focus adjustor to make the image fuzzy.

Procedure

1 Show students a selection of distorted images of cities and monuments from the CD-ROM (2.6A–E). Ask students to guess where the photos were taken (either the city or the monument, or both). Give them clues/prompts or introduce them to guessing language (*It could/might/may be*, *It seems to be*, etc.) where necessary or guide them as to whether they are 'hot' or 'cold'.

Answers: A Acropolis, Athens; B Christ the Redeemer, Rio de Janerio; C Hong Kong Harbour, Hong Kong Special Administrative Region, China; D Statue of Liberty, New York; E Zocalo Square, Mexico City.

2 Show the students the original photos (2.6F–J) and check students recognise the places and monuments. Students compare their guesses with the answers.

3 Students prepare distorted images from their own photos for the next class and follow the same procedure as above.

Variation 1: Fisheyes

An image can also look very different due to the camera angle, exposure, etc. Look at the Fisheye images on the CD-ROM (2.6K–O). (see also example Fisheye image on p. 61) Can the students identify the type of building or construction in each case?

Answers: K tunnel, London Zoo; L climbing frame, Hampstead Heath, London; M British Museum, London; N St Bride's Church, London; O St Paul's Cathedral, London.

See 2.11 How was it taken?

British Museum, London, © Nat Rea

Variation 2: Portraits

Instead of using photos of buildings and places, try portraits of famous people. You could even photograph members of your class or get the class to do so, and distort their faces. Students then have to find themselves behind the 'disguise'.

Note

If you or any member of your class has access to an Apple computer, the Photo booth feature allows you to take photos with a built-in web-cam, in different colours, and the images can be distorted in many different ways.

2.7 Tag it

Outline	Categorising images to find characteristic qualities. Giving students practice in tagging images. Providing practice in associating images with abstract concepts and moods.
Focus	Summarising skills. Adjectives of emotions, abstract nouns.
Level	Intermediate – Upper intermediate
Time	30 minutes
Materials and preparation	CD-ROM images 2.7A–D Four urban America photos: Bench, Homegoods, Phone, Structure. You can use many types of images for this activity, but it is a good idea to choose an image which communicates a mood or a particularly strong feeling. Links: Online

stock photo libraries which classify their images by tags include:
http://www.istockphoto.com
http://www.shutterstock.com
http://www.bigstockphoto.com
Access to the Internet for Variation 3.

Procedure

1 Show the students an image which would be easy to tag, e.g. CD-ROM 2.7 A–D. In other words, it should have a mixture of specific objects and at the same time transmit certain emotions, so that there is a balance between subjective and objective language.
2 Collect three or four photos from a photo archive that are linked generically and ask the students in groups to identify the differences between them and give them five tags each.
3 Each group comes to a consensus of five tags; then get students to report them back to the whole class. Remember to ask students to provide good reasons for their choices.

Sample answers: For the urban America landscape images, we could select: *Loneliness, emptiness, desolation, silence.*

4 In the case of the images taken from an online photo archive, you can refer the class to the website so that they can check if their answers match those chosen by archivers.

Variation 1: Matching tags

Provide the students with a variety of different tags which need to be matched with different images. You can introduce a few distracters here to make it more difficult. Make students justify their choices when possible.

Variation 2: Tag types

With higher-level groups, you could be more specific about the tags that they have to think of and demand that they attach five which must include an infinitive, an abstract/uncountable noun, a descriptive adjective, a countable noun, a past participle, etc.

Variation 3: Google™ Image Labeller

If you have access to computers in class, ask students individually to log on to http://images.google.com/imagelabeler/ Here they can practise giving tags to particular images with a random online partner. If they provide the same label, they receive points. The idea of the game is to improve Google™ Images search facility.

See 1.9 Flickr™ colours and 2.16 Concepts.

2.8 What's changed?

Outline	Finding differences between similar images. Contrasting and ordering photos in chronological order according to their differences.
Focus	Descriptive language: *in the foreground/background, on the left-hand side, in the top right corner*. Language focus could include the present perfect to describe (recent) changes, comparatives and the passive voice, e.g. *The roof has been destroyed.*
Level	Beginner–Intermediate
Time	30 minutes
Materials and preparation	CD-ROM images 2.8A–D Four photos: Autumn, Spring, Summer, Winter. CD-ROM image 2.8E One Thing, One Year.

Procedure

1 Find two or more different images of the same place in which there has been either a radical or a slight change. This change could have come about because of some natural disaster or urban development.

2 Students study the two images and write a text explaining what has changed. For example, if you show two different images of an Antarctic landscape, you could elicit sentences such as *The iceberg has melted*. If it is an image of a destroyed rainforest, you could elicit *These trees were cut down in 1980*.

3 Elicit ideas as to the changes and the causes of such changes. Discuss the ideas with the class.

4 Ask the class to think of a part of their town or city or any other place they know which has changed recently. Discuss the changes in small groups.

Variation 1: Tracking the date

1 Prepare a number of different photos of places that have (for whatever reason) changed markedly over the years. For example, you could select three different places and find three different photos of each, making a total of nine images.

2 Hand out the photos at random to the students, but without dates. Students mingle and have to describe their images, without showing them to each other. Although their image will have changed over time, it should

be easy for students to find the other students who have images in their sequence.

3 Once they have found their partner(s), they look at their images and identify the differences. They then put them in chronological order.
4 Students report back and reveal the correct order of each of the sequences.
5 This can lead to a discussion, the topic of which will depend on the images that you choose. For example, how man is gradually destroying the planet, the environmental problems that arise from such interventions, or the damage done by natural or other disasters.

Variation 2: Natural changes

It is not necessary to choose images of violent change which involve man's intervention. A memorable way of teaching the seasons is to show a photo of the same place in each month/season and ask students to match the photos with a particular time of year. They can then discuss the subtle changes that take place in the landscape. (See images 2.8A–D and 2.8E.)

Variation 3: Portraits / Past and present

1 Ask students to bring in photos of themselves, past and present. It is good if they can find ones of themselves as: 1) a baby or small child, 2) an adolescent, 3) an adult.
2 You can mix these up and post them up on the wall. The students have to match them to a particular person. (Obviously the people in the photo shouldn't help in any way.)
3 When students have grouped the images correctly, ask the students what has changed in each person 'over the years', e.g. *David's gone bald. He's not as slim as he used to be. He used to be blonder.*

See 2.9 Sequencing for another task which involves ordering images.

See 2.21 Is that you? for a task based on Variation 3.

See 7.7 Changing scenes for a related task.

2.9 Sequencing

Outline Students hypothesise about the next image, caption or punchline in a sequence.
Focus Modal verbs of supposition, narrative tenses, time adverbs: *next, then, finally.*
Level Elementary–Advanced

Time 30 minutes

Materials and preparation CD-ROM images 2.9A–L Photos showing different stages in a chocolate brownie recipe; 2.9M Complete chocolate brownie recipe. The images chosen should form some kind of narrative, either true or fictitious, such as a comic strip, photo stills from movies or a storyboard. Otherwise, the images should have an established order, e.g. illustrations from a technical manual giving instructions, images used to accompany a recipe, emergency instructions found on an information leaflet on a plane.

Procedure

1 Show a selection of four to six photos or images that make up a complete story, but out of sequence.
2 Students in groups put them in the correct order. (Keep the last image in the sequence back, even if that is merely the last image of a recipe showing the finished dish.)
3 Students report back their sequence, narrating the events.
4 In groups, they then imagine the last image in the sequence in order to finish the narrative. At this point you can reveal the last image.
5 Ask the class to write a narrative for the images in the form of a story or in speech bubbles / captions, depending on the image types.

Project to the class or distribute the 12 images (CD-ROM images 2.9A–L) which make up the sequence for a recipe. The students have to put these into the correct order and write captions for each step or narrate it orally. Then show the final image (CD-ROM image 2.9M) with the complete sequence for students to check their answers.

Answers: Sequence of images: (2.9) D, F, A, J, B, I, G, L, E, H, C, K.

Ingredients and instructions for the brownie recipe can be found at:
http://www.flickr.com/photos/smaky/262193604/

Variation 1: Broken sequences

Distribute three or four entire storyboards of images in class. Each student has one image which forms part of one four- or five-image sequence/ storyboard. Students have to find other members of the group that have images from the same story. They cannot show their images, but merely describe them. Once they have found all members of the group, they have to sequence the story in a logical order.

Variation 2: Sequencing image and text

Students read a story and then use this as a model to sequence a series of images. Remove an image from the story and ask students to find it by reading the accompanying text. Once they have decided on the image, they add the illustration themselves. You don't have to use a story for this Variation. The same task works well with a visual recipe.

Variation 3: Hold up picture story

Suitable for young learners and beginners. Each student is given a part of the story, e.g. CD-ROM 2.9A–L. They have to stand up, hold up their image and mingle, showing their image to everyone. The aim is for all the students to reposition themselves in a line, according to where their image fits in the sequence. Once they have formed the correct sequence, each student should read out what appears in their image, holding this up at the same time. Other students can interrupt and correct the description if and when necessary. Higher-level students can mingle and describe their images without showing each other their particular images.

Variation 4: Frozen moments

Show students a number of dramatic images from recent history. Ask students to contextualise the image: *Who can they see? Where are they? When was the photo taken?* Students then explain what happens next. Students can then research a particular image for homework and report back to the class.

Famous frozen moments could be: the image taken before President Kennedy's assassination, Diana and Dodi leaving the Paris hotel before their fatal accident, Maradona's 'hand of God' goal against England in the quarterfinals of the 1986 World Cup.

Variation 5: Students' own sequences

Students bring in their own images, e.g. a selection of photos of a wedding, a trip or a picnic, where it would be possible to work out the sequence. They could share these and challenge their classmates to order them.

Acknowledgement: *The ideas for Variation 3 come from* Pictures for Language Learning, *Wright, A., (Cambridge University Press, 1989).*

2.10 Is it real?

Outline	Students decide whether an image is a 'real' photographic representation, a 'manipulated' one, or simply a real photo of a fake object.
Focus	Fluency practice: negotiating about the authenticity of an image.
Level	Intermediate–Advanced
Time	30 minutes
Materials and preparation	CD-ROM images 2.10A Polar bear (fake); 2.10B Polar bear (real). A large number of digital images, only some of which have been distorted or manipulated.

Procedure

1 Show students two images, one of which is real and the other fake. For example, see the photos of the polar bears on the CD-ROM (2.10A and B).

2 Students in groups decide which one is real and which is fake. Ask them to justify their opinions, e.g. *It would have been too dangerous to take that photo. The scene looks manipulated. This image looks real because of the light / the colour / the position of the shadow.*

3 Explain to the class which image is real/unreal and why. You could then select other images that have been faked in other ways.

Answer: Image 2.10A is the fake one. The photographer – Hiroshi Sugimoto – took a stuffed polar bear and placed it into a naturalistic context. The seal seems to have just been killed by the bear. Sugimoto took his inspiration for this 'montage' from the dioramas in New York's Museum of Natural History. When looked at in museum cabinets, the animals seem totally fake, but change the context and the eye begins to play tricks.

4 Students draw up a list of reasons to 'fake' an image. Give prompts where necessary. This list will help give students the possibility of discussing more freely:

1) Using genuinely fake elements to trick the eye or make something more appealing as in advertising campaigns: inserting waxworks or stuffed animals, fake flowers.
2) Adding an image to 'improve' the overall effect, e.g. 'paparazzi photography', making somebody look slimmer / more attractive for aesthetic reasons (e.g. airbrushing in fashion photography).
3) Doctoring photos for political reasons, to grant a more positive or negative image to a person/situation.

Note

If you have students familiar with computer-generated imagery, ask them to brainstorm different ways that you can spot a fake image. You could focus on these criteria: illumination conditions (e.g. if one part of an image is taken at a different time of day from another, the shadowing will be different; or, if a photo is taken with a flash, that will create a different quality). Other issues could be edge sharpness, focus, resolution, colour, contrast, tone, scale.

Follow-up

1 Students can research famous fake images or historical hoaxes such as the Cerne Abbas Giant. A good source of these can be found at http://www.museumofhoaxes.com (this site includes hoax quizzes). Students report back to the class with their findings in the form of a question–answer session.

Another excellent source of images is to be found at http://www.snopes.com

2 Find an online spot the photo hoax quiz and ask students to say whether the images are real or hoax. Ask them to justify their reasons at all times. Try to give them the answers without telling them the circumstances in which the real photos were taken.

Variation 1: A real or a fake smile?

Students do this online quiz from the BBC which actually allows you to see a short video sequence of different smiles:
http://www.bbc.co.uk/science/humanbody/mind/surveys/smiles/index.shtml

Students can take photos of each other smiling and try to identify if the smiles are fake or not. How did they decide one way or the other? Which aspect in the face gives students the clue?

Note

Be careful not to offend sensitive students when doing this task.

Variation 2: Coursebook images

Students flick through their English coursebooks. Can they identify any *real* photos or do they all come from a photo archive? How can they spot the difference? In what way are some of the photos contrived or artificial-looking?

See 2.19 for a full activity on coursebook images.

2.11 How was it taken?

Outline	Giving students basic terminology to describe a photographic image: *long shot, close-up, aerial shot, mid-range shot, eye-level shot*, etc.
Focus	Fluency practice. Students negotiate and discuss how photos are composed and the effect this has on the finished image.
Level	Intermediate–Advanced
Time	20 minutes
Materials and preparation	CD-ROM images 2.11A–F Six photos: Extreme close-up, Aerial view, Low-angle shot, High-angle shot, Long shot, Eye-level shot. A selection of different photos taken from different angles and distances, such as those found in magazines and newspapers. You can use any other images of your choice for this task.
Note	There are excellent photographic examples from Flickr™ groups based on 'angles' such as: *What's your angle, buddy?; Angles, angles, angles; Alternative angle; Beautiful angles.*

Procedure

1 Elicit (or teach) the names of different kinds of shots that are used in film making, e.g. *a long shot* (which is regularly used in film as the 'establishing shot' to show surroundings and situation), *a close-up, an aerial shot, a mid-range shot.*

2 Students match the shots on the CD-ROM (2.11 A–F) with these descriptions:

1) long shot
2) close-up / eye-level shot
3) aerial / bird's eye view
4) low-angle shot
5) high-angle shot
6) extreme close-up.

Answers: 1 E, 2 F, 3 B, 4 C, 5 D, 6A.

3 Hand out a series of magazines or newspapers and ask students to identify the types of shots that are found there.

4 Ask students what kinds of shots are suitable for these contexts:
- showing the devastation of a hurricane
- highlighting the effects of cosmetic surgery on a nose
- examining the detail of a tattoo or a flower
- emphasising the height of a skyscraper
- reflecting the different colours of a landscape
- taking a photo of somebody secretly.

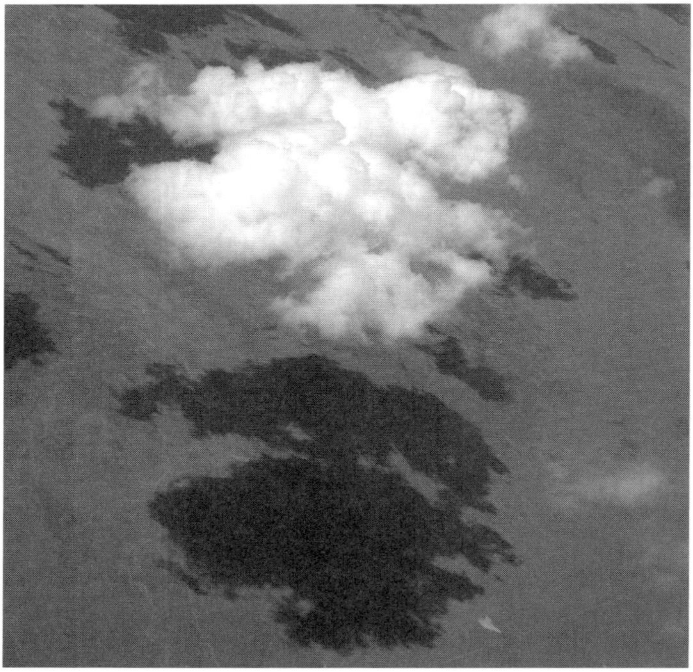

Aerial view, © Geoffrey Ingalls

Low-angle shot, © Lee Albrow

Sample answers: hurricane: aerial, nose: eye-level shot, tattoo: extreme close-up; skyscraper: low-angle shot, landscape: long shot, secretly: high-angle shot.

See 2.6 Out of focus Variation 1 for an activity on fisheye images.

Follow-up

Show students a film sequence which has plenty of action in it, e.g. a chase scene. Freeze-frame certain images and ask students to tell you what the different shots are. Discuss questions such as these:

- *Why did the director use these kinds of shots and for what effect?*
- *How do camera angles contribute to suspense and excitement?*
- *How are people and object profiles distorted by the camera angle used?*

Note

You could extend this specifically to look at different camera angles in moving images, e.g. *hand-held camera, panning shots*.

2.12 Where was it taken?

Outline	Checking students' ability to contextualise an image. Raising awareness of where a photo would appear in a real-world context and from where it was taken.
Focus	Fluency practice. Opinionating language and language of supposition: *It looks like . . .*, *It appears/seems to be . . .*, Passive voice: *It was taken by . . .*
Level	Intermediate–Advanced
Time	30 minutes
Materials and preparation	CD-ROM images 2.12A–E Photos: Medical, Surveillance, Space, Satellite, Web-cam. A selection of different photos taken in different contexts including photos of yourself. You could choose images from Google™ Earth for satellite images.

Procedure

1 Show photos of yourself taken in different contexts: in a passport booth, a formal photo (e.g. a posed university graduation photo), and an informal snap (e.g. a photo taken with a web-cam or mobile phone).

2 Ask the class questions about each photo, e.g. *Where was it taken? Who took it? A person – amateur or professional – or a machine? Is the photo posed or natural?*

3 Show students a variety of different photos or still frames from videos. Ask them to imagine their original context. (Although it may be obvious, it is important to ask learners why they have come up with these answers.)

4 For more controlled practice, you could dictate the following sentences and ask students to change them from the passive voice to the active voice.

This is an image/picture/photo taken from the air.
It was taken by someone in a plane or helicopter.
It's a satellite photo taken from space.
It's an image taken by a tiny camera inside a human body.

5 Students match the images on the CD-ROM (2.12A–E) with these genres:
1) Web-cam image
2) Surveillance (closed-circuit) image
*3) Satellite image**
4) Medical image
*5) Space image**.*
*(*images of earth)*
*(**images of planets)*

Answers: 1) E, 2) B, 3) D, 4) A, 5) C.

Follow-up

1 Surveillance photography
Set up a discussion on the issue of privacy and surveillance. For example, establish that, in the UK, the average person is recorded on CCTV cameras up to 300 times a day. Or dictate this quotation (and see if students can identify it):

> *There was of course no way of knowing whether you were being watched at any given moment. How often, or on what system, the Thought Police plugged in on any individual wire was guesswork. It was even conceivable that they watched everybody all the time.*
> (George Orwell, *Nineteen Eighty-Four,* 1949)

Group the class into two teams: A and B.

Tell group A that they feel the increase in surveillance will make us safer, and that the rise in the number of available images on the Internet, etc. will make us more knowledgeable about and aware of what's going on in the world.

Tell group B that they feel the increase in security cameras is an invasion of privacy. The sheer amount of new images available encourages us to lead sedentary lives in front of the computer.

Ask students to consider these issues in their groups among others:

1) *Surveillance cameras and issues of privacy (Is Big Brother watching you?). Are computer programs such as Google™ Earth also invasions of privacy?*
2) *The greater accessibility of images: we can see a foetus in the womb, our own house from an aerial shot on Google™ Earth, the ground underneath us as our aeroplane takes off.*
3) *We can take photos and send them instantaneously all over the world, using mobile phones and web-cams. What is the effect of this on human relationships?*

After students have discussed the issues in their groups, set up a class debate with students in group A arguing in favour of surveillance and group B arguing against. You may like to finish the debate by asking students which argument they agree with.

2 Google™ Earth
Students look at atlases or the Internet to choose a specific town or village in the world at random and then imagine what it is like: Is it green or built up? What are the streets like? They can then compare their mental image with the reality by looking at the town on http://earth.google.com.

Note

Google™ Earth may need to be installed before the maps can be viewed. It can be downloaded for free at the above address.

2.13 X marks the spot

Outline	Students study and learn to read different kinds of maps. Raising awareness about the nature of maps, and how they are able to distort reality. Questioning the objectivity of maps.
Focus	Fluency practice. Conditional forms. For Variation 3, a revision of comparative/superlative forms and present perfect.
Level	Intermediate–Advanced
Time	30 minutes
Materials and preparation	CD-ROM 2.13A Illustration-Cartographic symbols; 2.13B–E Cartograms; 2.13F Illustration – The world unites to aid Africa. A selection of different maps taken from different sources (see below). Choose images from Google™ Earth, etc. for satellite images.
Note	This activity fits in well with a cross-curricular approach, such as CLIL (Content and Language Integrated Learning), where students are studying school subjects through English.

Procedure

1 Find different types of maps (see below for types and sources) and ask students what they think they show or (if you cannot access these maps) brainstorm the different types with students.
Map types:
a) Population
b) Geological, showing type of soil/rock
c) Physical (colours are used to describe elevation)
d) Topographical (contour lines for elevation)
e) 3-D maps showing raised relief
f) Political maps marking countries
g) Time-zone maps
h) Weather maps or those of seas or tides.

Sources:
http://www.justmaps.org (for different types of maps)
http://www.worldmapper.org (for different types of cartograms)
http://www.world66.com/myworld66 At this site, students can create their own maps based on countries they have visited, those they would (not) like to visit, or any other criteria. Simply tick off the countries from a list and a personalised map will be generated.

2 Show students these roles and situations:

You are . . .
1) a driver in a traffic jam, looking for an alternative route home from work
2) a tourist planning a holiday itinerary
3) a hiker lost in the mountains
4) a traveller who has just arrived in a new city
5) a business person wanting to get from A to B in a busy city
6) an economist consulting global figures.

© Cambridge University Press 2008 PHOTOCOPIABLE

3 Ask students in groups to choose the best kind of map for each situation. Model an answer if necessary:
The best map for the driver in a traffic jam is a detailed street map so that he/she could look for a shortcut.
(Establish/elicit certain criteria that will make the task easier, e.g. scale, detail and legend of the maps and their boundaries or borders.)

Sample answers:

2) travellers' map showing major roads, tourist attractions, monuments, etc.
3) detailed mountain map showing walking routes, campsites, etc.
4) city map showing points of interest, hotels, etc.
5) detailed city street finder map
6) political map or cartogram.

4 Students report back their answers in open class.

5 Initiate a general discussion about maps to finish: Are the class good map readers? Are maps always necessary when you're sightseeing? Has a map ever let them down?

Variation 1: Guessing map symbols

1 Test students' knowledge of these cartographic legends/symbols (CD-ROM 2.13A) out of context:

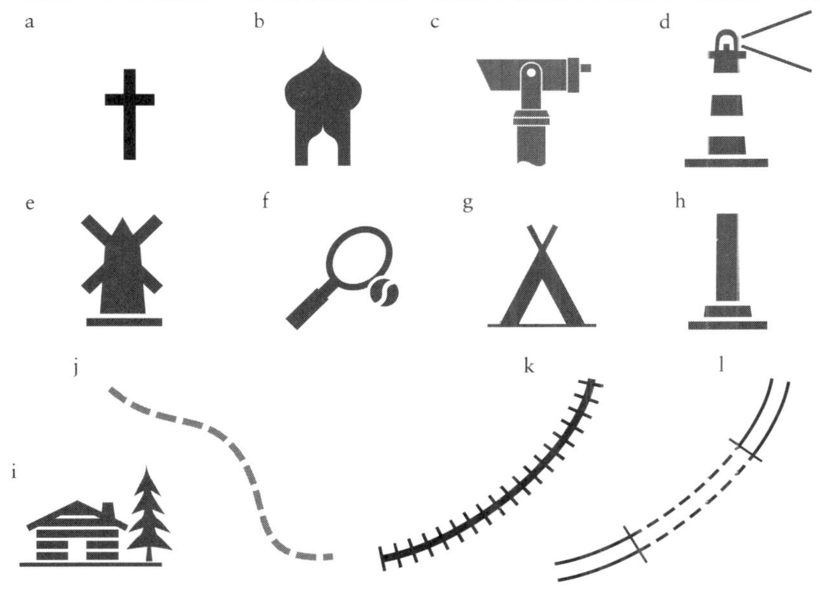

© Cambridge University Press 2008 PHOTOCOPIABLE

Answers: a church, b mosque, c lookout point, d lighthouse, e windmill, f tennis court, g campsite, h monument, i mountain lodge, j forest track, k railway, l road with short tunnel.

2 Students draw these symbols onto any map/template and test their partner on their significance.

Note

This task could also act as a lead-in for the main task above.

Variation 2: Find the route

1 Ask students what kind of maps they have at home. Tell them to bring some maps to class for the next lesson and talk about when and why they use them.
2 Make photocopies of one of the maps and give one to each student. Students work in pairs. One student selects a starting point and describes a route on the map without indicating where it is. The other student has to follow the route on the map to the final destination by listening to the directions.

Variation 3: Cartograms

Note

A cartogram is the presentation of statistical data in geographical distribution on a map. The Worldmapper website (http://www.worldmapper.org) features the maps themselves and PDF posters with all the background statistics as well.

1 Hand out or project the map based on population density from the CD-ROM (2.13B), but don't tell the students what it is.
2 In pairs, students identify the differences between it and a 'conventional' world map. Give them a prompt if necessary:

   In this map, India is much bigger and Australia is much smaller than usual. Brazil is about the same size.

   Students have to discuss these differences and guess what the map is depicting.

Example: *I think it represents population because the biggest countries in size are also the most populated.*

Show the class the same cartogram with its corresponding data (2.13C) for students to check their answers.

3 Distribute different cartograms (numbered or labelled with letters) among students in pairs. See 2.13D on the CD-ROM for another option.

Student A describes how his/her conventional map of the world has been distorted in each case and then guesses what is being represented, e.g. *The United States looks much bigger. Africa has shrunk.*

Student B knows the answer and can give clues or hints if Student A draws a blank, e.g. *It's something to do with money.*

Note

It's a good idea to choose cartograms which reveal surprising facts or are very different from the way conventional political maps represent the world.

4 Show the statistical information corresponding to each map (CD-ROM 2.13C and E). Students summarise the data, making comparative and superlative sentences about the different countries featured.

5 Show students this map, *The world unites to aid Africa* (CD-ROM 2.13F), or photocopy this smaller version. What do the class think it's called?

© Patrick Thomas

From *Working with Images* © Cambridge University Press 2008 PHOTOCOPIABLE

2.14 Abstracts

Outline Students study different kinds of abstract photos and have to identify the subject of each photo.

Focus Modal verbs of supposition (*It might be . . ., It may be . . ., It could be . . .*, etc.). Lexical sets of shapes, textures, materials.

Level Pre-intermediate–Advanced

Time 30 minutes

Materials and preparation CD-ROM images 2.14A–G Seven photos: Chinese lantern, Cucumber, Typesetting machine letters, Italian glass pen, Power switch, Tail light, Vacuum tube inverted. CD-ROM images 2.14H–O Eight photos: Balcony and Street, Wall of a house, Green fence and white wall, White lines on a football pitch, Surfboard, Football terracing, Ford Fiesta light, Ceiling. A selection of images in which the subject is not clear. This may be because the image is out of focus, taken from a strange angle or has been distorted with filters.

Procedure

1 Show students one photo from the CD-ROM (2.14A–G) as a model. Ask them to study the image and answer the following questions:

- *What is it made of?*
- *Is it natural or man-made?*
- *What would it feel like if you touched it?*
- *How much of the total object does this part represent?*
- *What is around this object?*
- *Do you think any photographic techniques have been used (e.g. filters) to distort the object?*
- *Having thought about these questions, what do you think it is? How do you know?*

Encourage the students to use modal verbs of supposition in their answers. Provide them with a model if necessary.

2 Ask students to feed back their answers in open class. Next tell students what the image is and ask them in what context they might find this image. In a magazine? On a website? What words/captions would accompany the image?

3 Show students the remaining photos and get them in pairs to answer the above questions for each image. Finally discuss students' answers in open class.

4 Ask students in pairs or groups to link the images in any way they think appropriate.

Answers: a Chinese lantern, b cucumber, c typesetting machine letters, d Italian glass pen, e power switch, f car tail light, g vacuum tube inverted.

Variation 1: Glimpsing images

Choose a selection of images in which the subject is not immediately clear. Flash up the images for a short while, allowing students to see them out of the corner of their eye. This makes the task more challenging and intriguing. You can then show them for a little bit longer until it becomes clearer what the image is. Also, if you are using any sort of projector (e.g. overhead, data, slide), the focus control can be used to make the image fuzzy.

Variation 2: Join the lines

Show the students abstract photos from the CD-ROM (2.14H–O). Students describe the number of lines, whether they are horizontal or vertical, the colour, the texture and in what context they were taken. Can they guess what the image is?

Example:

I can see one long dark vertical line running down the middle of the photo, and two short horizontal lines at the bottom. It looks like a door.

Answers:

2.14H Detail of balcony (in focus) and view of street (out of focus).
2.14I Outside wall of a house, with telephone and electricity cables. (The two horizontal side areas are boxes where the cables are kept.)
2.14J Green fence against the white wall of a football stadium.
2.14K White line measuring perimeter of football pitch and shadows of the fence alongside these lines.
2.14L Detail of surfboard.
2.14M Football terracing with stone steps, face-on.
2.14N Detail of front light of a Ford Fiesta.
2.14O Different levels of a ceiling with inset lighting.

See 7.2 Art fragments for how these images can be used in another task.

2.15 What's in your bag?

Outline	Students study the contents of different bags and pockets, and then match people's faces with their bags.
Focus	Revising or introducing the vocabulary of everyday objects. Present simple: facts, habits. *This person wears glasses / takes the bus / likes reggae*. Language of conjecture.
Level	Elementary–Advanced
Time	30 minutes
Materials and preparation	CD-ROM images 2.15A Photos of six people; 2.15B Photos of six bags; 2.15C–H Individual bag photos; 2.15I Answers; 2.15J–O Fridge magnets. You don't need any particular images for the first part of the task, just the contents of your bag or pockets. Make sure you have a range of different objects with you.
Note	For basic-level groups, choose high-frequency words such as *wallet, tissues, pen, shopping list*.

Procedure

1 This is a variation of 'Kim's game'. Take out the contents of your bag/wallet/pockets and place the different objects on the table in full view of the class. Elicit the vocabulary from the class or introduce the items yourself. You could remove the objects one by one with the students' eyes closed and ask them to remember the objects.

2 Ask students what things they carry with them on a daily basis. What do they use these things for? Do they like to carry a lot or a few things around with them? Why?

3 Show students the photos of the insides of people's bags (CD-ROM 2.15C–H). Give one photo to each group of three or four students. Ask them to identify the contents of the bag.

4 Students in groups then ascertain facts about the person and their habits, using the present simple tense, e.g. *The person likes chewing gum*. Encourage them to use other tenses as well: *I can see a bus ticket. Maybe they took the bus today*. Students report back their impressions to the class.

5 For higher levels, ask the students to imagine the personality of the person whose bag they are analysing. Model a sentence:

I think this person is quite (disorganised) because their bag looks really (messy).

6 Show students in their groups the six photos of different people and the six bags from the CD-ROM (2.15A–B). Ask them to study these images and answer the following questions:

- *What does each person look like?*
- *What kind of person do you think they are?*
- *Can you imagine their lifestyle and routines?*
- *Are you able to match the faces with the bags?*
- *What criteria have you used to do this task?*

7 Students report back the answers to the whole class. Look at all the bag contents and analyse in more detail what we know about each person from their things. Finally, reveal whose bag belongs to whom by showing students CD-ROM image 2.15I.

Bag 1, © Ben Goldstein

Variation 1: Fridge magnets

Follow the same procedure with fridge magnets. Show images CD-ROM (2.15J–O).

Ask students the following questions:

- *Do you or your families put anything on your fridge doors?* (Magnets, important information, sticky notes, postcards, etc.)

- *Why do people put things on fridge doors?* (To remind them of something or somebody every day.)
- *What can you tell about somebody's character from the way they decorate their fridge?*

Students can bring in photos of their fridges if they have interesting ones.

Variation 2: Bedroom walls

As above, students can take photos of their walls and exchange them with their partners. They can ask each other questions about what they have on their bedroom walls, where they come from and their significance.

2.16 Concepts

Outline	Analysing an image for how it communicates an abstract concept.
Focus	Fluency practice. Vocabulary: synonyms and antonyms, abstract concept nouns. Set structures: *It makes me feel . . . , I get a sense of . . .*
Level	Pre-intermediate–Advanced
Time	30 minutes
Materials and preparation	CD-ROM images 2.16A–J Ten photos of happiness: Relaxing, Double happiness Chinese symbols, Red sneakers, Ipod on the beach, Breakfast in an elegant hotel, Holiday, Feet of young girl on grass, A path in an oriental garden, Volkswagen van, Two people jumping on a beach. CD-ROM images 2.16K–P Six photos of silence: Water, Chairs covered in snow, Birds on a wire, Green path, Empty lake in China, Hotel room. CD-ROM images 2.16Q–ZH 18 children's illustrations of happiness.

Procedure

1. Write the word *happiness* in big letters in the middle of the board. Ask students to close their eyes and find an image in their mind's eye that they associate with this word. (It is important that they recall only the first image that comes to them.)
2. Ask the students, when they are ready, to come to the board and write a word next to *happiness* which they feel sums up the image that came into their heads.
3. The word *happiness* should now be surrounded by lots of other words. Ask the students to take another word which is not their own and imagine that word and *happiness* together. Ask the class: *When you merge the two words, what image comes to mind?*

4 Get students to report back their mental images. For example, a student who had chosen *happiness* and *sunshine* could say: *I see myself coming out of the sea and running along the sand to dry off.*
5 Show students a selection of images that capture happiness (CD-ROM 2.16A–J). Are they similar to their visual images?
6 Students find similarities between any of the 'happiness' images. They answer the following questions:

- *Which are the most direct and indirect expressions of happiness?*
- *Do you identify with them?*
- *What other words could sum up the images? Are they synonyms or antonyms of happiness?*
- *Which images of happiness do you find the most powerful / the most expressive? Why?*
- *Are there any images which you don't consider happy at all?*

Two people jumping on a beach, © Niro Taub

7 Show 18 images from the CD-ROM (2.16Q–ZH) of children's art, *Happiness is . . .* Ask students: *In what way are children's concepts of happiness different from our own?*

Sample answer: Happiness here seems to be associated with smiling and affection, pets, nature and open space, a frozen moment in time, holidays, music, objects of desire (mobile, ice cream, transport) and hobbies such as football.

8 Follow the same procedure for the word *silence* by looking at the six photos on the CD-ROM (2.16K–P). What mental images come to the students' minds when they hear the word *silence*? What do they think of these images?

Note

Other good concepts to choose are: *solitude*, *peace*, *pride*. Also, for lower levels, adjectives connected with the senses are good (*soft, sweet, blue*, etc.).

See Chapter 4 for more tasks on visualising images and imaging.

2.17 Cartoon captions

Outline	Matching words and images using cartoons. Understanding visual jokes, wordplay.
Focus	Writing and analysing captions for cartoons. Spoken and idiomatic language.
Level	Pre-intermediate–Advanced
Time	30 minutes
Materials and preparation	CD-ROM images 2.17A Illustration – Talk fast. I'm roaming; 2.17B Illustration – Sometimes I feel so empty inside; 2.17C Illustration – Maybe there was something to that whole global warming thing; 2.17D Illustration – Hey, what's up; 2.17E Illustration – Uh oh. We're in trouble; 2.17F Illustration – Isn't he cuddly; 2.17G Illustration – You're too strict!; 2.17H Illustration – No water for me, thanks! 2.17I–P Same cartoons without speech bubbles. You will also need a selection of photos from newspapers / magazines.

Procedure

1 Show examples of how images and words are related, e.g. a photo from a newspaper, and ask students to think of a possible caption.

2 Explain that an image in a photo library can have one or many 'tags' (key words) to identify the particular characteristics of the image. Show any image and ask the class to come up with some particular tags for it.

See 2.7 Tag it.

3 Find a series of cartoons or any other images – six to ten is a good number – with a short accompanying text (the shorter the better) in the form of either a caption or a speech bubble. These are easily found in the daily press or in comic books alternatively see CD-ROM (2.17A–H).

Note

The text should not be simply descriptive, otherwise the task will be too simple, but should allude (in an indirect way) to the image. However, this can be varied according to level.

4 If you are using your own images, erase the text but keep a copy of the text you have erased. If you have accessed the image digitally, you can do this with Photoshop®; if not, simply blank out the text with correction fluid or place a sticky note over the words. Alternatively see CD-ROM (2.17I–P) where the text has been removed from the cartoons.

5 Collect all the captions / speech bubbles and write them out in a list (see below). Then gather together the images without text.

6 Seat the students in groups of three or four and distribute the images and texts which the students have to match.

7 Set a time limit and ask a certain group of students to report back to the rest of the class with their opinions.

Speech bubble texts from CD-ROM (2.17A-H):

1) No water for me, thanks!
2) Hey, what's up?
3) Sometimes I feel so empty inside.
4) Maybe there was something to that whole global warming thing.
5) Uh oh. We're in trouble.
6) You're too strict!
7) Isn't he cuddly?
8) Talk fast. I'm roaming.

© Mitra Farmand

From *Working with Images* © Cambridge University Press 2008 PHOTOCOPIABLE

8 Elicit what makes the caption funny/strange/unusual. Clear up any ambiguities with the class and ask for alternative captions if necessary. Can the students improve on the ones given?

For example, *Sometimes I feel so empty inside* is normally said by someone who is feeling depressed or sad, not by a doughnut!
Explain that the humour in these particular cartoons comes from the fact that animals or inanimate objects are humanised in this way. The cartoons also use 'play on words' for comic effect, e.g. *to roam*, which can refer both to mobile phones and to an animal wandering around a field.

Follow-up

Students are given pictures/cartoons and have to invent captions – these could then be written on strips, and the pictures and the captions be displayed on the board or around the room for the class to match up.

Note

A great way for students to add captions and speech bubbles to photos is to go to http://www.bighugelabs.com/flickr/ and then choose the 'captioner' option. Students can upload their own photos to the website and can opt for speech balloons, thought bubbles or single-word captions. They then drag these captions and place them anywhere on the image.

See 1.7 Speech bubbles.

2.18 Room with a view

Outline	Students describe the view from their house in as much detail as possible, and then look at different people's views and imagine where they are from.
Focus	Basic vocabulary for describing views: *There is / There are . . .*, *I can see / make out . . .*, etc.
Level	Elementary–Advanced
Time	30 minutes
Materials and preparation	CD-ROM images 2.18A View from room 1; 2.18B View from room 2; 2.18C View from room 3.

Procedure

1 Students close their eyes and imagine the view from their bedroom in as much detail as possible. Ask them to think of how they would describe this with the language they have at their disposal. Let them think about this for a few minutes.

2 Students, in pairs, describe the view from their bedroom. Make sure they do not add too many details about the location of their house. For lower-level students, provide a prompt or describe your own view.

From my window I can see / make out . . .
There's / There are . . .
I have a view of . . .

(This activity clearly works best if the students do not know where their partner lives.)
As Student A describes the view, Student B can ask any questions to help them get a better impression of the place:

- *Can you see people from your room?*
- *Can you see the street?*
- *How much sky can you see?*
- *What colour are the buildings, the roofs?*

3 Once the students have finished their descriptions, their partners have to guess the location. If students live in the same city, Student B has to guess which neighbourhood / part of the city his/her partner lives in. If students come from different cities/countries, Student B has to build up a mental picture and imagine the area and report back his/her images to Student A.
Ask students to reverse roles, Student B now describes their view and Student A asks questions about his/her partner's view.

Examples:
You live on top of a hill. That's why you have a panoramic view.
You live in the centre of town. That's why you can see lots of shops.
You live in the middle of the country. That's why you can only see green.

4 Direct students' attention to the three photos on the CD-ROM (2.18A–C). Explain that these were taken from three different people's bedroom windows. Students describe each view and try to imagine where each one is.

Note

With lower levels, it is a good idea to do stage 4 at the start of the procedure. This way, the images themselves act as a prompt to model the necessary language.

Variation: Change your view

In addition to describing the views from their rooms, students discuss what they would do to improve the view or make it different. Establish some sentence stems according to level.

Examples:
I'd make the road narrower.
I would like to put a green hill there.
I'd prefer there to be a lower building.

See 1.8 Minimal differences and 4.7 Hotel rooms for similar tasks.

2.19 Coursebook images

Outline	Students interpret images or illustrations from language coursebooks (old or current).
Focus	Raising awareness as to how images relate to tasks in language-learning materials. Fluency practice: students discuss the role of images in class. Descriptive adjectives.
Level	Pre-intermediate–Advanced
Time	30 minutes
Materials and preparation	Your current coursebook or a number of different coursebooks.

Procedure

1 In pairs, ask students to discuss criteria for good coursebook artwork using this sentence frame:

The pictures in a coursebook should be . . .

If necessary, prompt students with certain descriptive adjectives to help them: *up-to-date, contemporary, eye-catching, memorable, attractive, interesting*; or concepts: *similar to those we see outside the classroom, make me interested in a topic, help me learn a particular structure, be not merely decorative.*

2 Students report back their opinions in open class. As a class, devise criteria for judging coursebook artwork, e.g. must be up-to-date and attractive.

3 Students look at their own coursebook or you can distribute other coursebooks if available. Students then evaluate the artwork according to the criteria the class has devised.

4 Students report back with their favourite images or coursebooks and explain why they like them.

Variation 1: Memorable images

Ask students to go through their coursebook and analyse the images. Which are their (least) favourite and why? Which are the most memorable and why? Which of the images will help them remember a structure or an item of vocabulary? How many images are merely decorative and not required for a particular task? Would they have been able to learn the structure, etc. as well without the image?

Variation 2: Image survey

Ask students to go through a given coursebook and classify the images in more detail. Ask students to answer the following questions:

1 *How many images of . . . are there?*
   1) *people*
   2) *landscapes*
   3) *interiors*
   4) *buildings*
   5) *objects*
2 *What is the ratio of illustrations to photos?*
3 *How would you describe these images in more detail? For example, regarding people:*
   - *Are they stereotypical? Western-orientated? Multicultural? Monocultural?*
   - *Do they represent different ages? Social classes?*
   - *Are the images real or airbrushed (Photoshopped)?*
   - *Are they models or real people?*
   - *What percentage of the people are smiling?*
   - *What makes them similar to or different from images of people you find in other media?*
   - *Where do you think the images were sourced?*

Finally discuss students' answers in open class.

2.20 Found images

Outline	Students guess the context of found images.
Focus	Practising the language of supposition and description: *It could be . . . , It looks like . . . , It seems to be . . .* Revising vocabulary of description/position.
Level	Elementary–Advanced
Time	30 minutes
Materials and preparation	CD-ROM images 2.20A–H: Wedding photo, Framed portrait, Landscape, Holiday snapshot, Interior, Passport photo, Stock photo, Vintage photo.

Procedure

1 Show the students the different images on the CD-ROM (2.20A–H). Tell students to imagine that they were found somewhere and have no owner. Perhaps they were found in the street, an antiques market, a junk shop or a charity shop.

2 Ask students to match each photo with one of the eight descriptions (1–8) below. You may need to pre-teach some of this vocabulary. If students need prompting, do the first as an example.

1) interior
2) landscape
3) vintage photo
4) passport/ID photo
5) formal photo (e.g. wedding or group photo)
6) framed portrait
7) holiday snapshot
8) stock/archive photo

3 Students report back their answers. Ask them to use the language of supposition (modals) where possible, or synonyms.

This ***is clearly / must be*** *a passport photo because you can see the blue curtain in the background.*

Answers: 1 E, 2 C, 3 H, 4 F, 5 A, 6 B, 7 D, 8 G.

4 In open class, ask the following questions:
- *Were they posed or spontaneous? How can you tell?*
- *Are they contemporary or old-fashioned?*
- *Have you taken a photo similar to one of these? When and for what reason?*

5 Group the students and ask each group to select a photo which they then have to describe in more detail.

For students who have not seen this language previously, ask them to look at snapshot 2.20D on the CD-ROM and complete the description.

This is a a) ______. The quality of the image isn't very good. In the far b) ______, you can see some modern buildings against the skyline. On the right, in the c) ______ , you'll find some other modern buildings. In the d) ______, you can see a man wearing a red T-shirt standing on a walkway of a modern building. On the e) ______, there is an old building with stone columns and f)__________ the building, there are some tourists with cameras.

© Cambridge University Press 2008 PHOTOCOPIABLE

Answers: a) holiday snapshot, b) distance, c) background, d) foreground/centre, e) left, f) in front of.

6 Students report back their descriptions to the class.
7 Ask the class if anyone has ever found a photo or discovered one which was not their own. What was it a photo of? Do they still have it? Did they ever find its owner?

Variation: Story-making

Note

http://www.isthisyou.co.uk and http://www.picturesifoundonthestreet.com are collections of found photos. The sites publish these photos online and thus attempt to reunite them with their owners.

Students can access site http://www.isthisyou.co.uk and choose a photo. They make up stories about the photo, its owner and where it was found. Remember, the photo could have been lost, dropped, stolen, left in a photo booth or thrown away. Students can decide for themselves. In some cases, they can then check where the photo was really found and then keep track of its history online, to see if the owner has been reunited with it.

2.21 Is that you?

Outline	Spotting likenesses in photos to establish their identity. Matching text descriptions to selected photos. Writing captions for photos.
Focus	Language of explanation and reasoning (*This is the same person because . . .*), language of physical characteristics (*bald, blonde,* etc.)
Level	Intermediate–Advanced
Time	45 minutes – 1 hour
Materials and preparation	CD-ROM images 2.21A Six passport photos; 2.21B–G Individual passport photos; 2.21H Photos of the people at different ages; 2.21I–N Answers. You will also need two old photos of yourself in which you appear with other people.

Procedure

1 Ask students if they have many photos of themselves. Where do they keep them? In a photo album, on their computer, in a drawer, organised or disorganised? Are there any on display, on the wall, in frames? Do they have a favourite photograph of themselves? Why is it their favourite? How has digital photography changed the way we look at / store these photos?

2 Show one or two old photos to the class in which you appear with other people. Can the students identify you? Was it easy or difficult to do this?

3 Tell students that they are going to look at six passport photographs on the CD-ROM (2.21A–G). In pairs, they decide how they would describe each one. Students report back their descriptions in open class.

4 Show the class the other 18 photos on the CD-ROM (2.21H) or print these out. Students, in pairs or groups, match the captions opposite with the images.

Answers: 1) B; 2) C; 3) F; 4) D; 5) Q; 6) H; 7) N; 8) K; 9) I; 10) R; 11) L; 12) O; 13) G; 14) P; 15) A; 16) E; 17) M; 18) J.

Focus attention on different expressions used to describe the images (e.g. *This is . . ., This (must have been / was) taken . . ., This must be . . ., I was only x when this was taken.*

WORKSHEET

1 My sister and me in the bath. I was only a few months old and had very fat cheeks!

2 This was me on holiday in Andalusia, 1991. I made the flower out of candlewax and put it in my sunglasses to match the silly hat!

3 On a work camp, at 16 years old. I was helping to rebuild an abandoned town in the mountains. A whole month of digging!

4 Taking the ferry 'cross the Mersey, on a trip to Liverpool. I was visiting my first 'real' boyfriend there.

5 At the age of four, it was easy to find me on top of the most incredible places.

6 My first days in Europe, feeling very happy, showing the 'thumbs up'!

7 This one is of me on the kibbutz in Israel where I was born – I learnt to speak in Hebrew and my first word was 'Tractor'.

8 Here I am sitting in the fields on a family picnic just outside Leeds, where I grew up. Music was my first love . . .

9 Here I am pretending to fly and laughing in my grandfather's garden

10 We played for hours on this rocking horse. It's the only toy I remember . . .

11 Eating and sleeping have always been my favourite activities.

12 This was taken during the Edinburgh festival – in the early nineties, I think. I did some work in a theatre venue there.

13 My first experience in front of the camera. The promise of 'Look at the birdy' seemed to work, but I was then disappointed that no birdy appeared.

14 This was the beginning of my 'New Romantic' phase – I let my hair grow!

15 At the age of 18, I also had 'my own private Idaho'.

16 This is me on holiday in Quintero (Chile) with my parents when I was seven.

17 We had many cats in our family, but this one was a friend's. I must have just got back from travelling around Asia because I'm wearing an Indonesian shirt.

18 Christmas holidays with my folks. Every day lying on the sofa without doing anything, when I really had to study! My first and only attempt to let my hair grow long.

© Cambridge University Press 2008 PHOTOCOPIABLE

5 Students then match each of the six people in the passport photos with three of the older photos. They can discuss in small groups and then check their answers with others. Students report back in open class.
6 The class can then discuss the links between all the photos and the written descriptions / photo captions. Show the answers (CD-ROM 2.21I–N). Ask in open class if there were any surprises.

Follow-up

Ask students to bring into class old photos of themselves taken at various ages. They can play the same game as above. To finish, they can choose particular images and practise writing captions for the photos.
This could become an interesting writing class on 'describing a photograph', comparing formal and informal descriptions of portraits and snapshots.

See 1.12 Written descriptions for similar tasks.

Acknowledgement: *The original idea for this task comes from the book* it's personal (*iT's Magazines, 2007*).

2.22 Paired images

Outline	Students distinguish, through images, the difference between two contrasting grammar items.
Focus	Any grammatical structure that you would like to introduce or review. It is useful to choose areas which can be easily confused and which represent a clear dichotomy, such as active versus passive voice, countable versus uncountable nouns, *to do something* versus *to have something done*, stative versus dynamic verbs.
Note	The difference between structures may be quite subtle. As such, the image acts as a convenient shortcut both for presenting and for testing understanding of these differences in meaning.
Level	Pre-intermediate and above (depending on the targeted structure).
Time	30 minutes
Materials and preparation	CD-ROM images 2.22A–G Seven paired illustrations. Project the drawings in class or print them out for use in class. Prepare some questions before the class, based on the illustrations which incorporate the structure that you wish to target.

Procedure

1 Focus students' attention on the first two drawings, of Ken and Brock (CD-ROM 2.22A). Ask in open class the prepared questions to make sure the students have understood the distinction between the two structures (the active and passive voice). Ask the first question and elicit the answer from the class:

Who left his girlfriend?
Ken left his girlfriend.

Then ask the second question and elicit the answer:

Who was left (by his girlfriend)?
Brock was left (by his girlfriend).

2 Show the students at least three more sets of drawings from the CD-ROM (2.22B–D) and follow the same procedure as for the first pair of sentences.

3 Students complete the task by asking and answering the same questions about the remaining pictures (CD-ROM 2.22E–G). To finish, tell them to write out the sentences which describe each of the drawings. Monitor carefully to check that they have done this correctly.

Sample answers:

2 Thelma drove (the car). / Linda was driven by the taxi driver.
3 Keith stopped (to tie his laces). / Leo was stopped by the police.
4 Glenda passed the other two runners. / Diana was passed by the fastest runner.
5 Nemo ate (the plankton). / Goldie was eaten by the big fish.
6 Craig forgot (something). / Philip was forgotten on his birthday.
7 Tracey taught (him to play the guitar). / Maria was taught by the teacher.

6 Encourage the students to expand upon the sentences so that they get more practice, e.g. *Ken left his girlfriend because he didn't love her any more. Brock was left because his girlfriend didn't love him any more.*

7 Students report back their sentences in open class. Listen to the different ways that they have completed the sentences and correct accordingly.

© Cambridge University Press 2008 PHOTOCOPIABLE

3 Creating images

This unit gives students the opportunity to interpret images and create their own. An important concern here is to reassure those students who may be reluctant to draw in class because they feel that they lack technical skill. Students should be encouraged to produce something (even if that amounts to a matchstick-man sketch) which is personal and particular to them and which can be used as a springboard for conversation and comparison with others. In contrast to many other tasks which are teacher- or text-led, here the learner is at the centre of each activity. As such, the teacher should take a reactive approach where possible, responding to the unexpected directions in which the students' images might take the class.

Students begin by creating their own collages, before drawing caricatures of themselves (3.2 Staring at yourself). This is followed by a look at photo stories in which learners analyse the relationship between text and image in order to create their own narratives. As such, they have to consider how the two disciplines combine to create the overall meaning and how they expect a viewer to interact with the photo story. Another task which works at this level is 3.7 Movie storyboards. This activity takes us a step further in the process of visualising a story by asking students to be engaged in different disciplines at the same time. Here, learners have to imagine the setting, soundtrack or sound effects, a possible voice-over and the action that takes place within each frame. To do this, they need to consider the camera angle, lighting and sound to create an overall effect.

Equally challenging, but on a less ambitious scale, students are also encouraged to think of important symbols in 3.6 Visual biographies. Here, they create a personalised template of images, communicating important aspects of their life visually. Such a task is suitable for the start of the course, providing an original way for students to get to know each other.

Two other tasks are more game-like in nature, in that the images form a kind of code which needs to be cracked in order to unravel a text (3.5 Visual limericks and 3.10 Draw a sentence). In the first, a limerick is presented pictorially and the images are used to help students reconstruct the text from memory. In the latter, images act as a prompt for practising a particular grammar structure – in this case, the present continuous tense. External images also act as models for the students in a number of tasks. These are provided in the form of Makeovers (3.11) and Pastiches (3.9).

3.1 Create your own collage

Outline	Students describe the objects, people, events and places that are important to them and display them in the form of a collage.
Focus	Speaking practice (explanatory monologue and asking questions). Writing short accompanying texts.
Level	Pre-intermediate and above
Time	1 hour (over two classes)
Materials and preparation	In the lesson prior to this one, you should ask students to bring to class photos, drawings, memorabilia and souvenirs which can be used to form a personal collage. Card, glue and scissors are also necessary.

1 In a previous lesson, ask students to think of one place, two events, three people and four objects which are important to them. (Or you can vary this if you like, e.g. two places, one person, etc.) Ask them to write these down in a list form. Give them a good ten minutes for this. Also create a list yourself.

2 Seat the students in pairs. Ask the class to explain to each other why these things are significant. Encourage them to ask additional questions where appropriate.

Present examples from your own list to the students as a model: *Dungeness is the name of the beach that I love on the south coast of England. It has special associations for me because I used to go with friends every summer . . .*

3 Ask students to report back information about their partners, e.g. *George has chosen his best friend, Isaac. He met him when he was four and they've known each other ever since . . .*

4 Tell the class that, in the next lesson, they will prepare collages that illustrate their choices. Remind them to bring pictures, photos or any other memorabilia, no matter how small or irrelevant.

5 In the next lesson, students work individually to prepare their collage. The more images they bring to class, the better. Monitor carefully as the students prepare their collages, asking questions and making sure students know how to describe all the different visual elements and can explain their significance.

6 Seat students in groups of three, ensuring that students are not with their partner from the previous lesson. They take turns to ask and answer

questions about their collages. Students describe what they have learnt about their partners.

7 Students then write a brief text about some or all of the images in the collage, explaining their significance. These can be posted along with the collages on the classroom walls. Students go around the room looking at the collages and discovering what they have in common. Students report back any coincidences in open class.

Note

Students are more likely to remember facts about their partners through these visuals than via a text. As such, this is a good task to do as an alternative 'getting to know you' activity.

Variation: Homemade collages

Students make the collage as a homework task, rather than in class. Those that have access to computers can prepare their collage using tools like Google™ Image Search and Photoshop®. This variation would be suitable if you wanted to set the task as project work.

See 3.6 Visual biographies and 5.10 Favourite things for other tasks which use students' personal information.

See 7.2 Art fragments.

3.2 Staring at yourself

Outline	Students draw caricatures of themselves and describe them to each other.
Focus	Fluency practice. Vocabulary of the body, physical characteristics and gesture. Comparatives and superlatives.
Level	Pre-intermediate and above
Time	30 minutes
Materials and preparation	A3 blank pieces of paper and crayons or felt pens.

Procedure

1 Explain/elicit the meaning of the word *caricature*.
Caricature: To draw or describe someone or something in a way that makes some aspects of them seem funny.

2 Draw on the board or show the class a caricature image of yourself. Ask the class to describe it.

Example: *You have big lips, a large nose, thick eyebrows*, etc.

3 Ask students to draw a self-portrait as if it were a caricature, highlighting their most characteristic physical features. They should focus on their faces only. Ask them to treat this as a fun task and not to take it too seriously. They should not show their caricatures to any of the other students.

Note

Another way to take the seriousness out of the task is to ask students to draw with the hand they wouldn't normally use for writing or drawing.

4 Collect all the sketches and rearrange them. Redistribute the pictures randomly, one caricature to each member of the class. Be careful that a student does not receive his/her own caricature.

5 Each student tries to identify the self-portrait that they have been given. They should look carefully at all their classmates. When they think they have found their 'partner', they should approach them and attempt to describe the portrait together. During the mingling, all students approach each other and carry out the task in this way, describing and comparing each other's caricatures.

6 Display the most interesting and/or funniest self-portraits. The students can practise the target lexis here (vocabulary of face and gesture) and comparatives and superlatives to discuss the different images.

Variation: Celebrities

If you have a class that enjoys drawing, students can then draw famous people, following a similar procedure to the above.

Follow-up

Explain or elicit the fact that caricatures have existed as a way to ridicule public figures and that they are still used in the media to poke fun at politicians, celebrities, etc.

Famous caricatures from the past can be seen at http://www.greatcaricatures.com

Sources:

Additional tasks could be based on the following websites:

1 William Hogarth: Characters and Caricatures, 1743:
http://en.wikipedia.org/wiki/Image:1743_caricaturas_280.jpg
For advanced-level groups, students select one caricature from the above image and describe it. His/her partner has to identify the exact caricature from a sea of exaggerated faces.

2 Political caricatures were a feature of *Punch* magazine, until it closed in 2002 (see examples at http://www.punchcartoons.com).
Students choose different caricatures from different sections of the website and research them.
3 There are some original caricatures at http://www.flickr.com/groups/caricatures/pool/

See 3.4 Wanted.

3.3 Teenage photo stories

Outline	Students analyse photo stories from teenage magazines and create their own storyboards of 'cringe' stories.
Focus	Reading and writing practice. Narrative tenses: past perfect, past continuous, past simple, present perfect.
Level	Intermediate and above
Time	1 hour
Materials and preparation	A photo story from an adolescent girls' magazine (good sources are *Mizz*, *Bliss*, *Seventeen*) or simply 'cringe' stories* from the same sources. Ask students to come to class with a camera or a mobile phone with camera facility.
Note	If you do not have the facility to print out images in class, ask the students to follow the procedure from step 6 at home as project work.

Procedure

1 Ask students if they know of any photo stories in teenage magazines. Have they ever read these stories? What kind of dramatic events occur in them?
2 Students read the following story which comes from *Bliss*, a UK magazine for teenage girls.

My friend had just brought me home from school, and our mums were having one of their chats. My friend loves horses and there was a field opposite my house with four horses in so I took her over to see them whilst our mums talked. The field was right next to where my crush lived and he had just got home from school too so I was trying to play it cool by sitting on the fence and rocking backwards and forwards. However, I lost my balance and fell backwards, head-first into the horse's water bucket. I was drenched from head to toe in my school uniform and I don't think I have ever seen that boy laugh as much.

© Bliss Magazine
From *Working with Images* © Cambridge University Press 2008 PHOTOCOPIABLE

* Cringe stories are true tales which have an embarrassing outcome.

3 Students discuss how they could present this information visually. How many storyboard images would they create and what would each of them include?
4 Seat students in groups of four, and ask them to write out their own 'cringe story' of between 100 and 150 words. Point out the typical structure of such a story:
   1 *Opening: Past perfect to set the scene.*
   2 *Body: Combination of past simple and past continuous to describe events in the story.*
   3 *Closing: Present perfect or future* will, *to describe feelings at the time or predictions about the event happening again.*

   Explain that the story must be quite dramatic and the ending embarrassing in some way or another. Ask the students to set the scene in their homes or at school with not too many props, so that it is easy to 'film' or capture visually. Tell them to feature the same number of characters as there are members in their group.
5 Tell students they are going to turn their cringe stories into photo stories and they should think of approximately nine images to go in their storyboard.
6 Once they have agreed on the images for the story, students take photos of each other acting out the parts in the story. Next provide the students with large pieces of card so that they can print the images out and lay them out as a storyboard. Students can add speech/thought bubbles as necessary.
7 Students then present their work as posters. Alternatively, the groups can act out the drama in front of the class.
8 The whole class can then vote for the most embarrassing stories and discuss what they would have done in each case.

Variation: Using other genres and media

Other story types and genres, for example a crime or soap-opera episode, also lend themselves to this kind of photo story treatment. You could record an interesting soap-opera episode and play a section of it for students to turn into storyboards.

Note

Stories can also be shown as PowerPoint presentations if you have access to the technology.

See 3.7 Movie storyboards.

3.4 Wanted

Outline Students analyse and design 'Wanted' notices with photos of each other.

Focus Fluency and writing practice. Vocabulary: crimes and offences.

Level All

Time 30 minutes

Materials and preparation CD-ROM images 3.4A Wanted poster (old); 3.4B Wanted poster (contemporary); 3.4C Illustration – Free to good home poster. Blank pieces of paper, size depending on the size of the image. Ask students to bring to class a photo of themselves. This could be a passport-size photo, but the larger the image, the better. Make sure you bring some photos of yourself if students fail to do so. Alternatively, if you have a small class and the necessary technology, students can take photos during class time. Ask them beforehand to bring digital cameras and pictures of pets.

Procedure

1 Establish the concept of a Wanted poster by encouraging students to picture one in their mind. Establish the following information that typically appears on such posters:

A mug shot or a facial composite image done by a police artist, the word 'Wanted', a reward, the reason why this person is wanted by the police, a telephone number to ring in case you spot this person or have information about them, the person's last known whereabouts and a physical description to match the photo. Any other extra information about this person (e.g. 'armed and highly dangerous').

2 Show students an old-fashioned-style Wanted poster, such as the one on the CD-ROM (3.4A) and a more contemporary one (3.4B). Ask: *What is the difference between the two posters?*

Note

You can find any number of such images online by keying in 'wanted poster' in Google™ Images.

Sample answers:

Contemporary poster: There is no reward for capture in the contemporary poster. The description is laid out in a list. The photos of the wanted man show him in different guises, with and without facial hair/glasses. It's not entirely clear what his crime is.

Old-fashioned poster: The description, written in one paragraph, includes some subjective or vague language (*sulky appearance, looks like a blacksmith*, etc.). Photos include background, whereas the contemporary images look like passport shots.

3 Collect face photos from your students (include some of your own if students fail to bring them to class) and redistribute them randomly, giving out one per student / pair of students. Ask the class to design a poster with the photo of their classmate, in either the contemporary or the old-fashioned style.

Note

Remember to ask students not to take the task too seriously. Rather than include serious crimes, it is probably better if they make up 'fun versions', e.g. *Wanted for arriving late to class every day this week.*

4 Students stick up the posters around the room and vote for the best one. Students report back to the whole class on what were the most common crimes committed.

Sources:

You can create 'cowboy'-style Wanted posters at:
http://www.glassgiant.com/wanted/

Variation 1: Wanted poster template (young learners / lower levels)

If you are reading a novel or watching a film in class, a fun activity is to get students to complete a Wanted poster for one of the characters. Students refer to the text or film to complete information about:

- last known whereabouts and/or address
- physical description
- particular information we need to know
- who to contact in case the person is spotted.

Variation 2: 'Free to a good home' posters

Get students to bring in pictures of pets. Explain to students the concept behind 'Free to a good home' posters. These are posters which offer a pet to the general public because the owner cannot maintain it.

Get students to prepare their own posters by describing their pets to try to encourage people to take them in. Direct students to the poster on page 105 or the CD-ROM (3.4C). Elicit why it is original/funny.

© Cambridge University Press 2008 PHOTOCOPIABLE

3.5 Visual limericks

Outline	Students analyse and create their own limericks both in words and in images.
Focus	Listening comprehension practice and writing verse.
Level	Pre-intermediate and above
Time	45 minutes
Materials and preparation	Prepare a sample limerick to show to the class as a lead-in model. CD–ROM image 3.5 Illustration – Visual limerick.

Procedure

1 Write the following limerick on the board:

There was an old man from Peru
Who dreamt he was eating his shoe.
He awoke in a fright

In the middle of the night
And found it was perfectly true.

2 Explain to / elicit from students the basic characteristics of the limerick:
   – *It tells a little story.*
   – *It is humorous (and based on one character).*
   – *It follows a particular rhythm and rhyme pattern (AABBA).*
3 Read out the limerick again and ask students to indicate the stressed words. (They should hear the marked intonation on the last word of each line.)
4 Tell students to draw a short storyboard of the limerick to help them remember it.

Note

If your students are not keen on drawing and you have access to computers, ask students to log on to Google™ Images and find a sequence of images that match the limerick. They can copy these and create their own storyboard that way.

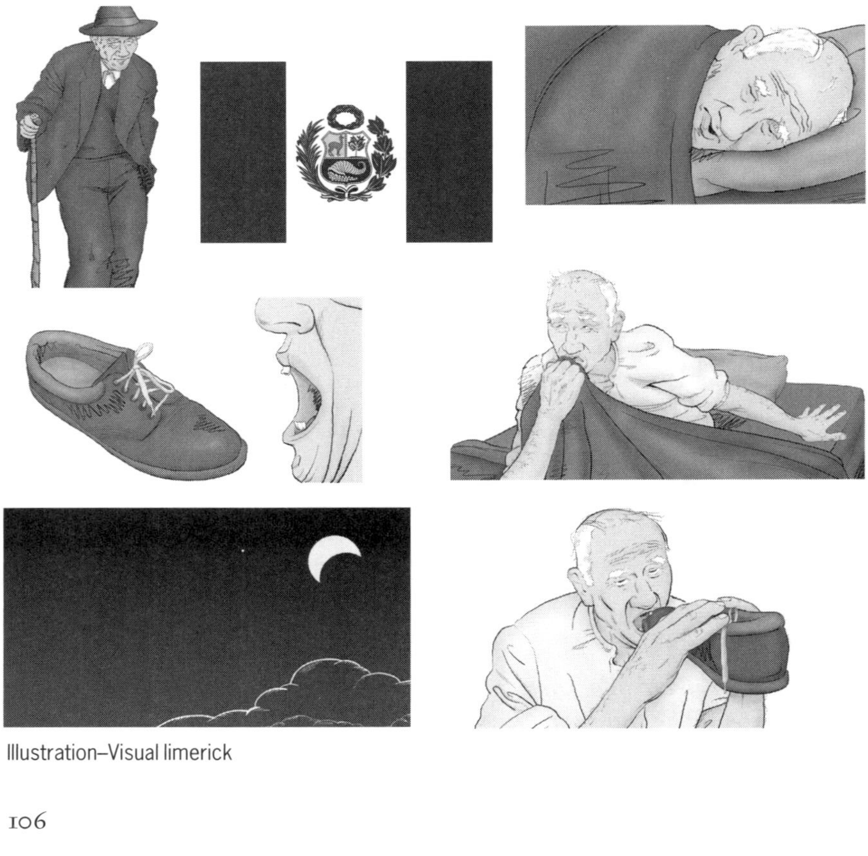

Illustration–Visual limerick

5 Students report back, showing their basic storyboards. Select one and show it to the rest of the class. Compare it with the version on the CD-ROM (3.5).
6 Write this limerick template on the board:

There was a ________________
Who ____________________
He/she ______________
____
And ____________________

7 Students look at the same images on the CD-ROM and complete the gaps in the template, using the images to help them reconstruct the limerick.
8 Students report back their versions. Correct and/or help the class reconstruct and reformulate phrases where necessary.
9 In pairs or small groups, the class write their own limericks using the template and then find or draw a few images to accompany their verse. They show the images in the correct sequence to the class and the others have to reconstruct the whole limerick.

Notes

1 Some limericks can be quite offensive, so be careful when selecting examples, especially with classes of children or adolescents.
2 Remember to choose limericks which are relatively easy to illustrate.

Follow-up

Follow the same procedure with different limericks. Here is another one which is (relatively) easy to draw:

There was a young soldier called Edser,
When wanted was always in bed, sir.
One morning at one
They fired the gun,
And Edser, in bed, sir, was dead, sir!

(Spike Milligan)

Source

From *One Hundred and One Best and Only Limericks of Spike Milligan.*

3.6 Visual biographies

Outline	Students describe their lives in terms of symbols and pictures to create a life map.
Focus	Fluency practice. Simple past tense and asking questions.
Level	Pre-intermediate and above
Time	30 minutes
Materials and preparation	CD-ROM image 3.6 Illustration – Visual biography.

1 As a lead-in, explain the notion of a *landmark moment* – often used to describe a memorable experience in the past. Give some examples from your own life and elicit a few more from students to check that they have understood the concept.

2 For example, write down facts like these on the board:
I moved to Italy in 1999. / My daughter was born in 2003. / I lost my job as a photographer. / I bought my first flat in 2006.

3 Next to each sentence draw a symbol or a thumbnail sketch to explain these four facts or refer to the images below or on the CD-ROM (3.6).

© Cambridge University Press 2008 PHOTOCOPIABLE

4 Students draw symbols or sketches for six landmark events, individually. Explain that they can use any symbols they like (e.g. street signs, pictograms, emoticons).

5 Seat students in pairs or small groups and ask them to interpret and compare each other's symbols and pictures.

Variation 1: Year by year

Hand out a chart/template like the one below to each student. This should be related to one specific year. Each student goes around the class, getting information about landmark events in different people's lives. Encourage them to ask for extra information about these events.

They then report back individually about some of the students' experiences.

Example: *Gary put a heart for this year because he met his girlfriend in January.*

Template: 1998

	Name	Symbols
1	Gary	❤

© Cambridge University Press 2008 PHOTOCOPIABLE

Acknowledgement: *The idea for this Variation comes from* Stories: Narrative Activities for the Language Classroom, *by Wajnryb, R., (Cambridge University Press, 2003).*

Variation 2: Other symbols

Students can represent their lives visually in different ways: as a line graph with scales indicating peaks and troughs, or as a pie chart indicating different aspects of their life. Select a year and ask students to create a chart to represent it.

See 5.10 Favourite things.

3.7 Movie storyboards

Outline Students read a narrative and break it down into a movie storyboard, pulling out the most important images and discussing how it will be filmed.

Focus Reading comprehension. Listening comprehension (see Variation).

Level Intermediate and above

Time 1 hour

Materials and preparation CD-ROM images 3.7A Illustration – Storyboard; 3.7B Illustration – Storyboard panels. A copy of the film *Seven* starring Kevin Spacey, Brad Pitt and Morgan Freeman, if possible for the follow-up. Note: this film is rated 18.

Procedure

1 As a lead-in, elicit or explain what a storyboard is.

Sample answer: *A storyboard is a sequence of still pictures deliberately arranged to represent the events of a story which will then be filmed. It is like a comic strip, with film-language subtitles and the speech bubbles written as a sound-effects (SFX) panel (along with any other sounds made in that shot or scene).*

2 Show the students the following image of a storyboard panel or project it from the CD-ROM (3.7A):

© Cambridge University Press 2008 PHOTOCOPIABLE

Establish that the storyboard features three key elements: a) a pictorial representation of a shot, b) a written description of it, c) the sound effects that accompany that shot.

3 In open class, ascertain why storyboards are important when making a film.

Sample answer: *1) As a preview, it helps you to think about how your film is going to look overall in terms of narrative and continuity. 2) The storyboard breaks the film's narrative into 'key moments'. These are easier to follow in images than purely in words.*

4 Explain or review different kinds of shots and their abbreviations: *LS – long shot, MS – mid-shot, CU – close-up, Z – zoom in, HCA/LCA – high/low camera angle.* Check students' understanding of their meanings.

5 Students read the following text, an extract from a literary adaptation of the film *Seven*, which describes a chase. Explain that the main characters are a murderer called John Doe who is on the run (Kevin Spacey in the film adaptation), and the detectives Mills (Brad Pitt) and Somerset (Morgan Freeman).

> John Doe's apartment was on a narrow street in a poor part of the city . . . Mills knocked hard on the door. Somerset heard a noise, but it didn't come from inside the apartment. He turned and saw a dark shape in the shadow of a door at the end of the corridor.
>
> Then he saw the gun. 'Mills!' he shouted. They both hit the floor at the same time. The noise hurt Somerset's ears . . . Then Mills pulled out his gun and ran after Doe, before Somerset could even think of stopping him.
>
> Somerset followed Mills down the stairs. Doe was standing on the floor below, his gun in his hand. Mills jumped back just as Doe fired. The bullet hit the wall close to Somerset.
>
> Mills waited for another shot. Instead he heard a door close. As fast as he could, he ran through the door and saw Doe running. Doe pushed a woman away and ran into her apartment.
>
> 'Police!' Mills shouted as he followed Doe into the apartment. He saw Doe climbing through a window onto the fire escape. Mills ran to the window. Doe fired again, breaking the glass. When Mills looked again, he couldn't see Doe, but he could hear him running.
>
> Out on the fire escape, Mills ran and jumped to the ground. When he reached the street, he wanted to scream. There were people everywhere. In this crowd, he would never see Doe. Then, suddenly, impossibly, he saw him. Doe was waiting to cross the street, looking for a break in the traffic . . .
>
> Doe ran through the traffic and disappeared into a narrow, dark street. Mills was close behind him, running fast.

Suddenly something hit Mills in the face. He dropped his gun – he heard it hit the ground – then he fell. The pain made him weak. A board, he thought, a piece of wood. He didn't see it coming, but that was all he could imagine. Doe had hit him with a board.

© adapted extract from *Seven*, *Penguin Readers Level 4* by Anthony Bruno. Reproduced by permission of Pearson Education Ltd.
From *Working with Images* © Cambridge University Press 2008 PHOTOCOPIABLE

6 Working in pairs / small groups, students turn this text into a 12-frame storyboard. To do this, they need to select what they consider the most important scenes in terms of narrative, location and atmosphere. Ask them to underline the different places described in the text and then any other key dramatic moments.

Show the first two storyboard panels in more detail (CD-ROM 3.7B) as a prompt.

Storyboard panels

Note

Reassure the students that they do not need to be expert artists to do this and that they should not include all the details of the story, as they will not fit this into 12 frames. Remind them that storyboards are very rough sketches and that they can write a few notes to help support their sketch.

7 Allow students sufficient time to do the storyboard. This could take up to 30 minutes. Monitor carefully during this time, indicating key vocabulary in the text and aiding the groups in selecting the best images to draw.
8 Students stick their storyboard posters on the wall. The class vote on the best version.

See 2.11 How was it taken? for a closer look at different kinds of camera shots/angles.

Follow-up

Students watch the same scene from the film itself and compare with their own storyboards. Alternatively, instead of following the procedure above, the students simply watch the sequence and break it down to fit the storyboard sequence.

Variation: Dictate the storyboard

For advanced-level groups, don't show the text but rather dictate it a couple of times. This will make the task much more challenging.

See 3.3 Teenage photo stories for another way of telling stories visually.

3.8 Image salad

Outline	Students choose and draw their own vocabulary lists in context.
Focus	Revision of targeted vocabulary. Lexical sets and word families.
Level	Elementary and above
Time	20 minutes

Procedure

1 Identify a lexical area which you have recently taught. Challenge students to brainstorm different words related to this area. Write these on the board (or ask the students themselves to come to the board and write them) in an 'image salad'. For example, if the topic were the beach, these words would be appropriate ingredients:

ice cream . . . wave . . . sand . . . deckchair . . . sunshine . . . parasol . . . beach bar . . . blue sky . . . boat . . . flip-flops . . . swimsuit . . . children . . . suntan lotion . . . sunbathing . . .

2 Students, in pairs or individually, look at the words on the board and attempt to draw a sketch to include all of the items. Remind the class that the artwork does not have to be of the highest standard, but that the images they produce should be enough to trigger the word in their imaginations.
3 Rub the words off the board. Ask the students to compare their pictures and identify the items they have drawn without consulting the vocabulary list. Students, in pairs or groups, exchange drawings, label them and then return them for 'checking'.

Note

This is a good activity for mixed-ability classes and for exam revision of vocabulary.

Acknowledgement: *The idea is based on the activity 'Choose Your Words, Draw Your Picture' (Mixed-Level Classes) in* Dealing with Difficulties *by Prodromou, L. and Clandfield, L., (Delta Publishing).*

3.9 Pastiches

Outline	Students transform well-known artworks by adding details to them.
Focus	Fluency practice. Practising conditional sentences. Giving explanations. Discussing 'altered images'.
Level	Pre-intermediate and above
Time	30 minutes
Materials and preparation	CD-ROM image 3.9 Painting by Edward Hopper – Nighthawks. Images can be easily manipulated using Photoshop®.

Procedure

1 Show the students the painting *Nighthawks* by Edward Hopper. (The class may be already familiar with this image from having done task 1.5 Who am I?) Explain that this iconic painting has been parodied/copied by many different people for many different reasons. For example, it has been used as an advert for Starbucks®, CSI, as well as in a Simpsons™ movie. It has also been transformed by the 'guerilla artist' Banksy in his work *Are you using that chair?*

http://www.artofthestate.co.uk/Banksy/Banksy_crude_oils_are_you_using_that_chair.htm

2 Ask students the following questions:
   - *If you could add an element to this painting, what would you add? A character, an object, a detail, a building?*
   - *Would you add any words, speech bubbles, graffiti, captions?*
   - *Would you turn the image into an advert, a magazine cover, part of a cartoon or a different genre altogether? If so, where would you place the advert?*

3 Students work in pairs or small groups and discuss what they would do with the image. If they have difficulties, you can show one or two examples of how the image has been transformed at: http://en.wikipedia.org/wiki/Nighthawks

4 Ask the students for homework to create an altered version of the painting. This can be done either as a JPEG file, using clip art, Photoshop® or any other means that students have at their disposal. Alternatively, students can print out a large version (A4 is big enough) of the painting and ask them to glue different elements to the paper.

5 In the following class, ask students to talk about the images they have created. Display them around the class. Students can vote on their favourites or the ones they consider the most original.

6 If you have access to a computer, prepare a PowerPoint presentation of different versions of *Nighthawks* available on the Internet.

Follow-up

1 Students, either individually or in pairs, choose their own image to be transformed. They can do this at home and bring it to class the next day. In class, they should show their created images, explaining their meaning and the reason they chose to transform them in this way.

2 Establish that other iconic images have been parodied or distorted over the years for various reasons. Ask the class to find such images on the Internet and talk about them in the next class.

Note

The most parodied portrait of all is Leonardo Da Vinci's *Mona Lisa* or *La Gioconda*. A great website http://www.studiolo.org/Mona/MONASV01.htm gives you access to many versions of the *Mona Lisa* separated by type/genre. Ask students to select one of the images and read about it. In the next class, they should describe the artwork, and summarise in their own words what the parody means and their opinion of it.

See 1.5 Who am I? for another task featuring Edward Hopper's painting. See 6.8 Subvertising for parodies of adverts.

3.10 Draw a sentence

Outline Students practise targeted grammatical structures by 'drawing the sentence' in a competitive/race-type activity. Making students aware of how whole sentences can be pictorially expressed.

Focus Any grammatical structure that you would like to review.

Level Elementary–Intermediate (young learners)

Time 15–30 minutes

Materials and preparation Prepare half a dozen sentences which include the target structure and which are not too difficult to draw. Write the sentences on separate pieces of paper or card. For example, to practise the present continuous for future planned events, write the following sentences:
My boyfriend/girlfriend's having a party tomorrow night.
My class is meeting at six to go to the cinema.
My grandparents are moving house next month.
My friends are going fishing tomorrow.
My parents are going to Paris next weekend.
My wife's having a baby in June.
CD-ROM image 3.10 Illustration – Draw a sentence example.

Procedure

1 Elicit a sample sentence using the structure that you would like to revise. For example, to elicit the sentence *My parents are going to Paris tonight*, draw two matchstick people on the board and an image to represent Paris, e.g. the Eiffel Tower. Draw today's date and a clock to indicate the time. To indicate the relationship ('my parents'), you may need to draw further stick figures or design a mini-family tree which includes yourself. Once the students have correctly guessed the sentence, write it on the board to act as a model.

2 Put the students into groups of about four. One member of each team comes to the front of the class. They will be the 'illustrators'. Show all the illustrators one of the sentences written on a card (e.g. *My girlfriend's having a party tomorrow night*), taking care to ensure that their teams cannot see the sentences. The illustrators then return to their groups where they have to draw the sentence as quickly as possible. The first group to guess the full sentence correctly is the winner.

Important note: No miming, speaking or writing is allowed. Younger learners will need to be monitored carefully.

Example: My girlfriend's having a party tomorrow night. (CD-ROM 3.10.)

3 The process is then repeated and the game continues with another illustrator coming forward from each group and being shown a different sentence.

4 When all the sentences have been exhausted, ask the students to use their drawings to reconstruct the correct sentences. Write these on the board, and highlight any features of grammar that you consider relevant or useful.

TIP

Remember that most students are not born artists and some are resistant to drawing. Reassure the class that the drawings themselves need not be 'artistic' and that the sentences can be drawn even by somebody who finds illustration difficult.

Variation 1: Grammar revision

For a more general grammar revision class, especially before an exam, make different sets of sentences all grouped according to the structures you wish to target. Each group then takes responsibility to illustrate their set of sentences. Once illustrated, the sentences can be exchanged. The groups then try to work out what the original sentences were.

Variation 2: Instructions and error correction with images

You can also use images as signs or mnemonics (visual reminders) for instructions in class or as a way to remind a class of errors. These can be designed in the style of road signs, displayed around the class and referred to when appropriate. An S-sign, for example, can remind the students to add the third person *s*. A diagram of two students face-to-face can be used to represent pairwork. Develop a series of cards like this for common errors and instructions, and students will get used to their presence in the classroom.

Acknowledgement: *The original idea for this activity comes from 'Picasso Sentences', from Resource Books for Teachers:* Grammar *by Thornbury, S., (Oxford University Press, 2006).*

3.11 Makeovers

Outline	Students look at photos of rooms and attempt to improve them.
Focus	Students practise conditional sentences: *I would paint that wall blue and I would get rid of that sofa*, etc. and present perfect for changes: *They've changed the carpet*, etc. Imagining where and how things can fit into a space.
Level	Pre-intermediate–Advanced
Time	20 minutes
Materials and preparation	CD-ROM images 3.11A–C Living room before, Kitchen before, Bathroom before. 3.11D–F Living room before and after, Kitchen before and after, Bathroom before and after. CD-ROM images 3.11G–L Six photos of different wallpaper designs for Follow-up task.

Procedure

1 Ask students in open class if they or their families have made any changes to their home recently. Which rooms were redecorated? What has changed? Do they like the changes or do they prefer how it was before? You may need to pre-teach some relevant vocabulary here.

2 Show a sample photo of a room that needs renovating (CD-ROM 3.11 A–C). Ask students in open class what needs to be changed. Ask them to consider various criteria: paint, furniture, walls, etc. Write an example sentence on the board as a prompt.

Example: *I would paint the walls white. It's very dark at the moment.*

3 In pairs students practise redesigning the room. Students could draw a picture to illustrate their ideas.

4 Students present their makeovers. The class can decide, for example by class vote, whether the makeover was successful.
5 Show students the makeover of the same room (CD-ROM 3.11D–F). Do students like what has been done? In pairs, students describe the changes that have been made. Encourage them to use the present perfect tense or the present perfect passive here (depending on your students' level):

They've painted the walls blue. / The walls have been painted blue.
The table has changed position.

6 Students report back all the changes they can see. Make sure you monitor and correct the verb tenses where necessary.

Variation: Correcting a makeover

With higher levels, students practise altering the makeover image, using phrases in the third conditional, e.g. *I wouldn't have knocked that wall down.*

Follow-up

Continuing the theme of interior design, students look at some wallpaper designs on the CD-ROM (3.11G–L).

1 Ask students if they have wallpaper at home. Do they like it or not?
2 Students describe the designs. What do the images remind them of?
3 In groups students discuss in what room they would put the wallpaper and why.
4 Students discuss for what other purpose the designs could be used, e.g. textile design, bed covers or tablecloths.

Furnishing catalogues are excellent sources of images for these kinds of tasks.

4 Imaging

Howard Gardner's theory of multiple intelligences has established the concept of the 'visual learner'. For all language users, though, whether 'visual' or not, words evoke images. For example, when we say a word such as 'world', an image flashes through our mind. One person's mental image of that word may be quite different from another's: the 'world' may be seen as a satellite picture, an old-fashioned globe or a conventional map of the world on a classroom wall, divided into different countries. At the same time, such mental images can be very powerful. One of the reasons that film adaptations of books are often so disappointing is that our imaginations have created something richer and we are disappointed by another person's vision that doesn't coincide with our own.

By triggering mental images, it is believed that learners retain language items and can then recall them more easily. In fact, those learners who can generate a lot of mental images have been found to perform better in certain memory tasks and achieve better academic results[1]. Numerous experiments have proven that subjects learn and remember material that is concrete (imagery-related) better than that which is abstract. One of our tasks as language teachers then is to help those students who are less visual and have more difficulty in picturing experience. Some of the tasks in this unit aim to do just that. Such work becomes more challenging when considering the intense diet of visual images that many of our younger students receive on a daily basis. We are bombarded by so much visual stimuli that it has been claimed that attention spans among young people (the so-called 'digital natives') are becoming alarmingly short. Faced by this intense visual exposure, it is refreshing to give students a chance to look inwards. In many cases, our imaginations conjure up far richer images from within (from our mind's eye) than the ones we receive externally. In this way, we can take a step back from the need for sensory overload and expand our students' horizons. We are perhaps moving from talking of 'a short attention span to a broader attention range'[2].

[1] *Imagine That!* Puchta, Rinvolcuri, Arnold (Helbling/Cambridge University Press), 2007 is a useful resource book on using mental imagery in class.

[2] This quotation from Rushkoff I first came across in a talk by Herbert Puchta on teaching adolescent learners.

In many respects, this chapter includes tasks which attempt to activate the mind's eye. For more sceptical or less visual students, the first task (4.1 Photo association) leads us in gently, introducing students to the notion of image association. Here, they have to find unexpected links between different mental images and order them in a logical sequence. This kind of image association is often used by advertisers (for example, a 'car' is often associated with 'freedom') as a marketing technique. In other tasks, external stimuli are provided: in 4.2 Questions to a portrait, students aim questions at a person on canvas, and, as they do so, they create an ever-stronger mental image of this person's identity. Other tasks are more game-like in nature: in 4.4 I am . . ., students are required to personify abstract objects, and in 4.6 Holding the image, students test their memories, retaining as many details as they can. We return to external stimuli in 4.7 Hotel rooms, in which the learners conjure up mental images regarding rooms and paths. The path is a particularly evocative image here, inviting learners to take separate journeys and describe where their particular paths are taking them. Such inner visualisations can be very powerful and profound. As in many other tasks in this book, the viewer is encouraged to interact fully with the image to create multiple meanings.

4.1 Photo association

Outline	Students practise 'image' association, finding unexpected links between images and ordering them into a logical sequence.
Focus	Vocabulary sets according to the chosen lexical field.
Level	Intermediate–Advanced
Time	30 minutes
Materials and preparation	Images to be accessed from: http://www.flickr.com/groups/gameofphotoassociation/ This is a group of photographers who regularly upload images into a sequence. One image reminds one photographer of another; in this way a chain of images is created. A selection of images from the above website link will be needed. Generate two PowerPoint presentations using these, one with the images in sequence and the other with the images mixed up. A computer and projector will be needed to display these in class.

Procedure

1 Explain to students what word association is: *A game in which one word leads to another through association.* Write the following chain on the board to give them an idea:

DOG → CAT → MOUSE

2 Explain that we make these associations because words frequently co-occur in real language use (like *fish and chips*), and because words of similar or related meaning form semantic networks in the mind (like *fish, fin, scales*).
3 Practise with students, giving them the first and last word in a chain of three. They have to complete the word in between. Write on the board these sequences. What do the last two have in common?

APPLE → ______ → EVE
FARM → ______ → EGG
PARTY → ______ → FLIES
FOOT → ______ → PARK

Answers: Adam, hen, time, ball. The last two examples in the sequence feature a word which acts as a hinge between two others: *football – ball park*.

4 Seat the students in groups of three. Ask each group to put the words below into a logical sequence. Establish that there is not necessarily one correct sequence, but they have to justify their order.

doctor teeth apple white dentist

One sequence could be:

APPLE → DOCTOR → DENTIST → WHITE → TEETH

Reasoning: An apple a day keeps the doctor away – A doctor looks after people as does a dentist – A dentist wears a white jacket – Your teeth should be white if you go to the dentist regularly.

5 Explain that the same game can also be played with images. Show students a selection of approximately 20 photos from the image association group in flickr.com. The best way to present the images is by downloading them one by one and inserting them – with the order mixed up – into a PowerPoint presentation. (Remember to make another presentation with the images in the correct order so that you have a record of the original sequence.)
6 In groups, students sequence the images, looking for a visual link between them.
7 Students report back their sequences in open class. Show the PowerPoint presentation in the original sequence. Did the students' suggestions match? Emphasise again that there is not one 'correct' sequence.

Note
A way of exploiting the PowerPoint format called *Pecha Kucha* was devised in 2003 by two architects in Tokyo. *Pecha Kucha* is Japanese for 'chit-chat'. Such presentations consist of 20 PowerPoint slides, each shown for 20 seconds. Therefore each talk lasts just under seven minutes. The idea is to create a series of concise talks (there are usually 14 presenters) in a given evening. Ask advanced learners to show their image/word associations in this *Pecha Kucha* format. This will add a competitive and fun element to their PowerPoint presentations.

Variation: Advertising
Word and image association lies at the heart of many successful advertising campaigns. Consider the images that you associate, for example, with cars (e.g. power, strength, elegance, open space, desert, wilderness, freedom). How has this image association been influenced by advertising campaigns and trends? For project work, students can collect images from different adverts, bring them to class the next day and ask their classmates what kind of product they belong to.

4.2 Questions to a portrait

Outline Students imagine and conduct a 'conversation' with a portrait.

Focus Fluency practice. Practising question forms.

Level Elementary–Advanced

Time 30 minutes

Materials and preparation CD-ROM images 4.2A Painting by Edvard Munch, self-portrait. The Night Wanderer; 4.2B 'Roman' portrait. You can choose any portrait for this. I have chosen a painting and a photograph to exemplify the idea. However, it is a good idea to choose portraits of an enigmatic nature.

Note It is important for students to realise that there are no correct answers to their questions. They are asking the questions to an image of a person who cannot answer back. The idea is for the questions to create mental images about the identity of a person based on their own imaginations. In order for the images to remain enigmatic, remember not to give the names of the paintings or the painters to the class.

Procedure

1 Show the self-portrait of Edvard Munch (CD-ROM 4.2A) to the students. Tell them to look at the image for about a minute without saying anything. Do not give them any other instructions at this stage.

2 In open class, students come up with questions, aiming them directly at the portrait, as if they were having a conversation with the person.

Note

Depending on the level of the class, the complexity of the question can vary, from *Where are you?* to *What have you been up to?* Be careful not to prompt at this stage. Let the questions emerge naturally from the group but make sure that all questions are asked in the second person.

Painting by Edvard Munch, self-portrait. *The Night Wanderer*,
© Munch Museum / Munch–Ellingsen Group, BONO, Oslo / DACS, London 2008

3 Students listen to each question, study the portrait closely, and imagine (but do not articulate) an answer in the voice of the person in the portrait.

4 Carry on in this way, asking students to volunteer questions, pausing and then imagining the answers. Correct any errors. Make a note of the questions yourself.

Sample questions (based on the Munch image) could be :

– *How old are you?*
– *Are you at home?*
– *What are you thinking?*
– *Where have you been this evening?*
– *How are you feeling?*
– *Why are you standing in that corridor?*
– *Are you looking at somebody or at yourself?*
– *What are you going to do next?*

5 Put the students in pairs or small groups. Ask them to recall the questions (prompt if necessary) and report back the answers that occurred to them. It is important for the class to answer in the first person, as if they were the person in the painting.

6 Each group then selects the best 'answers' and constructs a mental image of the person and how he/she is feeling at that time.

7 Students report back their mental images of this person to open class. How many of their mental images coincide?

Sample answer: The Munch portrait seems to sum up the artist's anxiety, restlessness and loneliness. We get the idea of a person wandering aimlessly around his house at night, unable to sleep, and catching sight of his own reflection. The bare room and windows emphasise this sense of loneliness even more. Munch painted a number of different self-portraits, each of which reflects a different mood.

8 Students repeat the exercises with image 4.2B.

Variation: Adopting the voice

Ask one student to sit beside the portrait. He/she is responsible for adopting the voice of the person in the portrait and has to answer the questions from the whole class as if he/she were that person.

Acknowledgement: *The original idea of asking questions to a still portrait who 'answers back' comes from* Imagine That!, by *Arnold, J., Puchta, H. and Rinvolucri, M., (Innsbruck: Helbling, 2007).*

See 4.4 I am . . . for a task which involves the personification of inanimate objects.

4.3 Flashbacks

Outline	Students get into the mind of a character and write up their mental storyboard, which builds up to a final image.
Focus	Writing practice. Narrative tenses for story-making (past simple, past continuous, past perfect).
Level	Intermediate–Advanced
Time	40 minutes
Materials and preparation	CD-ROM image 4.3 Four thoughts. Alternatively, find any image that has four people in it and prepare a short text to accompany it.

Procedure

1 Show the image *Four thoughts* (CD-ROM 4.3) to the students. It is better if you can project this onto a screen, but otherwise a photocopy will do. Ask the students to establish the relationship between the four people.

Four thoughts, © José María Cuéllar, http://www.josemariacuellar.com

2 Read out the following text at a gentle pace. Ask the students to close their eyes while they listen to the thoughts of one of the four characters in the photo. Ask students to match it to the thoughts of one of the four people. With lower levels, hand out the story, and allow the students to read and listen at the same time. Get students to discuss their answers.

> *It's six in the morning. I can't remember it being night-time. Everything's a blur now. It's very light out here, so light that I have a headache. It's going to be hot today, but right now it's cool. I look around me, at the sea, at the sand, at the others – I don't even know how we ended up here. At least we're safe, though – that's the main thing. I stare at the sea and lose myself in it. Now gradually the images are coming back to me. The images of last night . . . and it all begins to make sense.*
>
> © Cambridge University Press 2008 PHOTOCOPIABLE

3 Tell the class that this photo is the final image of a story or the last scene of a movie. The students individually reconstruct the story of that night in their imagination.

4 Ask your students, individually, to draw a set of four picture frames (model on the board if necessary). This can include matchstick figures and symbols, to make it easier.

For example, you could simply draw a picture of a bar, suggesting that this is where the four people started the evening, and a happy face suggesting how they were feeling then.

5 Monitor the students' drawing until they have completed the four squares in the storyboard.

6 Seat the students in small groups. Each member of the group now tells his/her story to the rest of the group. Ask them to consider the narrative tenses as they are telling the story and use the first person singular/plural to make the flashback more real.

Example:

At the start of the evening, we were all sitting in our favourite bar, when suddenly there was a tremendous noise that sounded like an explosion . . .

7 A volunteer from each group narrates their flashback story to the rest of the class. What similarities and differences are there between the stories? Are the stories tragic or comic?

Variation: Comic strips
This same task can be done with the final vignettes of comic strips, which may be more suitable for younger learners.

See 1.5 Who am I?

4.4 I am . . .

Outline	Students create a mental image of an object, describing it in the first person to others who have to guess what it is.
Focus	Practising various lexical fields: materials, function, etc. Adverbs: *sometimes, often, usually*, etc. and their position in the sentence.
Level	Elementary–Pre-intermediate (young learners)
Time	20 minutes
Note	This personification of objects is something students enjoy because it allows them to conjure up a number of different and unexpected images.
Materials and preparation	CD-ROM images 4.4A Illustration – All 12 objects; 4.4B–M Separate illustrated objects: Pyjamas, Flipflops, Keys, Flowers, Toothpaste, Remote control, Candles, Soap, Chips, Cereal, Kettle, Saucepan. Alternatively, prepare a set of flashcards for any lexical set you would like to cover/revise.

Procedure

1 Prepare a set of flashcards based on a lexical set you want to revise, e.g. *furniture*, *animals*, *buildings*, *food*, *everyday objects*, or use the 12 images provided (CD-ROM 4.4 A–M).

2 Read the text below as an example, asking students to listen and guess the object:
I'm sometimes made of plastic.
I'm usually round.
I have many different shapes.
But I'm often quite small.
I have numbers.
I often sit next to the bed.
You usually use me during the week.
You need me but you don't like me.

Answer: Alarm clock

3 Seat the students in groups and hand out different cards to different groups. Students work together to describe the image by imagining it in the first person. Remind them that, for their descriptions, they should

consider these factors: material, size, shape, location, before going into greater detail, as they may give too much information away too quickly.

4 Students in each group take it in turns to read out their descriptions. The other groups try to imagine what is being described.

5 Monitor accordingly to check that the descriptions correspond accurately to each image.

Variation: A Martian sends a postcard home

For higher levels. Ask students to think of an object from the point of view of a Martian. Use Craig Raine's poem, *A Martian Sends a Postcard Home*, as an example. Give the class the extract from the poem below and ask them to guess the object:

In homes, a haunted apparatus sleeps,
that snores when you pick it up.
If the ghost cries, they carry it
to their lips and soothe it to sleep with sounds.
And yet, they wake it up deliberately, by tickling with a finger . . .

© Craig Raine, 1979. Used by permission of David Godwin Associates
From *Working with Images* © Cambridge University Press 2008 PHOTOCOPIABLE

Answer: Telephone

Explanation: It's a machine that does not do anything (it *sleeps*) until you pick it up. The *cries* of the *ghost* are when it rings. Then you talk to it (*carry it to* [your] *lips*) or answer it and when you have finished put it back to *sleep* or hang up. We *wake it* and [tickle it] *with a finger* when we answer it or want to call someone else.

4.5 Drawing with words

Outline	Students create a mental image of a place, using words instead of illustration.
Focus	Practising various lexical fields depending on the context of the image.
Level	Elementary–Advanced (young learners)
Time	30 minutes
Materials and preparation	CD-ROM image 4.5 Illustration – Drawing with words.

Procedure

1 Show students image 4.5 from the CD-ROM. Explain to the class (if necessary, in their mother tongue with monolingual groups) that this is an image made up almost entirely of words.

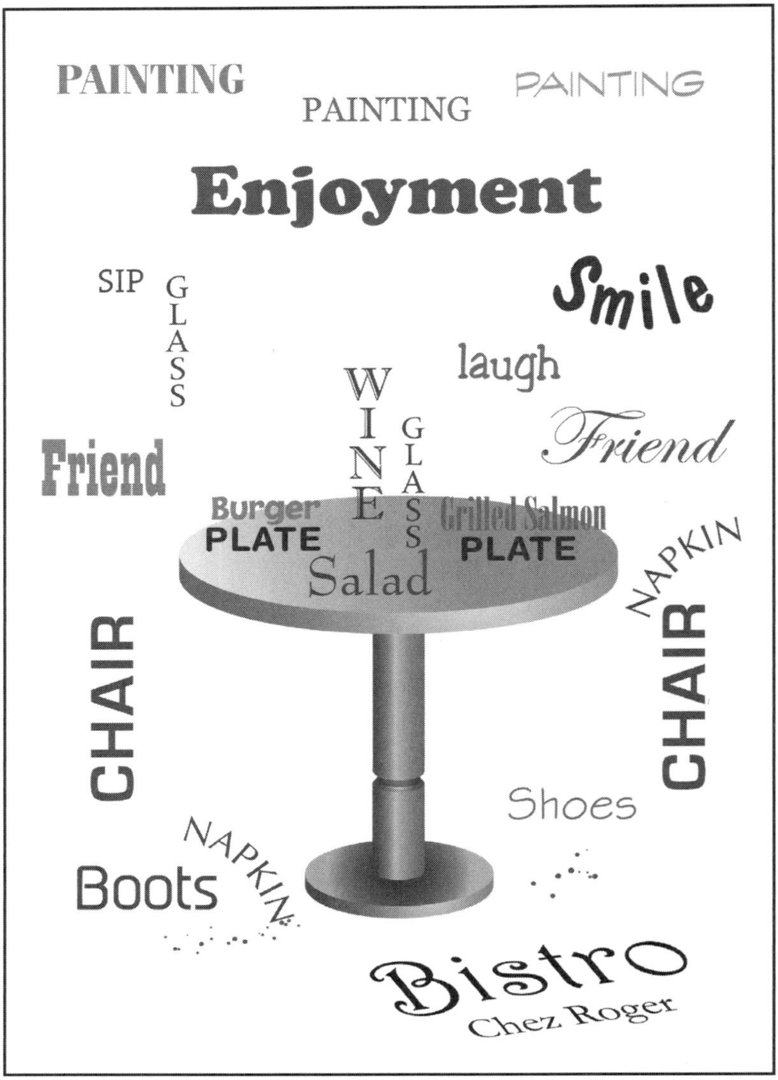

Drawing with words.
Based on an idea by Tibor Kalman.

2 Students look at it carefully and try to imagine the overall image from the word cues.

Pre-teach any vocabulary or ask students to group the words into categories, based on either nouns (e.g. foods: *salmon*, etc.), or verbs (e.g. *sip*, *laugh*).

3 Students take it in turns to describe the image in groups, using complete sentences, e.g. *There are two friends eating at a restaurant. One is eating grilled salmon. Somebody's dropped a napkin on the floor.*

4 Students think of a place that they know very well – better if it involves people – and which they can easily visualise. Tell them to draw their 'visualisation', following the model. Ask them to start by drawing only one object (like the table in the model) and gradually surround it with words.

Note

Remind the students: 1) to write the word exactly where the object would normally appear, 2) to be as specific as possible about the place. For example, they should not draw any restaurant, but a specific place they know well, including details of decoration and furniture.

5 Once students have finished their drawing, seat students back in pairs or small groups. Student A shows the image to Student B, who has to describe what they can see and guess the exact place that Student A had in mind. Then get students to change roles.

6 Monitor, making corrections where necessary. Choose one or two entertaining examples to be shown to the whole class.

4.6 Holding the image

Outline	Students practise holding a visual image in their minds.
Focus	Writing/speaking skills: descriptive statements and questions.
Level	Elementary–Advanced (young learners)
Time	30 minutes
Materials and preparation	CD-ROM images 4.6A Bedroom; 4.6B All the living people version 1; 4.6C All the living people version 2; 4.6D All the living people complete photo. You will also need a computer and projector to display these images in class. Alternatively, if you choose your own image, make sure there is plenty of descriptive detail, which students will need to assimilate.

Procedure

1 Seat students in pairs. Show image 4.6A to all students for about ten seconds.
2 Ask Student A to remember as much detail as possible about the image by holding it in his/her head as carefully as they can.
3 Meanwhile, ask Student B to write down a few true/false questions and a couple of open questions about the image.
4 Cover the image. Student B asks questions to Student A, testing his/her memory of it. How well have they held the image in their minds? Have they invented any details that are not there?
5 Repeat the procedure with another image, but reverse the roles.

Note

The more detail in the photo, the longer you should allow the students to see the image.

Variation: Jigsaw pictures (suitable for mixed-ability groups)

1 Show an image (e.g. CD-ROM 4.6D) to the whole class for a few minutes. Ask them to remember as much detail in it as possible.
2 Hand out two versions of the same photo to Students A and B. Student A's copy should have a large number of details removed (e.g. CD-ROM 4.6C). Student B's should have fewer details blocked out (e.g. CD-ROM 4.6B).
3 Students work in pairs to compare their versions of the image and attempt to bring the original picture back to life, completing any missing elements in their mind's eye.
4 Show the whole class the image with more details blocked out (CD-ROM 4.6C), using a projector. Elicit the missing elements and then compare with the original.

Example: *There's a large group of people in the right-hand corner who are missing.*

Alternatively, use an illustration rather than a photo. Provide two templates of the same images, as in step 2, but allow students to add the missing elements by drawing these details onto the templates.

See 1.6 What's missing? and 2.10 Is it real?

Acknowledgement: *The idea for the Variation is based on the activity 'Jigsaw Pictures' (Mixed-Level Classes) in* Dealing with Difficulties *by Prodromou, L. and Clandfield, L., (Delta Publishing).*

4.7 Hotel rooms

Outline	A guided imagery activity explaining a journey around the world. Students visualise the places and the journey in their mind's eye. Getting students to develop an intercultural awareness of different 'worlds'.
Focus	Listening practice. Lexical field of travelling. Verbs of seeing.
Level	Intermediate–Advanced
Time	45 minutes – 1 hour
Materials and preparation	CD-ROM images 4.7A–F Six photos of views from hotel rooms: Turkey, Egypt, Kenya, Japan, New Zealand, Brazil. 4.7G Answers. CD-ROM images 4.7H–M Six photos of paths for Variation. One photocopy of the texts for each student. A large piece of paper (A3) for the students to draw a six-square grid.

Procedure

1 As a lead-in, ask if students have ever stayed in a hotel. When was the last time? Do they remember the view? Ask them in pairs to describe the best view from a hotel, or another place, that they can remember.

2 Establish that you are going to tell students what happened on a round-the-world trip. Explain that the commentary is based around six views from different hotel rooms. Ask students to draw a six-square grid in their notebooks, or on pieces of A3 paper and number the squares accordingly.

Note

For a shorter class or lower level, choose four views rather than the full six.

3 Read out each text, describing the six views. Students listen and draw a very rough sketch of each one in their grids. Allow them to write one or two key words as well, to help them remember the image. Remind them that the sketch can be a simple matchstick-style drawing.

4 Pause after each description to allow ample time for the students to hold the images in their mind's eye, and to complete their sketches.

5 After reading the six descriptions, ask a few questions, e.g.

– *What country/city do you think it is?*
– *Do you think the view is beautiful or mundane?*
– *What clues were provided?*

6 Show the students the images of the views (CD-ROM 4.7A–F), ideally projecting them through a computer. Hand out photocopies of the six

texts. Go through them with the students, pointing out the details and vocabulary items. Concentrate the class's attention on the different verbs of seeing (*see, glimpse, make out*, etc.). Explain that they are all real views taken from real hotel rooms. Can the students guess in which places the photos were taken? Give the first country, Turkey, as a prompt.

1 Day 1
I wake up in a cave. My hotel's called the *Kelebek*. That means 'butterfly' in this country's language. I look out in the morning and the view is amazing. In the background there are lots of caves built into the sand. They say there are 300 cave churches and 30 underground cities near here. In the foreground, there are houses mixed in with caves. It's very dry here.

2 Day 42
I've been in this continent for about a month now and this is the best view I've seen so far. I'm on the ninth floor looking out on the Nile river, one of the most famous rivers in the world. The river is very wide at this point. There are two hotel towers – one on the left in the foreground and a great big white building on the right, which is the Grand Hotel. It has a revolving restaurant, 42 storeys high. No sign of any pyramids, of course.

3 Day 90
The Continental Hotel. I can't sleep. It's 6.30 am. I walk to the window, open it and look down. There's not much of a view. All I can see is a maid sweeping the pavement outside. There's a piece of lawn very neatly cut, the clean pavement, and the flags of the hotel are very still. There's no wind. Next to the maid, the porter is checking his mobile phone. The city's still asleep. For a minute, it doesn't look like Africa.

4 Day 221
This time I'm *in* the Grand Hotel, not looking at it. But it's a different city, of course, and this really is a panoramic view. I took the picture from the top floor, and you can see that the city doesn't stop – there's no end to it. It just goes on and on. This is the Shinjuku area, a great place to go out at night. Crazy! It's dusk. You can see all the lights just going on way down below. Usually, with the pollution, you can never see Mount Fuji, but that evening you could glimpse it, right in the background. Can you see it?

5 Day 278
After so many days in cities, I needed to see nature. And this country is maybe the most distant and the most beautiful in that respect. Look at this amazing landscape. How I found this hotel, I'll never know. I love this view – the trees in the foreground in flower, the lake and then more trees and those incredible snowy mountains in the background. I love it because there seem to be four different seasons all in one here.

© Cambridge University Press 2008 PHOTOCOPIABLE

6 Day 321
Right at the end of my trip, I needed a beach and so I headed for one of the most famous in the world, Copacabana. But as you can see, my hotel room didn't have much of a view. I had no money left for a place on the front. All I have in front of me are two apartment blocks. But look – you can just make out the beach between those two buildings. A tiny glimpse of sand. Sorry, but you'll have to imagine the rest!

© Cambridge University Press 2008 PHOTOCOPIABLE

7 Show students CD-ROM image 4.7G that matches the photos with the countries.

Answers:

1 Turkey (Cappadocia)
2 Egypt (Cairo)
3 Kenya (Nairobi)
4 Japan (Tokyo)
5 New Zealand (countryside)
6 Brazil (Rio de Janeiro)

Follow-up

Students can create their own travelogue of texts and photos for their summer holiday. The same task could work equally well with train or road journeys across one particular country like the US, China or Russia. Students could also produce such texts with the aid of image banks like Flickr™.

Variation: Paths

Show students the images of different paths (4.7. H–M) and ask them to write their own travelogue, inventing the countries and places where you can find these paths and where they might lead to. Students can design a route from one path to another.

The answers to some of these questions will act as prompts:

– *How would you describe the path? Friendly, scary, mysterious, narrow, wide, dark, light?*
– *Where do you think it leads to?*
– *Is it somewhere you want to go?*
– *How do you imagine your walk down the path? Silent, noisy, solitary, spiritual, uplifting?*
– *What noise do your footsteps make on the path?*
– *What would you do if you got lost?*

See 2.18 Room with a view.

4.8 Opposites

Outline	Students attempt to conjure up visual images for certain words. Raising intercultural awareness.
Focus	Key lexical items which express opposites.
Level	Intermediate and above
Time	30 minutes
Materials and preparation	Access to the following website: http://www.yourpointofview.com/hsbcads_print.aspx

Procedure

1 Lead in by explaining that there are often two opposite ways of looking at the same topic. For example, show, or ask the class to imagine, a photo of an attractive golf course full of people playing or watching the sport. Elicit from the class answers to the following questions:

What visual image of this sport and what single word would come to mind if you a) were a big golf fan, b) really disliked the game?

2 Still on the same task, ask the class to think of two opposite nouns or adjectives for the same image.

Elicit, for example:

A: exciting, fun, relaxing, heaven, green landscape and fresh air
B: dull, boredom, stressful, hell, environmentally unfriendly.

3 Explain to students that these are personal points of view. Suggest to them that golf can also be seen from a broader perspective. Make the point that in some societies, golf is played by everyone and is cheap (e.g. in Spain), and in others, it is rather expensive and played only by the upper/middle class or holidaymakers (in Scotland). Elicit the words: *popular/elitist*.

4 Ask the class what other images could be chosen to express the words *popular/elitist*.

Sample answers:
a glass of red wine / skiing / the opera / a pineapple / an image of a new school.

Note

A glass of red wine would be considered a normal beverage in Spain or France, while it is a luxury article and considered to have great therapeutic qualities in China and is, of course, forbidden in many other countries.

5 Suggest to students that two images can also represent two different viewpoints of the same topic. For example, ask students what image comes to mind when they hear the word *driving*.
   Elicit a positive image of innocent fun: *open space, freedom, comfort, glamour*, and a negative image: *traffic jams, stress, roadworks, pollution*. Ask them to explain these mental images in as much detail as possible.
6 Show the students one advert from the HSBC website: http://www.yourpointofview.com/hsbcads_print.aspx For example, you could choose the images of the water tap and the glass of water to explain that in some countries it is a luxury and in others a commodity.
   How does the accompanying text help communicate the advert's overall message?
7 Students visualise their own 'double images' for these word combinations:

wise/old	*work/play*
information/invasion	*love/loathe*
scary/reassuring	*leader/follower.*

8 Students report back their answers. Refer them to the same HSBC website for the 'official versions'. What is the basic idea behind the campaign? Ask the class to vote on their favourite / the most effective images.

See Chapter 6 for more tasks on advertising.

4.9 An image for a word

Outline	Students attempt to conjure up mental images for certain words. Encouraging students to question why they retain certain lexical items through guided visualisation.
Focus	Word networks / word families. Idiomatic expressions with *world*.
Level	Intermediate – Upper intermediate
Time	30 minutes
Materials and preparation	CD-ROM images 4.9A Cartogram – Population; 4.9B Illustration – The world unites to aid Africa.

Procedure

1 As a lead-in, ask students to think of a word that they really like in English. Do they like the form of the word, or its meaning, or both? Give them a couple of minutes and then tell them to visualise an image of this word. (Students can close their eyes as an option.) As they see the image in their mind's eye, instruct them to say the word to themselves silently or under their breath. Ask them if they can see any other images related to their word.

2 Students report back their words and images in pairs or small groups. Monitor, passing from one group to the next. Did any words coincide? What do the words and images have in common, if anything?

3 Elicit one at a time from students any expressions they know which include the word *world*. Pause after every expression, allowing plenty of time for the students to visualise an image.

If your students do not provide many expressions, begin with these five:

a *To watch the world go by*
b *It was out of this world*
c *The World Cup*
d *The outside world*
e *World-class.*

4 Students report back their impressions. Explain the images that you see when you hear these expressions.

Examples:

a *I'm in a busy station in a big city, drinking a coffee, looking at everybody rushing to get their trains.*
b *I'm coming out of a concert that I've really enjoyed, with the music still ringing in my ears.*
c *Me as a baby with the rest of the family all around me watching a black-and-white television. The year I was born England won it.*
d *An ape looking through the bars of a cage in a zoo.*
e *A gold medal on an athlete's chest.*

6 Ask the students to close their eyes (again this is optional) while you dictate the following six expressions. Choose half of these for a shorter lesson. Tell them to visualise images for each. Once again, remember to pause a good time between dictating each expression.

The world is your oyster
The World Bank

To go up in the world
A world of good
To be in a world of your own
Worlds apart.

7 Tell the students to open their eyes. They should now take a pen and paper and write down the expression(s) that conjured up the most images. Clarify any doubts as to the meanings of the expressions as you go.
8 Group the students in pairs. Students compare their mental images. The point is to allow the students to create their own meanings through these images. Once they have spoken about their image, you can then explain how the phrase is usually used and in what context.
9 Students report back in open class. Which phrases conjured up the most vivid images in general?
10 Other representations of the world can be found in the following images on the CD-ROM: 4.9A and 4.9B. Students discuss their different meanings. In what way is the world distorted in each?

Note

You could use any high-frequency word for this task. The examples can be varied according to your class's level. Use dictionaries or concordance lines from the British National Corpus to find contextualised examples: http://www.natcorp.ox.ac.uk/

Consult also the *Cambridge Advanced Learner's Dictionary* for other examples. For *world*, there is a collocation box that includes these items: *the real/whole/wide world, travel the world, change/rule/save the world, across / all over the world*. There are also many idiomatic expressions listed in the entry itself.

Acknowledgement: *This task was adapted from an original idea in* Imagine That! by *Arnold, J., Puchta, H. and Rinvolucri M., (Helbling, 2007).*

4.10 Stereotypes

Outline	Creating images from verbal cues. Imagining a scene and the characters within it. Raising intercultural awareness and challenging stereotypes.
Focus	Writing and using conversational snippets.
Level	Intermediate – Upper intermediate
Time	30 minutes
Materials and preparation	CD-ROM images 4.10A Illustration – Sunday lunch (no text), 4.10B Illustration – Sunday lunch.

Procedure

1 Lead in to this task by asking questions to the class about another country's or culture's customs. For example, elicit responses to the following questions in order to establish a stereotypical image of British eating habits:
  – *What do you know about British food?*
  – *Do you know any particular recipes?*
  – *Does British food have a good or a bad reputation?*
  – *Do you know what a traditional Sunday lunch is?*

2 Write the following utterances on the board. Explain that these are statements made by different members of a family having Sunday lunch. (Do not give any other clues about the setting or the characters.)
  1) Urrrgh! What's that green stuff? I'm not eating that!
  2) We'll have ours here, on a tray, Mavis.
  3) What's all this? You know I'm a wheat-intolerant vegan.
  4) Don't bother about me. I'll get a takeaway after the match.
  5) I'm O.K. I had a satsuma earlier.

3 Seat students in pairs or small groups. Instruct them to contextualise the statements, character by character:
  – *Which member of the family is speaking?*
  – *How old are they? What do they look like?*
  – *What kind of person are they? Where are they in the room?*
  – *What are they doing?*
  – *Who is Mavis?*

4 Focus on the key words in the first three statements: *stuff*, *that*, *ours*, *all this*, etc. and ask students what they refer to. Give/elicit an example as a prompt.

Example: *A fussy child could say statement 1 – the 'stuff' could be some horrible green food which is on the kitchen table.*

5 Students report back their ideas in open class. Get the whole class to agree about a visual image of the five characters.
6 Show students the image *Sunday lunch* with the text rubbed out (CD-ROM 4.10A). Students quickly match the statements with the characters. Were their characters similar to or different from their visual images?
7 Show the complete image (CD-ROM 4.10B). Conclude by asking general questions about the cartoon:
   – *What does the cartoon say about the great British tradition of Sunday lunch?*
   – *What does it say about stereotypical family life in Britain?*
   – *How does that compare with the stereotypical family in your country?*
   – *Were your mental images similar to this impression?*
   – *Are such stereotypes valid?*

Note

This activity is based on a particular comic drawing, but the above procedure could be used with many other images. It is interesting, however, to focus on visual stereotypes and challenge mental images. In this task, students are able to question some of these clichéd images or to see others reinforced. They can compare these with their own culture. As such, this works at raising intercultural awareness.

B Image types

5 Signs, symbols and icons

This chapter begins the second half of this book, based on image types rather than activity types. Symbols are a useful image type in the language classroom for a variety of reasons. They are culture-bound: one symbol may have a completely different meaning in one culture than in another, and its meaning may change radically over time. When we see the Nazi swastika today, for example, it is hard for many of us to believe that this was originally an Indian religious sign signifying peace. Secondly, symbols are context-bound: an 'x' may signify 'love', 'multiplied', 'incorrect', 'censored' or 'vote here', depending on where you see it. Finally, symbols can be easily created and are highly resonant. One of the symptoms of this digital age is the way in which a face splashed over a million different websites or newspaper front pages can become transformed into a symbol for a movement, a generation, a series of beliefs or a social phenomenon. Icons, whether they be people (footballers, missing children, film stars) or objects (the iPod® or the Walkman® that preceded it) are extremely powerful images in themselves. If introduced in creative ways in the classroom, their impact is undeniable.

The images explored here come from a very broad canvas. There are a number of tasks which explore the symbols' relation with a country's culture: the first task, 5.1 What is an icon?, looks at symbols which the British general public voted as being representative of their country. Elsewhere, students look at a wide range of different image types, including stamps and banknotes, analysing how cultures opt for a certain image to promote their country (5.2 Stamps and banknotes).

The chapter also looks at pictograms and street signs to find differences in what should be internationally recognisable images. However, even when these formal constraints apply to the designing of such symbols, there are subtle differences which are fascinating to explore with students. Take the example of the Olympic pictograms (5.4): in each case, the host country has decided to opt for designs which have to be internationally recognisable but, at the same time, say something about their culture (for example, the Sydney Olympic symbol features a boomerang). As such, the activity serves as a useful exercise in raising intercultural awareness. Perhaps for this reason there was such controversy related to the London 2012 Games logo. Many British people may have felt that the image was not culturally accurate or was referring to a culture which they couldn't possibly identify with. Connotative (what is conveyed indirectly) and denotative (what is indicated explicitly) meanings are also analysed when studying street signs. Such signs can communicate very different messages in very subtle ways, just by altering a pictogram convention or two.

The chapter looks at a number of other image types, from flags to masks, from alphabets to hands. In a digital world in which communication often revolves around a shorthand of computer icons and text-messaging symbols, the penultimate task aptly looks at the universal smiley icon (5.13 Smileys). This approach encourages students to create their own symbolic language with all its corresponding codes and nuances.

5.1 What is an icon?

Outline	To understand the concept of an 'icon', to analyse and group icons, to select icons for the class's own country/culture.
Focus	Fluency practice. Lexical sets according to chosen icons, e.g. sports, books. Cultural input.
Level	Elementary–Advanced
Time	30 minutes class time, 30 minutes homework
Materials and preparation	See http://www.icons.org.uk/theicons for the icons featured in this task.

Procedure

1 Use the following examples to establish: a) the different meanings of the word *icon*, and b) that the word in its computer-icon sense is nowadays the most frequent usage.

If you want to get online, just click on the Internet ***icon****.*
Friendly and lovable, the giant panda has become something of a national ***icon*** *for the Chinese people.*
Many religious homes in Russia have ***icons*** *hanging on the wall.*

2 Use a data projector or interactive whiteboard to display certain icons from the http://www.icons.org.uk/theicons website. Alternatively, print out

some of the icons and photocopy them for your class. Explain that the icons are all associated with the United Kingdom. In groups students look at the icons and try and group two or three icons into categories, e.g. food and drink.

3 Students compare with other groups. Ask the groups to defend their choice of categories. Individual students report back in open class, and you can then reveal the identity of each icon and agree on the best category headings. Good examples are buildings: Big Ben, Stonehenge; food and drink: cup of tea, fish and chips; sports: rugby, cricket; cultural icons: Sherlock Holmes, Monty Python; books: *Pride and Prejudice*, *King James Bible*; geographical features: The Thames, White Cliffs of Dover.

4 If students have an Internet connection at home, tell them to access the icons website (http://www.icons.org.uk) individually. Ask them to select five of their own favourites. Each student then compiles information about each icon from the website and reports back in the next class. Which did they find the most interesting/surprising? Which icons have equivalents in their country/culture?

Variation 1: Categorising icons

For Advanced-level groups, ask students which icons from the website were:

a) easy to identify, due to the clarity of the image
b) clear enough to get a general idea of the icon, due to the image's universality
c) difficult but not impossible to guess, due to the image's ambiguity
d) impossible to identify or guess, due to being culturally over-specific.

Variation 2: Top five

For Intermediate-level groups, students choose five icons to represent their country/culture. Ask them to be prepared to defend their choices. You could organise a vote to find the most popular icons in the class.

Variation 3: Icon webquest

If you have an Internet connection, base another class around the icons website http://www.icons.org.uk. (Alternatively, prepare the material for students to do at home.) Encourage the students to read some background material about selected icons, or the Icons Timeline or Icons Atlas, and prepare a quiz based on this information.

5.2 Stamps and banknotes

Outline	Developing cultural awareness of a country through chosen symbols – banknotes and stamps.
Focus	Descriptive language of colours, patterns, design, etc.
Level	Pre-intermediate–Advanced
Time	30 minutes
Materials and preparation	CD-ROM images 5.2A–B Brazil 10 Reais banknote, UK Prince William 68 pence stamp. Collect some banknotes and stamps from different countries. It is a good idea to choose a combination of conventional ones (stamps with representative fauna and flora or natural resources from that particular country) and more contemporary images. You do not need to have originals – such images are easily available on the Internet.
Note	Try sites such as http://www.banknotes.com (click on 'Currency Museum' to get a run-down of different countries' money) or a whole host of websites devoted to stamps, including very specific ones such as http://www.bird-stamps.org/ Otherwise, do a Google™ Image search and key in (for example) 'New Zealand stamps'.

Procedure

1 Write the name of a country on the board, e.g. *New Zealand*. Ask students – in pairs / small groups – to think of and note down any images they associate with this country.

Sample answer: *Mountains, kiwis, the Maoris, All Blacks, yachting.*

2 Hand out a photocopied worksheet with different stamps or banknotes, some of which are from the country/countries that you selected. You could choose from the two images on the CD-ROM (5.2 A–B).

3 Students in pairs focus on one stamp or banknote. Then present the following questions for them to answer:
- *What is the main image?*
- *What else can you see on the stamp/banknote?*
- *What cultural values are represented? Choose ideas from this list: equal opportunities, economic power, solidarity, flora and fauna, representative figures, pride, education.*

4 Students report back in open class. Widen the debate to include the following questions, where possible:
- *Why do you think the country chose to represent itself in this way?*
- *What message is the country sending by using this image?*
- *Which stamp/banknote do you find the most original/impressive? Why?*

- *What is the traditional role of stamps/banknotes? In what way have some of these examples subverted this?*

Sample answers 5.2. A–B:

England: This stamp was issued to mark Prince William's 21st birthday. The image is daring within its conventional format as it represents William in a very modern, sophisticated way, dressed in a serious but fashionable suit. A possible interpretation is that this image represents a new-look, contemporary Royal Family with an impressive, serious and attractive heir to the throne or, as the BBC put it, here is a 'reticent royal icon'.

Brazil: This banknote was issued in 2000 to commemorate the 500th anniversary of Portuguese sea captain Pedro Álvares Cabral's arrival in Brazil. The traditional front shows a representation of one of the earliest drawings of the country and an image of Cabral and ships from his expedition. The other side, however, represents a stylised map of Brazil with photos depicting the ethnic variety of the Brazilian population (white, black, Indian and mixed race). Such images of 'real' people are not commonly found in official designs such as stamps or banknotes.

5 In open class, students discuss how their country is traditionally represented in stamps and banknotes.

Variation 1: One country, one icon

Students research a particular country of their choice and bring an example of one stamp/banknote to present to class. Individuals should explain why they have chosen these particular examples and what the images represent about a particular country.

Variation 2: Design your own stamp/banknote

Students choose a country and design their own stamps or banknotes for it – this is an ideal task for younger learners as project work. Make sure that:

1) they choose an image clearly associated with this country – a famous person, building, etc.
2) they make it clear how much the note is worth and that it cannot easily be forged.

In the next class, students present their image ideas to the rest of the class, who then vote on the best ones.

5.3 Street signs

Outline	Interpreting, deciphering and creating signs.
Focus	Paraphrasing signs. Functional language in sign language, different registers (formal/informal).
Level	Intermediate–Advanced
Time	20–30 minutes / 1 hour with Variations
Materials and preparation	CD-ROM images 5.3A Illustration – Five street signs; 5.3B–F Individual street signs; 5.3G Illustration – Six dog signs; 5.3H–M Individual dog signs; 5.3N Wait for me! sign.
Note	You can use different types of street signs for many activity types. I have chosen to focus on function and register, but you may prefer to use signs as speaking prompts for lower levels (see Variations).

Procedure

1 Distribute or project the different signs (CD-ROM 5.3A–F) to the students in pairs or small groups. Check first that students know the following different sign types: 'warning', 'security', 'advertising', 'request', 'road safety', and their concepts. Present the class with the following questions:

- *What kind of sign is each and where would you find it?*
- *How could you communicate the message of each in one simple sentence? e.g. Sign 1: Don't even think of parking here → It is illegal to park here.*

Answers:

B Parking/warning sign: this is commonly seen on the streets of New York City.

C Advertising sign: on a shop window when selling sale products or because the shop is closing down.

D Warning sign: outside a private property.

E Local government/community 'advice' sign: on the street – or in a residential or commercial area.

F Request / road-safety sign for drivers: on street, perhaps on leaving a town.

2 Students choose adjectives from this list to identify the style of each sign. (Note that more than one adjective can apply.)

1 *polite*
2 *threatening*
3 *humorous*

4 *insistent*
5 *friendly*
6 *official*

Answers:
B threatening/insistent/official/humorous
C insistent
D threatening/humorous
E friendly/polite
F friendly/polite

3 Ask students: *In what way are these signs unconventional or original? What would a conventional equivalent look like, in each case?*
Answer: They are unconventional because they don't use the wording that we typically associate with signs. They are more colloquial in register. For example, sign 5.3F would normally appear at the entrance of a town and its wording would be 'SLOW DOWN' or 'DRIVE SLOWLY' with a speed limit attached.
4 Ask: *Why could signs C and E be considered the odd ones out?*
Answer: Sign C is different because its purpose is to sell, not instruct or warn. Sign E's design is 'un-sign-like' because of the small letters and lack of strong colour; it is not explicit but merely suggestive.

Follow-up

Show the students the following six signs from the CD-ROM (5.3G–M) which are all directed at dog owners. In what way does the illustration, design and wording alter the message of each? Follow the same procedure used to analyse the five previous signs.

I'll wait here

Variation 1: Creating signs

Suitable for lower levels. Students create signs for their classroom (e.g. *No eating or drinking*), which could then be displayed. Encourage them to make the signs humorous or different in some way, and to incorporate some of the new language they have just seen. Show image 5.3N as an example. This is a real sign found in a school library.

Students can also make their own signs from templates at:
http://www.victorystore.com/dyo/signs/index.htm
and their own street signs at:
http://www.streetsigngenerator.com/

Variation 2: Drawing signs

Put students in pairs. Ask Student A to draw the following common signs, but not to show the wording to Student B:

MEN AT WORK
ANIMALS CROSSING
FRAGILE: HANDLE WITH CARE
WARNING: WET FLOOR

Student B has to provide the equivalent wording for each sign. Student A then provides the correct answers. The two students can then change roles, using the following signs:

SILENCE PLEASE
NO MOBILE PHONES
DON'T DROP LITTER
NO T-SHIRTS OR SHORTS

Students finish by discussing where they might most commonly find these signs.

5.4 Olympic pictograms

Outline	Interpreting, describing and deciphering pictograms. Appreciating cultural differences between one set of pictograms and another.
Focus	Sports vocabulary. Descriptive adjectives. Reading-comprehension practice.
Level	Intermediate +
Time	45 minutes +
Materials and preparation	CD-ROM images 5.4A Mexico Olympic pictograms 1968; 5.4B Moscow Olympic pictograms 1980; 5.4C Tokyo Olympic pictograms 1964; 5.4D Barcelona Olympic pictograms 1992; 5.4E Atlanta Olympic pictograms 1996; 5.4F Sydney Olympic pictograms 2000; 5.4G Athens Olympic pictograms 2004; 5.4H Olympic pictogram answers.

Procedure

1 As a lead-in, establish how many cities have held the Olympic Summer Games in the last 50 years and which will hold them in the future. Alternatively, design a matching task with years and cities.

Answers: 1960: Rome, 1964: Tokyo, 1968: Mexico City, 1972: Munich, 1976: Montreal, 1980: Moscow, 1984: Los Angeles, 1988: Seoul, 1992: Barcelona, 1996: Atlanta, 2000: Sydney, 2004: Athens, 2008: Beijing, 2012: London.

2 Establish/elicit a number of different Olympic sports. Divide students into groups and tell them to think up four sports for each category: a) track and field, b) watersports, c) ball sports, d) winter Olympic sports, e) combat sports.

Sample answers: a) track and field: 100-metres, 400-metres hurdles, marathon, javelin, b) watersports: rowing, swimming, waterpolo, sailing, c) ball sports: football, hockey, basketball, handball, d) winter Olympic sports: ice hockey, skiing, ice skating, tobogganing, e) combat sports: boxing, wrestling, fencing, judo.

3 Write the word *Pictogram* on the board and establish the difference between a pictogram and any other sign or icon (see Sample answer on p. 151). What classic international pictograms are used all over the world?

Sample answer: A pictogram is a graphic element, a visual reference for a letter, word or phrase. 'Pictograms communicate through the associations that we attach to an image or group of images.'[1] Therefore, for a pictogram to be successful in an international context, it needs to be culturally neutral and give unambiguous information. Famous pictograms include street signs, airport/hospital/emergency information signs, which, by and large, are recognised the world over.

4 Present the following pictograms from the Mexico City Olympic Games on the CD-ROM (5.4A) and ask the following questions:
   a) *What can you see in each of the four pictograms?*
   b) *What sports do they represent?*

   For higher-level students:
   c) *Are they good pictograms? (i.e. Are they internationally recognisable/unambiguous?)*
   d) *Which decade do you think these Olympic pictograms come from? The 60s, 70s, 80s or 90s?*

Answers:
a) A boxing glove, football, swimmer's arm and pool, arm lifting a weight.
b) Boxing, football, swimming, weightlifting.
c) The ball could perhaps apply to another sport. The swimming pictogram is also ambiguous.
d) The pictograms come from the 1968 Mexico City Olympic Games.

5 Show the students the pictograms from the Moscow Olympic Games (CD-ROM 5.4B) for the same sports. What is the difference between the two sets?

Sample answer: The Mexico City pictograms symbolise each sport by means of the apparatus or the equipment needed. This creates a strong impact, as the pictograms require less detail. The Moscow pictograms also use white silhouettes, but they show the figures doing each sport.

6 Show the students the other Olympic pictograms (CD-ROM 5.4C–G) for the same four sports. What is the difference between them? Ask students to choose from these different adjectives for their descriptions.

classical	*detailed*
creative	*elegant*

[1] Ambrose, G. and Harris, P. *Image* (Lausanne: Ava Publishing) 2005, p. 146.

artistic	*stylised*
curved	*old-fashioned*
naturalistic	*statue-like*
abstract	*clear*
dynamic	*minimal*
geometric	*painterly*
free	*physical*

Students report back their answers in open class.

Note

Provide dictionaries for students to check meanings of the adjectives.

Football pictograms for all seven Olympic Games, © IOC / Olympic Museum Collections

7 Photocopy the following texts and ask the students, in pairs or small groups, to match them with the five Olympic cities:

Tokyo, Barcelona, Atlanta, Sydney, Athens.

A This is a more **abstract** approach. The symbol of the boomerang is used for the figure's two legs and two smaller versions for the arms, making this a **creative** and original concept. However, the boomerang symbol is also restrictive, because some of the sports are not easy to identify.

B The figures have no trunks and are drawn with **freer**, more **painterly** brushstrokes, used to create an **abstract** look. This reminds us of the **artistic** traditions in a city that has Miró and Picasso as its representatives, contrasting greatly with the geometric look of previous Olympic pictograms.

C This is not geometric at all, but rather **old-fashioned**. The bodies are much more **naturalistic**, with far more **physical** features, such as muscles, incorporated. The orange background and black figures remind us of the **classical**, **statue-like** figures of Ancient History.

D Some pictograms only show half bodies. The design is very **minimal** and **clear**, cleanly drawn. Although it is very **stylised**, it looks a little **old-fashioned** today.

E Scratched white lines are used with the black bodies to create very **detailed** figures. These are very **elegant, curved** and **dynamic**, with a softer, flexible look to their bodies.

© Cambridge University Press 2008 PHOTOCOPIABLE

Answers:
A Sydney, B Barcelona, C Atlanta, D Tokyo, E Athens.

8 Students report back their answers in open class. What clues helped them to make their decisions? Students comment on whether the adjectives in the texts coincide with their original descriptions. See all seven sets of Olympic pictograms on CD-ROM 5.4H.

Follow-up

Students research the cultural connections between the pictograms and the countries hosting the Olympics. This is worth studying, particularly in connection with Barcelona, Sydney, Athens, Beijing and London.

Note

The controversy over the 2012 London Olympic logo shows how important branding and image have become. The idea behind this symbol of a digital age goes against the usual classical icons associated with the Olympics. Find the logo on the Internet, show it to your students and ask them what they think it represents (many critics say it resembles a graffiti tag).

5.5 Guessing pictograms

Outline	Deciphering pictograms, hypothesising about images to guess their origin and/or meaning. Creating pictograms.
Focus	Functional language: *This pictogram means/represents . . .* Modal verbs of ability/obligation: *You can/can't/must*, e.g. *You must be careful. It's fragile.*
Level	Pre-intermediate–Advanced
Time	20–30 minutes
Materials and preparation	CD-ROM images 5.5A Two pictograms, 5.5B Six pictograms from the same place; 5.5C Similar-looking pictograms; 5.5D Pictogram – Growing old. Worksheet (all pictograms are also available on the CD-ROM).

Procedure

1 Photocopy the worksheet and distribute it around the class to students in small groups or pairs.

WORKSHEET

1 **Look at these two pictograms.**

a 

b 

– What do they mean?
– Where would you normally see them?
– How often have you come across signs like these?

2 **Look at this group of six pictograms (c–h) that were designed for the same place.**
– What does each of them indicate?
– Can you guess the place from the kinds of pictograms?
– What clues do the pictograms give you?

© Cambridge University Press 2008 PHOTOCOPIABLE

c

d

e

f

g

h

3 **Look at these four pairs of similar-looking pictograms (i-p).**
- What do you think each image represents?
- Where do you think they belong?
- How do you know?

i

© IIT Bombay

j

© IIT Bombay

k

© IIT Bombay

l

© IIT Bombay

m

n

© IIT Bombay

o

© IIT Bombay

p

4 **Subverted pictograms.**
Look at this collection of four pictograms in one.

© Patrick Thomas

- What do the four signs mean?
- Where would you normally see them?
- What has the artist achieved by putting them together in this way?

© Cambridge University Press 2008 PHOTOCOPIABLE

Answers to worksheet:

1 Pictogram a is a neighbourhood-watch sign. A neighbourhood-watch organisation is a joint venture by neighbourhoods, local government and the police, to curb crime. A sticker like this indicates to potential thieves that steps have been taken in the area to protect property, etc. You would normally see this pictogram in a private house, either stuck on the front door or on a visible ground floor window.

Pictogram b is a sign indicating where to dispose of food, paper and cardboard. It encourages you to recycle rubbish. You would normally see this pictogram by a waste-disposal bin in a public space.

2 Some of these pictograms are much easier to decipher than others. Students should have no problems with pictograms c, f and g. In pictogram d, the arrows indicate that the same bus returns to where it started from. Pictogram e indicates that people will be searched and have their possessions inspected by security staff. Pictogram indicates an area where people buy official merchandising.

c meeting point
d shuttle bus
e inspections
f ATM service
g baby-changing facility
h merchandise

These pictograms were all designed to be used in a large international sporting venue.

The pictograms give clues in that there exists specific, specially-designed 'merchandising' in the area, which suggests a theme park or at least some themed event. The ATM machine and meeting point suggest that it is a large area with many services. The inspections area suggests that there would be extra security for such an event. The baby-changing facilities would be available at any large public space, such as an airport.

3 This task shows that when pictograms are found out of context they can be confusing or difficult to interpret.

i Hotel information. Airport. Notice the comfortable bed.
j Isolation ward. Hospital. Notice the hospital-style bed on wheels.
k Arriving passenger. Airport. The passenger only has one bag and is not dressed in any particular way.

l Porter. Railway station, India. Notice the two bags which the man is carrying in an uncomfortable way, and the uniform which can be shown in the cuff detail.

m Fragile sign on a box. The glass is not attractively shaped and looks almost industrial.

n Bar in a public place. The glass reminds us of a cocktail glass. It looks like it has an olive in it. We therefore link the glass to leisure and entertainment.

o Drinking water available. In any public place.

p Hand wash only. On clothes label tag. Other clothes labels use the water motif.

4 The last pictogram is called *Growing old*. Perhaps it gives an impression of how society sees you differently as you grow old. Signs which never previously applied to you now do.

Follow-up

Ask your students to create their own pictograms. Alternatively, if they are not keen on drawing, they could always describe their ideas in words. To help, it is a good idea to give them particular contexts to work with. For example:

- a bottle-recycling bin
- a nuclear-free zone
- a veterinary surgeon
- a park-and-ride facility
- a place where street musicians are allowed to play.

They then show their work or describe their ideas to the rest of the class and explain their pictograms. Students then vote on the best, clearest and most original designs.

5.6 Unmasked

Outline	Students analyse and describe different masks, and then design their own one.
Focus	Explaining the function of different masks: *This is used for . . .* Adjectives to describe facial expressions.
Level	Pre-intermediate–Advanced (young learners)
Time	30 minutes
Materials and preparation	CD-ROM images 5.6A–D Four photos of masks: Mexican, Carnival, Ice Hockey, Gas mask. CD-ROM image 5.6E Template mask. Large pieces of paper or, preferably, cardboard, to design a mask with coloured pens, etc. If you want the students to wear the mask, prepare face-size pieces of card and string as well. You can print out the mask template (5.6E) and then enlarge the image on a photocopier.

Procedure

1 Lead in to the task by showing image 5.6A of a mask to the students. Elicit the function of the mask. Where do the students think it comes from? Is it contemporary or ancient?

Answer: This is a souvenir mask sold to tourists in Mexico. Similar masks were worn in ancient rituals thousands of years ago to represent gods, etc. So it is a contemporary representation of an ancient icon.

2 Students think of different types of masks or painted faces. Dictate the following questions:
- *What can they be used for?*
- *Who can use them?*

3 Students in pairs make a list and report back their answers in open class. Establish/elicit some of these functions:
- *Protective masks: dentists, surgeons, construction workers.*
- *In sports: ice hockey, baseball, wrestling.*
- *Gas/oxygen masks: in wartime, in emergency.*
- *Ritualistic/theatrical masks: from ancient Greece, traditional Chinese and Japanese drama.*
- *Festivals: Halloween, carnival in certain countries, most famously in Venice and Brazil.*
- *Kids' masks at birthday parties, based on famous cartoon or fantasy characters (such as the Incredible Hulk).*
- *Medical: masks are increasingly worn in some countries if you are ill and do not want to spread your infection, or if you are allergic.*

- *Death masks: in ancient Egypt, Rome and China, masks were put on corpses before burial.*
- *People wear masks in demonstrations, often as grotesque caricatures of politicians to protest against something.*
- *A facial (mud) mask is a substance you put on your face to clean your skin and leave it smooth.*

4 Students discuss the following questions in pairs:
   - *When was the last time you wore a mask?*
   - *What was the reason?*
   - *What kind of mask was it? Funny/scary, etc.*

5 Students look at three other masks (CD-ROM 5.6B–D), and answer these questions:
   - *When would you use these masks? Why?*
   - *What are the masks made of?*
   - *How would you look if you put this mask on?*

   Students report back their answers in open class.

6 Focus students' attention on the template for the mask (CD-ROM 5.6E). Draw a similar one on the board so that the class get the idea. Explain that they are all invited to a carnival party. Tell them that they have to design their own disguise for it.

7 Put the students in groups and hand out card (or copies of the mask template from the CD-ROM), string and coloured paints, crayons or pencils. Tell them that, before they begin, they should consider concept, colour, material, etc.

8 Students create their masks and put them on. Volunteer members of each group can walk around the class. The other students have to guess what everybody's mask represents.

9 Students report back in open class about the ideas for the masks. Which were the most popular models?

Note

If you want the masks to be presented as posters, get the students to draw on larger pieces of paper/card.

Variation: Hats and other clothes

You could follow a similar procedure, using hats/headgear, or other similar articles of clothing, costumes or forms of disguise.

See 1.13 What's it for?

5.7 Culture shock

Outline	Students analyse different street signs and try to imagine their cultural origin. They design their own street signs based on certain texts.
Focus	Deciphering and explaining: *This means . . ., This could refer to . . .*, shapes and colours to describe signs.
Level	Intermediate–Advanced
Time	30 minutes, plus 30 minutes for Follow-up
Materials and preparation	CD-ROM images 5.7A Five street signs; 5.7B Five unusual signs.

Procedure

1 As a lead-in, students describe what street signs they have seen on the way to class today, or which ones they usually see.

2 Ask them to describe a couple of signs from their mind's eye. (This is not as easy as it sounds.)

Example: *A STOP sign is usually hexagonal (it has six sides). It has a red background and letters in white.*

3 Seat students in pairs. Focus their attention on the five street signs (CD-ROM 5.7A), which all come from a particular country.
Ask these questions:

– *What is strange about these signs?*
– *What do you think the signs stand for?*
– *What clues do they give you about the country and its culture?*

Note

You may need to explain/paraphrase *rickshaws* and *hawkers*.

Answers:

– Because of their subject matter, you wouldn't often find these signs in many western societies.
– a) Warning: low flying aircraft; b) Warning: hippos; c) No hitchhiking; d) No rickshaws; e) No hawkers.
– The signs come from South Africa. We can guess this from the wildlife, the forms of transport and the street-selling, which is common in Africa.

4 Students look at the other signs (5.7B) in small groups.
– *Why would they look strange in your country?*

- *Where would you expect to see them?*
- *What do you think they mean exactly and in what society might you find them?*

f) *Frogs on the road:* frogs are not usually protected in this way. The sign might be found on the roadside to warn drivers, in a country with a tropical climate?
g) *No cannabis smoking:* cannabis is not legal in most countries. Perhaps you would find it in a public building, in a very liberal society such as Holland?
h) *Neighbourhood Watch:* quite common in some western societies like the US. The sign is used to raise awareness about burglaries. You would find it in the windows of people's houses. However, the image of the burglar here is quite humorous, like a cartoon character.
i) *Don't leave children unattended:* unusual to find this in school because most children are accompanied by teachers. You could find it in a library.
j) *No ice cream or guns:* in most countries it is not common for people to carry guns. The combination of the two prohibitions (ice cream is something children like) is startling. You may find this at the entrance of a bank?

5.8 Image history

Outline	Students analyse how symbols have changed their significance over the years. Matching texts and symbols.
Focus	Ways of contrasting the past and now, *used to*.
Level	Pre-intermediate–Advanced
Time	40 minutes, plus 30 minutes for Variation
Materials and preparation	CD-ROM images 5.8A Four symbols; 5.8B–I Eight images of hearts; 5.8J–O Six images of apples; 5.8P–Q Two Photoshopped images of apples. Collect as many different images of the symbols discussed (apples, hearts, etc.) as you can, using Internet image searches.

Procedure

1 Lead in by telling students that symbols and icons change their significance over time, according to the context and the moment.
2 Present the class with the following short texts about iconic images. Students read and guess what the images are. They discuss their answers in pairs.

1
Originally used to mark the entrances of Spanish cemeteries, this sign has come to indicate danger, and is still a standard symbol for poison. However, it is rarely used today for that purpose because of its negative marketing effect and connection with pirates. These associations may make the symbol attract rather than detract children. In pre-Columbian Mexico, people believed that part of this symbol represented life and not death. Today you can still find it made into sweets and papier-mâché figures on the Day of the Dead.

2
It is thought that this was an early symbol for the sun in Chinese art. Roof tiles dating back to the Tang Dynasty with this symbol have been found near the ancient city of Xian. But it also may indicate the swirl of smoke, a vortex of water or a mysterious pull of energy. It is also a symbol of hypnosis.

3
An unofficial symbol of Ireland, this symbol has three green leaves. It was traditionally used for its medicinal properties and was a popular motif in Victorian times. It is also a common way to represent St Patrick's Day and Irish pubs – immediately appealing to those on the lookout for an English-speaking establishment and warm welcome when travelling abroad. It is also said to bring good luck.

4
In European traditional art and folklore, this symbol is drawn in a stylised shape, typically coloured red. It suggests both blood and, in many cultures, passion and strong emotion. The shape, sometimes intersected with an arrow, is particularly associated with romantic poetry and is often used as a symbol for St Valentine's Day. It was famously used to promote New York and other cities.

© Cambridge University Press 2008 PHOTOCOPIABLE

3 Ask a volunteer to come to the board and draw the four symbols. Compare with the representations on the CD-ROM (5.8A).

Answers:
1 Skull and crossbones, 2 Spiral, 3 Shamrock (three-leaf clover), 4 Heart.

4 Dictate additional questions in open class to check comprehension:
– *Which symbol(s)*
  is/are the most mysterious? (spiral)
  can be easily misunderstood? (skull and crossbones)
  can make people proud about where they live? (heart)

has many negative connotations? (skull and crossbones)
is/are most commonly used on particular days? (heart/shamrock)
is/are identified with a particular country? (shamrock / skull and crossbones)
is/are usually a particular colour? (heart/shamrock)
can make you feel a particular emotion? (heart/spiral)

5 Students discuss different places where they can find 'hearts'.

Example:

- *On playing cards*
- *'I love NY'-type signs*
- *On Valentine cards*
- *On chocolate boxes*
- *As an icon for love or romance in many contexts*
- *On ancient coins*

Explain to the class that the photographer Moza Hantoush has produced a number of different photos on the subject of hearts. Students look at the images (5.8B–I) and think of captions for them on the subject of love. They can rewrite these captions in different ways: 1) with the word *love*, 2) with the word *heart*, 3) with neither.

6 Students report back their ideas and then match the images with the captions that Moza originally gave them. You can either dictate the captions below or photocopy them for the students.

Moza's captions:

1 Love is a gift
2 Served with love
3 A very special penny
4 Even when the heart stopped beating
5 Trapped
6 True inner beauty
7 You don't die of a broken heart, you only wish you did
8 With love comes pain

© Moza Hantoush
From *Working with Images* © Cambridge University Press 2008 PHOTOCOPIABLE

Answers:
1 H, 2 E, 3 B, 4 D, 5 C, 6 G, 7 I, 8 F.

7 Get students to discuss Moza's messages. By framing the heart in these different ways, what do students think she is saying about love?
8 Students think of another symbol – eagle, rose, cross – and play the same game in pairs, asking each other to visualise the same object in different ways.

Variation: apples

1 Explain to students that some symbols can take different forms. Ask the class to close their eyes and think of what they see (in their mind's eye) when you say the word *apple*.
2 Once the students have an image in their mind, dictate the following questions:
   - *What kind of apple do you see?*
   - *Is it red or green or a mixture of the two?*
   - *Is it large or small, sweet or sour, hard or soft?*
   - *What does it feel like?*
   - *Does your apple have a name? (e.g. Granny Smith)*
   - *Is it on a tree or somewhere else?*
   - *Do you touch it?*
   - *Do you take a bite out of it? Does it taste good?*
   - *What sound does it make when you bite into it?*
3 Students report back their answers. Ask students to explain why they think they chose that particular image. What particular associations do they have with it?
4 Show students six images of apples on the CD-ROM (5.8J–O). What is the connection with the word *apple* in each case?

Answers: 1 An apple for the teacher, 2 Adam's apple – a part of the body, 3 New York City – 'the Big Apple', 4 An apple a day, 5 Isaac Newton and the apple falling from the tree, 6 Apple® Computers is Bill Gates's (of Microsoft®) rival in this industry.

5 Show the last two images which have been manipulated or Photoshopped in some way. How do the students interpret these new images of apples?

Follow-up

For more advanced students. Students research a particular image or symbol and attempt to track its social history. Where did this image originate? How has its symbolism/meaning changed from one generation to the next? For example, you could choose an article of clothing which has become a fashion icon, such as the leather jacket, the mini-skirt, the bowler hat or the kilt.

See 1.10 Google™ it for another task featuring the apple.

5.9 Hands

Outline	Students analyse and translate gestures using hands, etc.
Focus	Key exclamations, colloquialisms, warnings, etc. Lexical set: jobs.
Level	Elementary +
Time	15 minutes
Materials and preparation	CD-ROM images 5.9A Perfect symbol; 5.9B Hand gestures; 5.9C Hand gesture answers; 5.9D Churchill's V sign; 5.9E Black Power salute; 5.9F Clinton's thumb.
Note	Be careful with younger learners that this task does not degenerate into a succession of rude gestures. Use your judgement to decide whether this activity would be suitable for your teaching context.

Procedure

1 Mime a few hand gestures and ask the students to guess their meaning. You could show students the 'perfect' sign on the CD-ROM (5.9A) but note that this sign is considered offensive in some countries, for example Brazil.

Other gestures also have different meanings in different cultures. For example, standing with your hands on your hips is a sign of being ready in western cultures but it could also be seen as an aggressive gesture. Open palms indicate sincerity and openness, which is why it is often a popular gesture with politicians.

2 Students mime different hand gestures to each other in pairs and see if they agree as to their significance.

3 Show students the different gestures (CD-ROM 5.9B). Ask them to match the symbols with their definitions:

peace	stop	offering
power	bad news	fingers crossed
framed	that's great	punch

Hand gestures, © IIT Bombay

Answers: A fingers crossed, B framed, C offering, D peace, E power, F punch, G stop, H bad news, I that's great.

4 Students report back their answers in open class. Show students the answer sheet on the CD-ROM (5.9 C). How else could they communicate each hand gesture in words?

Example: *fingers crossed / touch wood / let's hope so.*

5 Ask students how they would communicate the following statements using hand gestures. Do the 'air quotes' hand gesture as an example, used when you say something 'in inverted commas'.

Note

This can be dictated as a list, with the students standing up and doing the hand gestures spontaneously. This way, you can see immediately if everyone's interpretation is the same.

With one hand:

I'll phone you.
Come here. (beckoning)
Can I have the bill/check, please?
That's expensive.
Okay.
Slow down. / Be patient.
Look at that.

With two hands:
Time out.
High five.

Follow-up

1 Establish the fact that many different professions require the use of hand signals and gestures. Students compile a list in pairs or small groups.

Sample answers: traffic policeman, ground staff at airport, football referee/linesman, cricket umpire, orchestra conductor, photographer.

Follow one of two procedures, according to the level of your class:

Higher levels: Students describe gestures without miming (and/or give clues as to why the gestures are needed), and the rest of the class have to guess the profession.

Lower levels: Students mime the hand movements, and the class match a job to each.

2 Look at the photos on the CD-ROM (5.9D–F) – Churchill's V sign, the Black Power salute, and Clinton's thumb. Ask the students to name these people and ask what each hand gesture means and to tell – or guess – the story of its origin.

Students discuss and write captions for each of the images.

Answers: The '**V sign**', commonly known as 'sticking two fingers up' or 'flicking the Vs', is thought to have originated in the United Kingdom. It involves facing the palm inwards, while the index and middle fingers are extended vertically. This is the way that Winston Churchill initially indicated '**Victory**' at the beginning of the Second World War (often with a large cigar jammed between the two fingers), but he reversed the sign later in order to distinguish the 'V for Victory' campaign from a gesture widely considered insulting.

Black Power was a political movement among persons of African descent throughout the world, though it is often associated primarily with African-Americans in the United States. Most prominent in the late 1960s and early 1970s, the movement emphasised racial pride and the creation of black political and cultural institutions to nurture and promote black collective interests, advance black values and secure black autonomy. Tommie Smith (gold medal) and John Carlos (bronze medal) famously performed the **Black Power salute** on the 200-metres winners' podium at the 1968 Olympics in Mexico.

The gesture dubbed the '**Clinton thumb**' after its most famous user, Bill Clinton, is used by politicians to provide emphasis in speeches without pointing the finger. This gesture has the thumb leaning against the thumbside portion of the index finger, which is part of a closed fist. It does not exhibit the anger of the clenched fist or pointing finger, and so is thought to be less threatening. This gesture was likely adopted by Clinton from John F. Kennedy, who can be seen using it in many speeches during his political career.

(Source: http://en.wikipedia.org/wiki/Hand_gesture)

5.10 Favourite things

Outline	Students introduce themselves using a variety of symbols and images. Showing how images can be used to: 1) evoke a particular experience or feeling and 2) introduce oneself.
Focus	Fluency practice. Introductions, presentations and explanations.
Level	Elementary–Intermediate
Time	15 minutes (useful as a warmer)
Materials and preparation	Photocopy of template for each student. CD-ROM images 5.10A Illustration – Favourite things template; 5.10B Illustration – Favourite things example.

Procedure

1 Draw on the board six squares. In each square, draw a symbol, an icon or a small picture which expresses the following favourite things to you: *person, place, symbol, pastime, time*, hate* (see example (CD-ROM 5.10B)). Be careful not to explain the significance of each of these signs or symbols yet.

(* This could be interpreted in any way: as a year, a season, a time of the day, etc.)

Note

You don't have to take a long time over this or draw very well but merely come up with an image which, to your mind, represents these categories. It is better to be natural here. Students will appreciate the fact that you are opening yourself up in this way and return the intimacy.

2 Ask students in pairs to describe the six images as best they can. Tell them these represent six different 'favourites'. Students have to guess what the criterion for each box is.
3 Students report back their answers, which you accept/reject as appropriate. Explain the importance of each image.

Example: *I like this symbol because it represents hope and optimism for me.*

4 Give students a copy of the six-square template (CD-ROM 5.10A) or ask them to draw their own one. They could follow your example and draw a representation of their six favourites: *person, place, symbol, pastime, time* and *hate*.

Note

It is important that the students express their feelings in a spontaneous way when they draw. The pictures do not need to be accurate or professionally drawn.

5 When they have finished drawing, students in pairs show each other their images. They take it in turns to guess the significance of the symbols.
6 Students report back in open class what they have learnt about their partners.

Variation 1: Interviews

Suitable for higher levels. Instead of getting the students to do the activity in pairs, ask them to do the task individually and pin up the drawings around the class. Each student takes one and tries to find its owner by interviewing members of the class. This works well if you have a small group of students, and can be very amusing, as students may well interpret the symbols in many different ways.

Variation 2: Lonely hearts

Ask students to draw an image of themselves, in the form of symbols, as if the sketches were part of a lonely-hearts advert. The idea is that the drawings attract another person in the class who has similar tastes.

5.11 Idioms

Outline	Students analyse drawings which help recall idiomatic language. Raising awareness as to how visual stimuli and mnemonics can help when learning idioms.
Focus	High-frequency idioms with *like*. Fluency practice. Grouping idioms to allow them to be learnt as a coherent set.
Level	Upper intermediate – Advanced
Time	45 minutes
Materials and preparation	CD-ROM images 5.11A Illustration – To have a memory like a sieve; 5.11B Illustration – Six idioms; 5.11C Illustration – six idioms – answers; 5.11D Illustration – Burnt-out worker.

Procedure

1 Mime an action to open class. For example, *working very hard*. Elicit an idiom that we use in English when you are working very hard: *I work like . . . a dog*. Ask the students if they use the same image in their language. (e.g. in Spanish it is more common to say *to work like a donkey*.)

2 Show the illustration of the sieve (CD-ROM 5.11A) and teach the expression *to have a memory like a sieve*. Ask students if they have the same or a similar expression in their language for someone who is very forgetful.

3 Point out to the class that many idiomatic expressions use the word *like* as we are constantly making similarities with one thing and a particular image in our minds.

4 Show students the other illustrations of objects (5.11B). Ask what they think is the missing verb related to each of these images. Write a prompt on the board as follows:

to __________ *like cat and dog*
to __________ *like a chimney.*

5 Students report back their answers in open class. Correct where necessary and then show students the answers (5.11C).

Answers:

1) to fight like cat and dog
2) to smoke like a chimney
3) to drink like a fish
4) to know something like the back of your hand
5) to eat like a horse
6) to stick out like a sore thumb

6 Suggest to students that creating a strong mental image of an idiom can help them remember it. Write the following idioms (or a selection of them) on the board, and check that students know the meaning of each one.

to fit like a glove
to get on like a house on fire
to spend money like water
to go out like a light
to sleep like a log
to spread like wildfire

7 Ask the students, working individually and without writing, to make up a sentence that contextualises each idiom. They should then think of a strong mental image that captures both the meaning of the sentence and the literal meaning of the idiom. For example, *I went to the party dressed in a suit, but it was a very casual party so I stuck out like a sore thumb*. The image might be of a person at a party dressed as a bandaged thumb.

8 Erase the latter half of each sentence from the board (i.e. leaving *to fit*, *to get on*, etc.). Ask individuals to complete the sentences by recalling their sentences.

9 Use this exercise to demonstrate the value of strong mental images as mnemonics (memory aids). You can repeat this activity with any other idiomatic expressions, such as phrasal verbs. Show the students the example of a 'burnt-out' worker (CD-ROM 5.11D) and ask students if they can guess what the illustrated phrasal verb is.

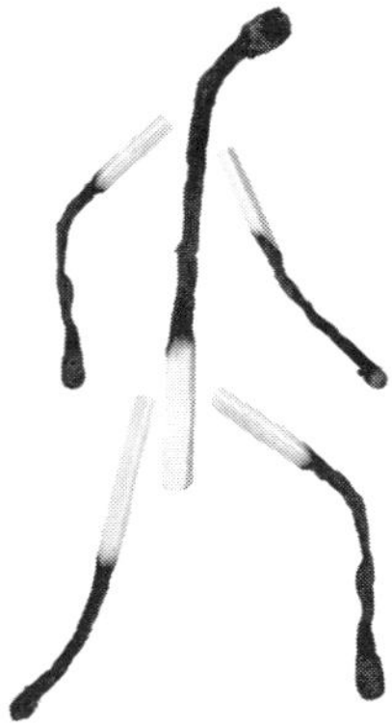

Burnt-out Worker, © Patrick Thomas

See 3.10 Draw a sentence.

5.12 Alphabets

Outline	Students study different alphabets and learn different lexical sets accordingly.
Focus	Specific and/or miscellaneous vocabulary depending on alphabet images chosen. Place prepositions and language of conjecture for Variation 1.
Level	Elementary and above, depending on the alphabet chosen. Young learners.
Time	20–30 minutes (depending on the Variation)
Materials and preparation	CD-ROM images 5.12A Urban alphabet; 5.12B–ZA A–Z Individual letters of the alphabet. You will need a computer with an Internet connection and projector for the main task and access to the other alphabets on the CD-ROM for the Variations.

Procedure

1 Play an alphabet game with your students. In open class, begin by saying *A is for . . .* and then ask the students to continue the chain, thinking of a word that begins with the following letter. If a student cannot think of a particular word in roughly ten seconds, anybody else in the group can volunteer a word. Try doing two rounds of the alphabet. Alternatively, take one letter of the alphabet and ask students, working in groups, to brainstorm words in different categories (e.g. fruit and vegetables, countries, clothes, sports) that begin with that letter. The group that comes up with the most words in a time limit (say, four minutes) is the winner.

2 Connect to http://www.flickr.com/groups/alphatheme/ and show students the home page through a projector. Explain that this group is formed by photographers who take pictures of objects beginning with a certain letter. Together they piece together 26 photos to represent each letter of the alphabet and then the alphabet and activity are 'closed'.

Scroll down the page until you reach 'Slideshow of our themed images' and then choose a letter from the alphabet. For example, the slide show for the letter 'g' would be: http://www.flickr.com/photos/tags/alphathemeg/show

Note

Make sure you know the words corresponding to each of the images before starting the slide show.

3 Students work in pairs or small groups. Show the slide show of images based on a particular letter, pausing after each to give students time to look at the image, and write down a word for *anything* in the photo which begins with the letter in question or which makes them think of a word beginning with that particular letter. Correct or give hints to the answers as you go along if the students are having difficulties.

4 At the end of the slide show, ask students to report back their answers in open class. Click on the top left-hand corner of the screen to return to 'tagged photos' and go through each photo to read the tag that was given by the photographer in each case. Students compare with their answers. At the end, the group with the most correct words wins.

Note

In some cases, it is interesting to read the comments made by the photographers about their images.

Follow-up

Choose a letter of the alphabet. Ask students to bring an image which corresponds to this letter to the next class, preferably a large colour picture.

Students can create a poster collage the next day of all the images and play the same game as above.

Variation 1: Alphabet city

Letters of the alphabet are to be found all around us: in nature, in the sky and in man-made objects. One Flickr™ group takes photos of anything that just happens to make up the shape of a familiar letter: a tree, a cloud or a detail of a building or household object.

1 Show students the Urban alphabet (CD-ROM 5.12A) and ask the class, in pairs, to try and make out what the original object is in each case.

Note
The images are available on the CD-ROM (5.12B–ZA) as individual letters as well.

2 Write up the prompts on the board where necessary and revise prepositions of place, such as *It's the end/side of a . . ., It's an aerial view of . . .*

Note
It is not important that students identify each of the 'letters' but at least say what they look like to them.

The B (etc.) *looks like . . . / seems to be . . . / is made of / belongs to . . . / was taken by . . .*

3 Students report back their answers in open class.

Variation 2: Cognate alphabet
John French's alphabet, available on Flickr™, http://www.flickr.com/photos/johnefrench/sets/72157600098012239/, is a nice way to teach cognates.

Show the students the alphabet and ask how many of the images in the alphabet are spelled with the same letter in their language(s) as in English. Students can create their own alphabets based on this model, thinking up other cognates.

Source
These activities have been inspired by the alphabet sites on flickr.com.

5.13 Smileys

Outline Students decipher emoticons and draw their own versions.
Focus Revision of targeted vocabulary. Lexical sets, verbs: *yell, wink*, etc., adjectives of feeling.
Level Elementary–Intermediate
Time 20 minutes
Material and preparation CD-ROM images 5.13A Illustration – Smileys; 5.13B Illustration – Keyboard.

Procedure

1 Draw a couple of similar-looking smileys on the board, such as a big smile or a laughing smile and establish their meanings.
2 Establish that the clues in the emoticon indicate its meaning (e.g. a 'D' looks like the image of big lips smiling).
3 Ask students if and/or when they use emoticons (in MSN Messenger, in mobile sms, in emails, etc.). How often and how many do they normally use?
4 Seat students in pairs or small groups. Students look at the smileys (see page 176) or on the CD-ROM (5.13A) and match them with the captions.

Answers: 1 c, 2 e, 3 f, 4 b, 5 i, 6 j, 7 a, 8 g, 9 k, 10 d, 11 n, 12 l, 13 m, 14 h, 15 o.

Note
For higher levels, to make the task more challenging and open-ended, only provide students with the smileys.

Teach more low-frequency vocabulary (e.g. *toupée*) where necessary.

5 Students report back their answers in open class. Explain certain details, such as the O referring to an angel's 'halo'. Provide the answers found above.
6 Students in pairs create their own emoticons using the keyboard below (CD-ROM 5.13B). Reassure them that these do not have to be serious in the least. Rather, encourage the class to create humorous examples where possible, using letters as well as punctuation marks.

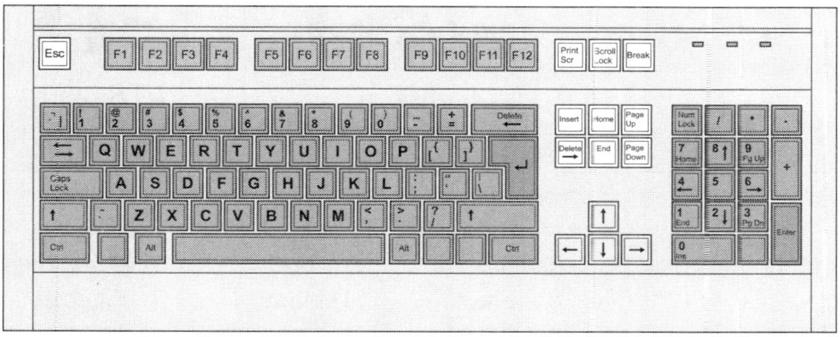

© Cambridge University Press 2008 PHOTOCOPIABLE

7 Monitor carefully and select some students to come to the board and draw their emoticons. The rest of the class have to guess what they mean.

If students run out of ideas, select some smileys from an entertaining list in the *Unofficial Smiley Dictionary*:
http://www.charm.net/~kmarsh/smiley.html

Smileys:

:-)	;-)	~:-)
1	2	3
:-*	:-{}	:-O
4	5	6
8-o	*<:-)	;^)
7	8	9
:-))	{:-)	o:-)
10	11	12
:-#	@:-)	:-D
13	14	15

© Cambridge University Press 2008 PHOTOCOPIABLE

Captions:

a) oh, my god!	b) kiss	c) happy	d) really happy
e) winking	f) one-hair	g) birthday	h) turban
i) lipstick	j) surprised	k) smirking	l) angel
m) my lips are sealed	n) toupée	o) laughing	

© Cambridge University Press 2008 PHOTOCOPIABLE

Follow-up

Students can research the history of the smiley face. Where did it originate and what has it symbolised over the years? What effect does inserting a smiley face into an email or text message have?

Sources

A list of emoticons used in messenger services can be found at:

http://messenger.yahoo.com/emoticons.php

For the difference between western and Japanese smileys (the latter are read vertically not horizontally), have a look at:

http://club.pep.ne.jp/%7ehiroette/en/facemarks/body.html

5.14 Flags and insignia

Outline	Students analyse and describe different flags and other insignia. They design their own flag (see Follow-up).
Focus	Listening and reading practice, reconstructing a text. Lexical sets: colours, shape and position of motifs on flags.
Level	Intermediate–Advanced
Time	30 minutes, plus 1 hour for Follow-up
Materials and preparation	CD-ROM image 5.14 National flag- Swaziland. Photocopy of text on Swaziland flag. Access in class to the flag identifier website http://www.flagid.org/ and a website showing examples of coats of arms for Follow-up.

Procedure

1 Lead in to the task by asking students to think of any flag, preferably not their own state or region's flag, which would be too obvious. Ask them to spend a few minutes picturing it correctly. Ask them to think of how they can describe it, going through each detail.

2 Teach any key vocabulary if necessary (*stripe*, *star*, *triangle*, *horizontal*, etc.). This will be essential with lower levels.

See 1.1 Describe and draw for flag vocabulary.

3 Group students in pairs. They take it in turns to describe their flag while the other attempts to draw it.

4 Establish with students the visual ingredients which contribute to making a flag. Group these into areas: *division*, *shape*, *colour*, *device*.

5 Show the flag of Swaziland (CD-ROM 5.14) as an example of a complex design and break down its description in open class. Next get the students in pairs to identify these five features:

1) three stripes of colour: red, blue and yellow
2) black and white shield
3) blue and red feathers
4) two spears
5) one staff.

6 Students read the text on the Swaziland flag and discover the significance of the different colours and symbols.

SWAZILAND

Red stands for the battles of the past, and refers to bloodshed. Blue stands for peace and stability. Yellow stands for prosperity and the natural resources that the country possesses.

There are two horizontal blue stripes on the edge of the rectangle and two smaller yellow stripes either side, going towards the centre. In the centre there is a thicker red horizontal stripe.

In the centre of the red band there is a black-and-white Swazi shield of the Emasotsha regiment, in a sideways position, as when carried walking. The black portion of the shield is towards the flagpole. The shield is decorated with some blue and light red *injobo* feathers which hang from the upper portion of the black part of the shield.

Behind the shield are two spears (*tikhali*) and a staff (*umgobo*) with tassels (also *injobo* feathers). The spears point away from the flagpole and are above the stick. All three of these tools lie horizontally and are in their natural colours.

These two symbols stand for protection of the country from enemies. The shield is black and white to show that black and white people live together peacefully in Swaziland.

Text adapted from http://www.flagspot.net
© Reproduced by permission of Flags of the World
From *Working with Images* © Cambridge University Press 2008 PHOTOCOPIABLE

7 Students report back a simplified version of this in open class. Go around the class, monitoring the description, and then ask various students to report back different details in open class. Make sure the students can see the flag clearly as they give their descriptions.

Note

Information about other flags can be obtained from http://www.flagspot.net

When choosing other flags, remember to select ones with plenty of detail and different colour, features, etc. according to your students' level.

See 6.7 Market leaders, and in particular CD-ROM image 6.7: Adbusters' Corporate America flag, for an example of a subverted flag. Discuss with students what this anti-consumerist organisation is saying by waving this flag.

Follow-up

1 If you have access to a computer room, ask students to log on to http://www.flagid.org/ Using the search tool, they can search for flags, design their own and find their favourites. Once they have found a flag they like, ask them to report back to the class with the details. This is a great resource and a good way to consolidate vocabulary.

2 Brainstorm different kinds of flags: political, institutional, etc. Consider flags such as the African-American flag, the gay rights flag, the pirate flag. Ask students: *In what contexts are these flags flown?*

Sample answers: Many flags are flown at half-mast when somebody important dies, beach flags tell you the state of the tide, flags are put on the top of a mountain to indicate achievement, people use flags in various protests, they are flown outside houses to indicate allegiance/patriotism, flags are also used as signals on train platforms.

3 For young learners, see: http://www.fotw.net/flags/ This site includes an online colouring book of flags for each country.

4 Show students a large group of coats of arms from: http://en.wikipedia.org/wiki/Gallery_of_sovereign_state_coats_of_arms
Ask the students, in pairs, to group these together in threes, finding any connections they like. They can do this categorisation by:
1) colour
2) shape/style
3) similar elements
4) number of elements.
Students report back what they have discovered in open class. Did any of the groups make the same connections?

6 Advertising images

'In the cities in which we live, all of us see hundreds of publicity images every day of our lives. No other kind of image confronts us so frequently. In no other form of society in history has there been such a concentration of images, such a density of visual messages.'[1] These words were written by John Berger in his seminal book on images, *Ways of Seeing*. If this was the case in 1972, how much truer are those words now. Advertising now appears in almost every form and bombards us from almost every angle imaginable and at any hour: as banners on websites, on the sides of taxis, or as unwanted cold calls in the middle of the night. As Berger went on to say (nearly 40 years ago), 'One has the impression that publicity images are continually passing us like express trains on their way to some distant terminus. We are static, they are dynamic, until the poster is posted over . . .'[2]

It is precisely that dynamism that makes them work so well in the language classroom. Their attention-seeking devices are recognised and appreciated by learners who have been exposed to so many of them on a daily basis. The advertisers' strategies and techniques can be easily analysed and learners respond well to such a procedure. This is explored in the first three tasks (6.1–6.3 Analysing ads: a basic procedure 1–3), which set up a basic set of questions and approaches that can be applied to any advert in the print media. This establishes a set of questions which will enable learners to interact with advertising on an engaging and critical level, to get to grips with this 'wallpaper of consumer culture'.

The essential question we return to when analysing adverts is: 'How do you get your message and campaign noticed when there is so much competition?' Certain companies, such as Benetton, Calvin Klein and Absolut, have done this by making their adverts iconic representations of a certain culture, fixing the gaze of viewers by subverting the conventions of advertising. Although ephemeral, their messages – like so much advertising – are able to reflect and construct cultural identities. As such, using these kinds of adverts in class is an invaluable and entertaining way to develop intercultural awareness.

Many of the tasks in this chapter explore the relationship between image and text in advertising (its multi-modal aspect). This can be seen particularly

[1] Berger, John: *Ways of Seeing*, p. 129, Penguin, 1972.
[2] ibid. p. 130.

in 6.9 Meet Alex and 6.11 I think, therefore I listen, which analyse the roles of captions and accompanying copy respectively, and study the visual layout of the adverts and their lexical reference at the same time. Other tasks look at how intertextuality[3] is at play in so many contemporary adverts. For example, in 6.6 Adverts everywhere, we look at ambient adverts which by their very nature refer to or imitate other non-advertising texts. In 6.4 The old and the new, students are encouraged to look at how an advertising campaign has changed over a generation. In 6.5 Campaigning, students evaluate the strengths and weaknesses of adverts which don't promote a product, but rather a series of ideas. In 6.8 Subvertising, learners unravel spoof adverts or visual parodies of well-known campaigns. Finally, the class can get to grips with a single campaign and product: an American radio station (WBUR) in the final task, 6.11 I think, therefore I listen.

6.1 Analysing adverts: a basic procedure 1

Outline The first of three basic procedures for teachers and students to follow when analysing an advertising image.

Focus Developing a visual literacy, enabling students to analyse advertisements that include images. Language of agreement and negotiation.

Level Intermediate–Advanced

Time 45 minutes

Materials and preparation CD-ROM images 6.1A Adobe advert part 1; 6.1B Complete Adobe advert; 6.1C Botox advert; 6.1D Porsche Design advert part 1; 6.1E Complete Porsche Design advert; 6.1F MINI Cooper advert part 1; 6.1G Complete MINI Cooper advert. Photocopies of worksheet and copies of CD-ROM images. Alternatively, project the images in class from your computer. A combination of images that have been used in adverts, preferably within the print media. Find examples of adverts, each with the main focus on one of the following: a) a person, b) a setting, c) an object.

Note When selecting adverts, either remove the text from around the product, or find a double-page spread which has no text on one of the pages. It is crucial, at first, that the students cannot see the name of the product or the product itself. Note that the trade names *Adobe*®, *Porsche*® and MINI are visible, although in a very small typeface, in images 6.1A, D and F. Please cover these if you feel your students will see them.

[3] The way one text echoes another, either by lexical or visual references.

Procedure

Photocopy the worksheet and distribute it around the class to students in small groups or pairs. Remember this worksheet can be used with any adverts which feature people, places or objects. However, sample adverts are provided as models.

WORKSHEET

1 Look at the image of this person and discuss the questions below with your partner / in your group.

1. What do you think this person does? How do you know?
2. What is the person doing in the image? Where is he?
3. What is he looking at? At you, inside or outside the frame?
4. From where are you looking at him?
5. What do you think is his mood/attitude?
6. What values does this person represent? How do you know? Consider: background details, clothes, gender, class, nationality, ethnicity.

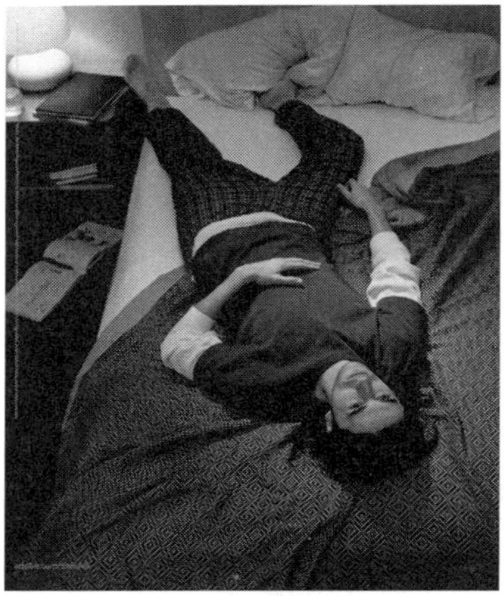

© Philip-Lorca diCorcia / Adobe®

2 Considering your answers to the above questions, try to identify the product.

3 Look at the whole advert (which your teacher will supply) and its accompanying text. Why was this particular person chosen to advertise this product?

4 Look at the image of this other person. How is this person presented to us differently? Consider: demeanour, attitude, naturalness, style.

© Image courtesy of The Advertising Archives

© Cambridge University Press 2008

PHOTOCOPIABLE

5 Look at the image of this place which represents half of another advert.

1 What kind of place is this?
2 Do you know or can you guess where it is?
3 What associations does it have for you? (e.g. mountains = freedom)
4 Is it a place you would like to go? Why? / Why not?
5 What do you think this landscape is helping to advertise? Why? What clues does the text give?

© Eterna SA/KW43 Branddesign, Germany

6 Look at the image of this object which represents another half advert (your teacher will supply the colour version).

1 What is it and what is its function?
2 What value/associations/ symbolism does it have for you?
3 What does the insect resemble? Why do you think the image has been photographed in this way?
4 What do you think this insect is helping to advertise? Why?

© 2008 MINI, a division of BMW of North America, LLC. All rights reserved. The MINI and BMW trademark, model names and logo are registered trademarks.

7 Look at all the adverts and their accompanying texts. How effective/original/ eye-catching are they?

© Cambridge University Press 2008

PHOTOCOPIABLE

Sample answers: Worksheet

1

1 He may work in a creative field – perhaps an artist, journalist, designer, architect. He is dressed in quite trendy clothes. He has a modern look about him. He has work with him.
2 He is lying on a bed. He looks like he is in a hotel room, judging by the decoration. Notice also that he has a book open on the floor and what looks like some work on the bedside table. Perhaps he would not work like this at home.
3 He is looking up at the ceiling, or at something outside the frame of the image. He is perhaps depressed and/or thinking about something serious. He seems almost paralysed.
4 We are looking down at him from above. He is upside down.
5 He may be depressed, tired or just thoughtful. His face is serious and this transmits a rather solemn mood to the image.
6 He seems to be in a nicely decorated place, perhaps an expensive hotel. He seems quite well-off (his clothes are quite trendy). Otherwise, he is a white, middle class professional. He may work in a male-dominated profession.

2 The product advertised is computer software for graphic design.

3

He is a graphic designer. He is young and trendy and many designers may identify with such a look. The fact that he is photographed in this unusual way – upside down and from above – attracts our attention and may appeal to people who work with images.

4

In contrast to the man in the other image, the woman here has a summoning gaze. She is looking directly at us, the viewer. In a way, she is inviting us to look more closely at the advert. She is wearing make-up and our gaze is focused on her skin and face. The rest of her body is not emphasised at all. She is also smiling and this adds to the overall image's artificial, airbrushed quality. We are therefore aware that this image has been designed for promotional purposes, whereas the Adobe® image may not necessarily belong to an advert.

5

1 A barren and inhospitable landscape, almost lunar. There is no trace of human presence.

2 It could be a desert, perhaps in the United States.
3 Freedom, open space, natural beauty, power, strength, eternity, distance.
4 It seems that it would be a difficult place to visit easily. The landscape is very dry and barren, so it does not appeal very much. However, the rock is very impressive and the whole scene is quite spectacular to behold.
5 It is perhaps advertising a tough, powerful car. Landscapes such as these are often used to promote cars which allow you to visit such places. Cars are often associated with open spaces of great natural beauty because they are equated with an idea of freedom. The word *engineers* in the text also calls cars to mind. However this advert actually advertises a watch.

6
1 It looks like the body of half a bee. The photo is focusing on the tail of the insect, where the sting is.
2 Despite the honey bee's painful sting and the negative stereotype of insects as pests, bees have a popular image. This is most likely due to their usefulness as pollinators and as producers of honey, their social nature and their reputation for diligence. Bees are one of the few insects used in advertisements, being used to illustrate honey and some other foods.
3 Students are unlikely to suggest that the insect resembles a car. However, it would be interesting for students to share their interpretations and discuss possible reasons why the image has be photographed in this way.
4 Students discuss their answers.

7
The more original and eye-catching adverts are the Adobe® and MINI Cooper ones. The former tells an interesting story which explains what the man is doing on the bed. The photo of the man is in itself interesting and encourages the viewer to hypothesise about what the product might be.

The image of the bee for the MINI Cooper is also highly original. It matches the MINI's paintwork perfectly. It also suggests that the MINI is a buzzy, dynamic vehicle. The bright yellow colour symbolises happiness and energy.

The Porsche® Design timepiece advert uses an image which is often associated with cars, which is understandable considering that Porsche® are best known for manufacturing cars. It suggests that the timepiece will last forever.

The Botox® advert is by far the most typical and direct advert. It doesn't work in the two-panel way as the other three adverts do and it is meant to be taken much more literally.

6.2 Analysing adverts: a basic procedure 2

Outline	Focusing on the target market and message of the advert.
Focus	Speaking practice. Language of agreement and negotiation.
Level	Pre-intermediate–Advanced
Time	30 minutes
Materials and preparation	Photocopies of worksheet. Copies of the adverts 6.1B and 6.1C. Students will also need copies of 6.1E and 6.1G for question five.

Procedure

Photocopy the worksheet and adverts and distribute them around the class to students in small groups or pairs.

WORKSHEET

1 **How do adverts persuade you to buy a product? Discuss in pairs or small groups.**

2 **Look at the images of the people in the adverts.**
   - In what way is the image attractive or persuasive?
   - What kind of viewer is the advert trying to attract? Consider: age, gender, class, profession.

3 **Look at the texts accompanying the images of people and how the whole pages are framed.**
   - How does our eye travel over the page? (i.e. What do we focus our gaze on first, what do we notice last, and what do we hardly read at all?)
   - What are the differences/similarities between how image(s) and text interact? Consider: position, type of text (headlines, subheadings, font), amount of text, additional information.
   - Why is there so much text to complement/enhance the image?

4 **Complete the following sentence for both adverts:**
   If you don't use __________ (name of product), *you* _______________.

5 **Look at the other adverts and answer these questions:**
   - What are the market, message and angle of each advert?
   - Why, in these cases, is no (or very little) text required?
   - With regard to the use of image, what do the two adverts have in common?

© Cambridge University Press 2008 PHOTOCOPIABLE

Sample answers:

1 They often feature attractive and appealing images which invite you in and seduce the gaze. In conventional adverts, these images may represent something or somebody that you desire. They can also work alongside text to attract your attention (as 'hooks').

2 – The image of the man in the Adobe® advert is not a typically persuasive one. He is not looking directly at us or smiling. However, the woman in the Botox® advert is obviously promoting a product. It is not a natural image at all.

– The Adobe® advert may be trying to attract professional creative people of a similar age to the man on the bed. The Botox® woman is attracting a particular client: a woman in her forties who is worried about her appearance and wants her wrinkles to disappear. The emphasis on youth in the woman's face suggests clearly that she is the role model for many potential Botox® buyers.

3 – In both adverts we focus on the faces of the people rather than the text, followed by the logos and, in particular, the highlighted text on the forehead of the woman in the Botox® advert. We would only stop to read the body of text if we were really interested in the product.

– There is a much more direct link between the text and the image in the Botox® advert and this text is intended to invite the reader in. Notice the use of the second person in *your toughest wrinkle* and imperatives such as *welcome*. The fact that this is placed on the woman's forehead makes it impossible to avoid. There is another catchy slogan: *it took forty years . . .*, which is also intended to help to encourage empathy on the part of the reader.

– Both adverts rely on lots of text for a variety of reasons. The Adobe® software is intangible and you cannot see it. Likewise, you wouldn't want to sell the Botox® product in a more literal way by showing the cosmetics. It simply wouldn't be as attractive. The texts help contextualise the product and explain its use. This is done in a relatively indirect way in the Adobe® advert (*it's everything but the idea*) and a very direct way with the Botox® (*it's not magic, it's …*).

4 If you don't use Adobe® software, you'll never be able to express yourself / your ideas.

If you don't use Botox®, you'll always have wrinkles.

5 The Porsche® Design timepiece is a status symbol and is aimed at an affluent and male market. The message seems to be that a Porsche® Design watch is eternal and solid and will last forever like the rock. The MINI advert would

seem to appeal to a younger market. The MINI is ideal for a young, modern professional who works in the city. The MINI is being sold as a dynamic, buzzy kind of vehicle that gets you quickly from A to B. The adverts for the Porsche® Design timepiece and the MINI Cooper work in a different way from the other adverts. One striking image – be that a mountain or a bee – is enough to attract the viewer and get the advert's message across. Any more text would simply get in the way of this message.

6.3 Analysing adverts: a basic procedure 3

Outline	Students focus on the different techniques that advertisers use with images to sell their products. Matching images with techniques.
Focus	Students identify advertising techniques in order to create their own adverts. Role playing workers in an advertising agency. Reading comprehension. Language of agreement and negotiation.
Level	Pre-intermediate–Advanced
Time	45 minutes
Materials and preparation	CD-ROM images 6.3A–F Six adverts: Aspro, Cif, Häagen Dazs, Pantene, Dettol, MINI. Photocopies of worksheet. You will also need a selection of different types of adverts from magazines.

Procedure

Photocopy the worksheet and distribute it around the class to students in pairs or small groups.

WORKSHEET

1 Think of a recent advertising campaign – it can be film or print media – that you particularly like, and one that you particularly dislike. Explain why.

2 Different advertising campaigns use different techniques to sell their products. What do you understand by the concept 'before and after'?

Example:

How is washing powder often sold to people?
What other products typically use this technique?

3 Read the short texts (a–e) about advertising techniques. Match them with the headings for each text (i–v).

i Association of ideas
ii 'Science'

© Cambridge University Press 2008 PHOTOCOPIABLE

iii The camera never lies
iv Ask the expert
v Story line

a The advert is in the form of a mini-drama, which helps attract our attention. In this way, the visual image of an advert often sticks in our mind for longer.
b Images are often used to trick customers. For example, the picture of a pizza in an advert bears no resemblance to the real thing you find when you open the box.
c We frequently link a certain product in our minds to a particular image or concept. For example, perfumes are marketed using images that will appeal to people who seek a glamorous lifestyle.
d Adverts often encourage us to buy a product because an authority or a celebrity recommends it. Their 'seal of approval' is a guarantee that the product is worth having.
e Advertisers often use technical details, jargon and complicated graphics to explain the 'state-of-the-art' nature of their product. We are persuaded by these images into thinking that we have the most sophisticated model available.

4 Discuss with a partner the techniques that these adverts use (your teacher will supply copies of the adverts).

1) Aspro (painkiller)
2) Cif (cleaning product)
3) Häagen Dazs® (ice cream)
4) Pantene (shampoo)
5) Dettol (antiseptic)
6) MINI (car)

5 Look at adverts in different magazines handed out by your teacher. In pairs, find adverts that employ at least one of the different techniques, including 'before and after'. (Bear in mind that some adverts may use various different techniques at the same time.) Report back to the rest of the class, holding up the advert in each case.

6 Concentrate on one advert and analyse the message, the target market, the relationship between image and text, the position of the image and how it is presented. Write this up for homework and report back your findings in the next class.

© Cambridge University Press 2008 PHOTOCOPIABLE

Sample answers:

2 Washing powder is often sold using the 'before and after' technique. You see an object which is dirty and old and then transformed into something clean

and new. This transformation happens fast and efficiently. Other products which use this technique are medicines, remedies and slimming products.

3 i) c, ii) e, iii) b, iv) d, v) a.

4 1 Aspro: storyline, before and after
2 Cif: before and after, the camera never lies
3 Häagen Dazs®: association of ideas (luxury, good taste), the camera never lies
4 Pantene: science, association of ideas (natural products – healthy)
5 Dettol: ask the expert
6 MINI: association of ideas (Union Jack: patriotic, symbol of the UK)

Follow-up

1 Some of these adverts (Aspro, Dettol) are quite old-fashioned. Ask students to explain how they are different from contemporary adverts. This provides a good link to the following activity, task 6.4.

2 Groups work as advertising agencies to plan a campaign for a product of their choice. They need to discuss the image they want to use (including the people, the setting and any objects), produce a text, and then present their campaign to the rest of the class. They will need to explain the rationale for their campaign, including its message, its angle, the target market, and so on.

The class votes on the best campaign and presentation. The results can be presented as posters and distributed around the class.

Instead of consumable objects, students could choose to advertise their own school or town, or some charity or worthy cause, e.g. recycling, animal rights.

6.4 The old and the new

Outline Students focus on how advertising has changed over a century, analysing the relationship between text and image in contemporary and archive adverts.

Focus Students create their own advert based on this analysis.

Level Pre-intermediate–Advanced

Time 45 minutes

Materials and preparation CD-ROM images 6.4A Coca-Cola advert 1930s; 6.4B Coca-Cola advert 1890s; 6.4C Coca-Cola advert 2000s; 6.4D Coca-Cola advert 1960s. These images are used from step 2 in the worksheet. Photocopy the worksheet. In addition to the Coca-Cola® adverts, you could choose any archive advertisements for this task. These can be accessed from:
http://www.advertisingarchives.co.uk/
http://www.flickr.com/groups/vintage_advertising/

Procedure

Photocopy the worksheet and distribute it around the class to students in pairs or small groups.

WORKSHEET

1 **Work in pairs or small groups. Think of an advert for Coca-Cola®. What image comes into your mind? What adjective is often used to sell this brand? What else can you remember about Coca-Cola® adverts?**
2 **Look at four archive adverts for Coca-Cola®. Try to put the images in chronological order, from the 1890s to the present day. What was it about the image that helped you decide the date?**
3 **In which advert is the Coca-Cola® product seen as:**

a) giving you energy
b) a medicinal substance
c) part of everyday life
d) something new
e) being associated with a particular moment/feeling
f) something different?

4 **Focus on the images themselves and discuss these questions.**

a) How is Coca-Cola® physically portrayed in each of the adverts?
b) Which adverts are associated with routine and which with pleasure/leisure?
c) How have the slogan / key words and accompanying texts changed?
d) Looking at the four adverts together, what conclusions can you make about the way advertising has changed in more than a century? In what way is the last advert so different from the others?

5 **Report back your answers to the class.**

© Cambridge University Press 2008 PHOTOCOPIABLE

Sample answers:

2 Chronological order of adverts: 6.4B (1890s), 6.4A (1930s), 6.4D (1960s), 6.4C (2000s). We can identify the chronology of these adverts from different visual clues: the type of illustration/photography employed, the typeface, the amount of text, the advert's concept (Coca-Cola® would now not be bought for its medicinal purposes and women would not be targeted as housewives).

3 1890s: a, b
1930s: a, b, c, f

1960s: a, d, e
2000s: c, e, f

4

a) 1890s advert: it is served in a cup. In the 1930s a hand is holding out the famous bottle. In the 1960s advert, we see people in the process of drinking from the bottle. In the 2000s advert, we only see the top of the bottle and the Diet Coke logo.
b) All of the adverts are associated with routine and the role Coca-Cola® plays in that routine, except the 1960s advert, which clearly shows an image of pleasure and leisure.
c) The key words have changed from *delightful* (1890s) to *wholesome (substances)* (1930s), to *refreshing* (1960s). The 1930s advert has the most text, explaining why Coca-Cola® is so different from other drinks. In the first two adverts, the emphasis is on Coca-Cola® helping you to overcome tiredness.The 1960s advert refers to its refreshing qualities. The last advert doesn't specify the drink's special quality – it just says that it is special. Notice that three of the adverts include slogans which have a short, catchy quality to them (partly due to the five/six syllables used in each): *the pause that refreshes*, *Coke refreshes you best*, *that certain something*.
d) Nowadays advertising requires less explanatory text and less information. You can sell a product via association of ideas or by using a more abstract concept which can trigger these associations. Furthermore, we have been bombarded by so many different advertising images that advertisers now try to do something different to attract our attention. Notice that the last advert includes no images of people, but rather lots of white space. However, its concept is deceptively subtle. It indirectly tells a story of a couple's life through the quotation, the idea being that the viewer conjures up the rest as a mental image. It is saying that Coca-Cola® forms a familiar part of people's everyday life like a 'hello' or a 'goodbye'. By not saying too much and leaving it up to our imaginations, the advert is perhaps more resonant and effective. This is a trend that many advertisers are following these days.

Follow-up

1 Students create their own advert for Coca-Cola®. Ask them to think first of the image. (Will it be a typical one, representing leisure time, or an image we normally associate with a different product?) This can be done as project work. The adverts can then be displayed in class the next day.

2 Design a similar activity yourself, using other well-known brands, such as Gillette®, Mars, MINI, Persil washing powder.
3 Make a comparison with Pepsi® and Coca-Cola® adverts and other rival companies' images and campaigns.

6.5 Campaigning

Outline	Identifying different advertising campaigns from slogans. Judging the strength of a campaign by analysing different messages. Ranking advertising campaigns according to originality and effectiveness.
Focus	Fluency practice. Language input: imperatives, questions, predictions, conditionals, warnings.
Level	Intermediate +
Time	45 minutes
Materials and preparation	CD-ROM images 6.5A–D Four adverts: Population awareness, Malaria awareness, Drug awareness, Global warming awareness. Alternatively, any current public-information campaigns.

Procedure

1 Through reference to some current advertising campaigns, establish the importance of having strong images and good catchphrases when advertising a product.
2 Seat the students in small groups and show them the different slogans below. (You will need to pre-teach the colloquial verb *to spike*, meaning *to add a drug to somebody's drink without them realising*.) Ask the class to categorise the slogans according to the sentence type / structures used, e.g. questions, emphatic statements, imperative, types of conditional, prediction.
   1 *Winter: You'll miss it when it's gone.*
   2 *Help! We are nearly out of space.*
   3 *Do you know the world's smallest "Weapon of Mass Destruction"?*
   4 *This is how easy it is to spike your drink.*

Ask: *What do all the sentences have in common?*

Answers:
1 conditional / prediction
2 imperative
3 question
4 emphatic statement

They all include a direct address to the reader, either with *you* or *your* or by using the imperative form.

3 In their groups, students match each slogan with a campaign below (A–D). Do the first as an example.

Campaigns:
A Population awareness
B Malaria awareness
C Drug awareness
D Global warming awareness

Note
You should remind students that these images are not selling a product as such, but are trying to raise awareness about important social issues.

Answers: 1 D, 2 A, 3 B, 4 C.

4 Students then compare with other groups of students before reporting back in open class.
5 Divide the class into two halves (A and B) and then ask them to form smaller groups within each half. Give students in Group A copies of the adverts for campaigns A and B (CD-ROM 6.5A–B). At the same time, ask them to imagine a suitable image for the other two campaigns, C and D.
Give students in Group B copies of the adverts for campaigns C and D (CD-ROM 6.5C–D). At the same time, ask them to imagine a suitable image for the other two campaigns, A and B.
6 Form pairs with students from the two halves (A and B). Each Student A reports their group's idea for Campaign C. Each Student B listens and compares with the finished advert and then shows Student A the original.
7 Ask students to do the same for all four adverts, taking it in turns each time to report back their campaigns and compare with the finished product.
8 Students report back, saying which adverts were the most surprising, effective or original. Ask questions in open class to ensure that students have understood the message of the campaign in each case.

Note
Bear in mind that the drug awareness campaign is not found in the print media. It is printed on a paper umbrella inserted in a cocktail. Does this make the campaign more or less effective?

See 6.6 Adverts everywhere.

Variation 1: Charities

For project work, students focus on one particular charity or organisation and analyse their different campaigns in terms of the images used.

Ask students to consult http://www.adsoftheworld.com and then search within the archive for company names and key words.

Organisations to choose from are: UNICEF, Greenpeace, Friends of the Earth, Oxfam, World Health Organisation, Amnesty International, Against Malaria Foundation.

Variation 2: World campaigns

The class focuses on a particular campaign (e.g. AIDS awareness, drink-driving, anti-smoking) and analyses a number of adverts from the images used. Students find examples from different countries/cultures in the world to see how the issue is treated differently. This is a useful intercultural awareness-raising task.

Access either http://www.adsoftheworld.com or http://www.advertisingarchives.co.uk with key words to help students find examples of different campaigns.

See 2.2 Ranking for an analysis of different anti-smoking campaigns.

6.6 Adverts everywhere

Outline	Raising awareness about the different places where advertising can be found in contemporary society.
Focus	Fluency practice. Locations and prepositions of place to describe where you can find advertising.
Level	Intermediate +
Time	45 minutes
Materials and preparation	CD-ROM images 6.6 A–B Two adverts: Help the Homeless, Lego crane. Example of drink-drive campaigns.

Procedure

1 Initiate a discussion about advertising by getting students to recall where they have seen adverts recently and establish that advertisements appear in such places as:

On the Internet (banners and spam), on your mobile phone, on television and radio, in the cinema, in print media (magazines/newspapers), in the street (on hoardings and billboards), on public transport (at bus stops, on buses, on trains, in taxis, etc.), on buildings, on the sides of lampposts, on flyers, bookmarks, beer mats, pens, etc., in lifts, on escalators, and anywhere you have to wait, as sponsorship on sportswear, hot-air balloons, Formula 1 cars.

2 Show the class the following poster (CD-ROM 6.6A) found on a litter bin and ask students to discuss the questions below.

Help the Homeless advert, © Permission of Marcus Kemp / BBDO Atlanta

- *Where would you normally find the words 'Nutrition Facts'?*
- *What is the effect of this text appearing on a litter bin?*
- *Why was this piece of paper placed here? For what kind of campaign?*

Sample answers: 'Nutrition Facts' normally appears on food packaging. On a bin, it gives the impression that you can find something to eat there. The paper is there to raise awareness about the sad fact that homeless people may need to look for food in bins.

3 Ask students to look at another ambient advert for Lego (6.6B) in groups.

Students look at the image carefully and discuss these questions:

- *Where is the advert?*
- *What is it selling? A campaign or a product?*
- *Can you see the name of the product?*
- *Do you think it is a good place for an advert? Why? Why not?*
- *In what way is the advert more or less effective because of its position/location?*

4 Students report back their ideas and then imagine a product and an interesting/effective place to advertise it. Ask the class to consider the kinds of people who will see the advert in that particular place (e.g. many adverts in airports are targeted at business people).

Example locations for adverts: *A billboard on the way to the airport; The side of a taxi; The back cover of a teen magazine; A sticker on a lamppost; A plastic bag; On the walls of a hospital maternity ward; In a tube-train carriage.*

6 Students discuss the best ideas for adverts and report back in open class.

Follow-up

Students take photos of any adverts that they see in the street or in unconventional places. They can bring them to class the next day and discuss the campaign, its location and its visual impact.

You can access more examples of ambient adverts at: http://www.adsoftheworld.com – select *ambient* in the media drop-down menu.

Variation: Drink drive campaigns

Focus on one particular campaign. Ask students to compare their impressions of ambient adverts on this topic. Initiate a discussion based on these questions:

To start an anti-drink-driving campaign, where is the best place to advertise it?

- *On a beer bottle or a beer mat in a bar?*
- *Painted on the street itself?*
- *On illuminated signs visible from the road?*
- *In the toilets of a bar?*
- *On the television or radio? (non ambient)*

Which of these campaigns is the most effective? Why?
In your country, how are these campaigns carried out? What do you think are the best types?

6.7 Market leaders

Outline	Students establish links between an image and a particular brand. Role playing marketing people.
Focus	Fluency practice. Practice in asking questions. Language of advice and persuasion.
Level	Intermediate +
Time	45 minutes – 1 hour (discussion and role play)
Materials and preparation	CD-ROM image 6.7 Corporate American flag for the Follow-up. Choose any well-known images that have become representative of a certain brand for the main activity. You will need a photo of two or three children from different ethnic backgrounds for step 1. Photocopy of worksheet.

Procedure

1 Explain the identity of a brand by showing an image of two or three children together who all come from different ethnic backgrounds (e.g. Asian, European, African). Ask students if this image reminds them of a well-known brand. Try to elicit 'Benetton'.

2 Photocopy the chart that follows or copy it onto the board. Establish the idea of 'brand identity' by getting students to complete it.

Note

An image here can refer to a logo, a trademark or simply a picture that frequently accompanies the product. There may be more than one image per brand.

BRAND	REPRESENTATIVE IMAGE/LOGO/TRADEMARK
Benetton	Multicultural kids
	Different representations of the same bottle
Marlboro cigarettes	
Ralph Lauren cologne	
Domino's Pizza	
	Black silhouette with headphones, and apple with a bite taken out of it
	Clown, yellow arches of an M letter
	Crocodile
Microsoft® Windows® / Vista®	
Rolls-Royce	

© Cambridge University Press 2008 PHOTOCOPIABLE

The expected answers are:

BRAND	REPRESENTATIVE IMAGE/LOGO/TRADEMARK
Benetton	Multicultural kids
Absolut vodka	Different representations of the same bottle
Marlboro cigarettes	Cowboy on horseback
Ralph Lauren cologne	American flag / polo player on horseback
Domino's Pizza	Two red domino pieces
iPod® MP3 player / Apple® computers	Black silhouette with headphones, and apple with a bite taken out of it
McDonald's	Clown, yellow arches of an M letter
Lacoste	Crocodile
Microsoft® Windows® / Vista®	Four coloured squares shaped like a flag
Rolls-Royce	Female figure (*The Spirit of Ecstasy*)

Note

If the students cannot describe the image in words, let them visualise it and draw the image in the gap provided.

3 Students report back their answers in open class and discuss the relationship between the brand and the image.

Give a sample response to prompt the students:

The McDonald's logo is seen to represent happiness (bright yellow and red are used). The colours appeal and are easy to identify from afar. The clown image represents fun and attracts children.

4 Initiate a discussion about these companies and their rivals in the market, establishing the importance of branding and corporate image. Why is this important?

Sample answer: To stand out from the competition, to appeal to certain customers, to maintain brand loyalty, etc.

5 Divide the class in half, and then divide each half into pairs. The pairs in one half of the class are *different companies*: you can assign the kind of company or they can choose from this list:

- *A takeaway pizza company*
- *A luxury car firm*
- *A soft-drinks company*

- *A clothes-shop chain (aimed at young people)*
- *A popular cologne company (aimed at both sexes)*
- *An electronics/computer company producing portable MP3 players.*

The pairs in the other half of the class are *advertising agencies*, competing to give each company a new brand identity. Each pair first prepares its case: the 'company' pairs decide what kind of brand identity they want for their product; the 'agency' pairs decide what characterises their agency's advertising style, e.g. shock, humour, mystery, surprise, cool, and what angle they are going to adopt to promote the companies, etc.

Each agency then 'visits' a company, to form a group of four. The company explains its goals, and the agency offers suggestions for logos and a new angle. Then each agency moves to the next company, and the process is repeated, until all the agencies have been 'interviewed' by all the companies. Each company then quickly decides which agency they will employ, and reports their decision – and reasons – to the rest of the class.

Present this useful language to act as prompts for the different roles:

Companies:
In five years' time, I'd like to . . .
I want to attract different kinds of customers.
My image needs updating/changing. What would you suggest?
We need to attract younger people.

Advertising agencies:
Your logo needs changing. I would suggest . . .-ing.
I think you should do . . . What you need to change is . . .
Why don't you . . .?
Haven't you ever thought of . . .?
The best colour for your product is . . .
I would place advertising . . .

Follow-up

1 One student describes a well-known logo and/or trademark and the others have to draw it and/or guess the product.

Note

Sometimes a very familiar logo, when described out of context, can be very difficult to guess (e.g. the Adidas® three-stripes logo or the Windows® 'flag'). This actually makes the activity more fun.

2 A good source for logos is the Corporate American flag produced by the organisation Adbusters[1] (CD-ROM 6.7). Get students to test each other on the logos on the flag.

See 6.8 Subvertising for an activity which features other adverts by Adbusters.

3 Ask students to research Benetton's advertising campaigns. They can access information about these at the company's website: http://press.benettongroup.com/ben_en/about/campaigns/list/

Students could think about some of these questions. Do they agree with the use of such controversial images to sell clothes? Which adverts do they remember, if any? Do these adverts truly make the public aware of such issues, or are they merely a sales gimmick whose only aim is to shock? What do Benetton hope to gain from such campaigns?

6.8 Subvertising

Outline	Analysing visual jokes inspired by advertising. Class create their own adverts.
Focus	Interpreting jokes through the use of subverted images. Finding an angle for students' own parody adverts.
Level	Intermediate–Advanced
Time	30 minutes
Materials and preparation	CD-ROM images 6.8A–D Four spoof adverts: VW, Nike, Calvin Klein, Prozac.

Procedure

1 As a lead-in, ask students if they can recall any adverts from VW, Nike or Calvin Klein. How are these products often marketed?

2 Show the class three images from Adbusters[2] (CD-ROM 6.8A–C). Explain that these are spoof adverts (parodies of conventional adverts). Pose students the following questions:

- *What aspect of the product is being criticised in each case?*
- *How is this done through the images, the text or a combination of both?*

[1] Adbusters is a Canada-based not-for-profit anti-consumerist foundation which runs a magazine of the same name. Their version of the Stars and Stripes flag makes a statement about the corporate powers that they suggest dominate US society today.

[2] Adbusters is a Canada-based not-for-profit anti-consumerist foundation which runs a magazine of the same name. Here, Adbusters parody adverts from different companies (to create 'subverts' or 'spoof ads'). They do this in order to critique our consumerist society.

Sample answer: The VW spoof advert criticises the fact that cars pollute the environment. It is saying that the planet would be a better place with fewer cars and more rivers and natural spaces. The car filled up with water provides a comic image which at the same time communicates a serious message about the planet. The VW logo has been tampered with so that it resembles a river.

Nike are being criticised in this advert for exploiting workers in Asian sweatshops (e.g. in Indonesia) to produce their goods. The text cleverly begins as you would expect in a Nike advert, but quickly subverts it by saying that it is not cool to wear Nike and that you should think twice before buying a pair of Nike sports shoes. The photo represents a barefooted, anonymous worker – a poignant reminder of people we don't normally see in adverts.

The Calvin Klein parody advert shows a muscled man looking disappointedly down at what is inside his CK underwear. This laughs at the fact that fashion companies only ever show models with perfect bodies to advertise their clothes.

3 Finally, show the Prozac® advert (6.8D). How is this advert different from the others?

Sample answer: Prozac® is not a product that anyone can buy but an anti-depressant and is therefore never advertised.

4 Students in groups choose another well-known company and design a spoof (parody) campaign for this firm. Ask them to consider the angle first, and then the image and the amount of text they will need to make the spoof obvious. If possible, they should try to imitate or make fun of a well-known campaign by this company.

To assist this task, you can provide the following prompts:

Your advert is for:	**Your angle is:**
A bank	It's easy to make money when there are bank charges for everything.
A furniture company	You are destroying the rainforests of the world by making cheap chairs and tables, etc.
A petrol company	Cars and planes pollute and contaminate thanks to you.
A computer company	You make people lead virtually reclusive lives; surfing is so dull.
A food/restaurant company	Your food is full of calories and makes people obese.

5 For students who don't mind performing, this still image could then be transformed into a television advert which certain groups could perform in class.
6 Students can present the adverts without revealing the actual company name, and invite the rest of the class to guess.

Note
For different kinds of spoof adverts and subvertising, visit the Culture Jamming links at Wikipedia: http://en.wikipedia.org/wiki/Culture_jamming

6.9 Meet Alex

Outline	Students explore the relationship between captions and images.
Focus	Vocabulary of names and forms of naming/addressing people, from formal to informal register.
Level	False beginner – Intermediate (young learners)
Time	15–30 minutes
Materials and preparation	CD-ROM images 6.9A Alex Raeburn photos; 6.9B Alex Raeburn answers.

Procedure

1 Project the image (6.9A) from the CD-ROM. This 12-image collage was inspired by a magazine advertisement.
2 Explain that the images represent 12 different ways of referring to the same person. In this case, the man's name is Alex Raeburn. Explain the activity by pointing to one of the photos.
For example, indicate the photo of the young child. Ask the following questions in open class:
- *Who is this?* (Alex's son)
- *How does his son address him?* (Ask students to choose from the list below. Elicit: *Daddy*.)

3 Students match the photos with the correct captions:
Darling, Alex, 237, Alexinho, Row 1 Seat 50, Groom, Mr Raeburn, Mister, Woof!, Daddy, Passenger Raeburn, Boss.
4 Students report back their answers in open class and determine which of these ways of addressing someone are formal/informal or personal/impersonal.
5 Students establish what each image represents. Students report back in open class and explain/elicit the expressions *They call him . . . / He's*

called . . . For answers, project or make copies of CD-ROM image 6.9B.

Example: *This picture shows a football stadium. He goes to watch the football with some friends. They call him 'Alexinho'. / Here, he's called 'Alexinho'.*

Note

It might be necessary to explain the meaning of *groom* and show that the destination on the bus says: *Wedding Special. Becky & Alex.*

6 In pairs / small groups, students ask each other questions to find out the different names they themselves are given, depending on the context and the person who is addressing them.

Provide a model yourself, eliciting questions from the class, and then encourage your class to do the same in groups.

Example:
What's your name at home? ***They call me*** *Dave.*
What's your name at work? ***I'm called*** *Mr Forbes.*
My mother ***calls me*** *Davey.*
My son ***calls me*** *Daddy.*
My wife calls me ***Forby*** *– it's a* ***nickname****.*

7 Tell students that the images were inspired by an advert for a car.

Follow-up

Brainstorm with the class other ways in which cars are commonly advertised. Ask students to collect different car adverts and compare and contrast them according to the following criteria:

- *message/angle*
- *target market*
- *text-type used*
- *association of ideas*
- *originality of concept.*

Variation: Create your own 'name mosaic'

Students make their own 12-photo mosaic, as if they were Alex Raeburn, but with images of their own. These could be photos of members of their family, workmates or even their pets, or some other context in which they find themselves. The idea is to do a version of the advert, by showing the different people and contexts that surround us all, and the names that each of us is known by in different situations.

6.10 Selling yourself

Outline	Students place themselves in an advert.
Focus	Conditional clauses (*If I were in an advert, I'd be advertising . . .*). Reading comprehension.
Level	Pre-intermediate and above
Time	20 minutes, plus 1 hour homework / next class

Procedure

1 Show students a Gucci advert from this website:
http://www.museumofhoaxes.com/hoax/forums/viewthread/3180/
Ask the following questions: *Is it a typical advert for Gucci? Is there anything unusual about it at all?*

2 Read out the newspaper article below. Alternatively ask students to read the article online at the above address. Tell students that the article is about the advert they have just seen. You may need to pre-teach these words: *prankster*, *fake*, *to con*, *to fall for*, *scam*, etc.

Swiss Newspaper Falls for Prankster's Fake Gucci Ad

Some people will do anything to appear in the papers. But few have the audacity of a man in Switzerland, who conned one of the country's biggest media companies into publishing a two-page ad he created of himself posing semi-naked beside a bottle of Gucci perfume. The man, who claimed to represent the Italian fashion giant, called up the Swiss weekly *SonntagsZeitung* last week to book the expensive colour spread in Sunday's edition, a spokesman for the paper said.

Christoph Zimmer told *The Associated Press* on Tuesday that the man asked for the 60,000-Swiss-franc (about $50,000) bill to be sent to Gucci.

'We've spoken to Gucci and apologised for the mistake,' Zimmer said. 'We're going to try and get the money back from this guy, but we don't rate our chances.'

The Milan, Italy-based Gucci could not be reached for comment.

Zimmer said the paper fell for the scam because the call arrived too late for the advertising department to check whether it was genuine.

© *Associated Press*, 27 February 2007. Reproduced by permission of YGS Group

3 Check understanding of the text by asking students questions, for example:
   - *How did the man manage to get away with his prank?*
   - *What does it say about our ability to create images these days?*
4 Students imagine themselves in an advert in the colour magazine of a big Sunday newspaper. What kind of product would they like to advertise/represent?

   Model a sentence yourself, using a conditional clause, and ask them to continue the visualisation.

Example: *If I were an advert for a drink, I'd be a Coca-Cola® advert. I'd be sitting on the beach, drinking from the bottle, with a beautiful view of the sea behind me.*

5 Invite students to produce their adverts in the next class. They should bring in photos of themselves, the product they are advertising and any other images they might want to include in their advert. They can thus create a collage advert, working individually or in pairs or small groups. Alternatively, students can create their adverts for homework and bring them to the next lesson.
6 Once the adverts have been completed, post them up around the class. Students can vote on which is the best / most convincing. Are any as convincing as the Gucci advert?

Variation: A television advert

If students have access to cameras or camcorders, they can film their own advert (set a maximum of 60 seconds for this) or take photos of each other posing with a particular product, and then add the corresponding text.

6.11 I think, therefore I listen

Outline	Students study an advertising campaign for a radio station.
Focus	Reading comprehension, matching image and text. Media vocabulary and promotional language.
Level	Upper-intermediate +
Time	30 minutes
Materials and preparation	CD-ROM images 6.11A–F Six magazine adverts without texts – Coffee cup, Kitchen, Polar bear, Politician, Soldier, Windmills; 6.11G–L The same adverts with texts. You can either project these or print them out as photocopies.

Procedure

1 Show the students the six different images from the CD-ROM (6.11A–F), without the texts. Students describe each image in turn.

Example: *There are some dancers in a coffee cup . . .*

2 Seat students in pairs. Explain that the images are part of a campaign for a radio station. Students establish the different categories of news that the images could represent.

Answers: 1 coffee cup: arts and culture, 2 kitchen: global issues / poverty, 3 polar bear: nature and environment, 4 politician: politics, 5 soldier: wars, foreign news, 6 windmills: technology.

3 Ask the students to try to make a connection between the image, its location and the news category. Discuss ideas in open class.

Example: *Coffee cup with dancers: the image is there because you are having a coffee and a croissant, reading the newspaper and listening to a radio report about dance.*

4 Write the headings below on the board. Students match them with the images. Tell them to look for connections between the titles and the photos (e.g. wordplay).

Empowering perspectives
Putting a face on the news
A robust blend of diversity
Perspectives that hit home
The quest for truth
The spirit of exploration

Example: Empowering perspectives: windmills (explain that the wordplay with 'power' refers to wind power in the image).

Answers:
Putting a face on the news: Kitchen window – refers to faces staring.
A robust blend of diversity: Coffee cup – play on words with *blend*.
Perspectives that hit home: *To hit home* means *to make an impact*. The photo of the soldier and his child is certainly a powerful one.
The quest for truth: Do politicians tell the truth?
The spirit of exploration: Image of polar bear suggests adventure and exploration.

5 Show students the complete adverts (6.11G–L). Ask them to find more connections between the images and the accompanying texts.

Example: *The mention of 'global warming' and 'inquisitive nature' in the Polar bear text.*

6 Present the text below to students and highlight characteristics of promotional language, such as:

- Positive adjectives (*inspiring, engaging*), verbs (*to transcend*) and nouns (*wealth*)
- Imperatives (*Discover*)
- Linking expressions (*That's why . . .*)
- News vocabulary (*viewpoints, movements, coverage*)
- Communication vocabulary (*tune in, stream, podcast*).

A ROBUST BLEND OF DIVERSITY. The world today is full of inspiring voices, viewpoints and movements. That's why WBUR offers a wealth of engaging options, including cultural, community and arts-oriented coverage that transcends traditional genres. Discover what it's like to be truly informed. Tune in at 90.9 FM, stream or podcast at wbur.org.

© RDW
From *Working with Images* © Cambridge University Press 2008 PHOTOCOPIABLE

Students read the other texts at the bottom of the adverts and identify similar characteristics.

7 The class can then create their own adverts for this particular campaign. This can be done for homework. Tell the students to consider:

1) the kind of image and what type of news it will reflect
2) what type of 'frame' the image will appear in, e.g. a coffee cup, a mirror
3) an accompanying text to connect with the two previous ideas.

7 Art images

Stock photography has created a globalised and digitalised visual-content industry which has inevitably blurred the boundaries between publicity images, news media and fine art. You can now find artworks on stock-photography websites and download them for a small fee. When you visit any of today's major art galleries, your favourite paintings will be magically transposed onto fridge magnets, stickers, coffee cups and the like.

The merchandising industry surrounding fine art has led us to question what is 'authentic' and what is 'fabricated', what is 'real' and what is 'fake'. Partly for this reason, this chapter is not limited to art images with a capital A. The chapter also attempts to remove these artworks from the hallowed gallery or museum space. Essentially, the intention is to ask similar questions of these images as of any other image in this book, to take high art down from its pedestal. For that reason, many very well-known artworks appear throughout the book alongside the banal or mundane. For example, the very first activity (1.1 Describe and draw) uses an 'eternal' Cézanne still life alongside a simple line drawing and an utterly ephemeral digital avatar. The same is true of classical photography, which also features in this chapter, although such photos are not traditionally considered as 'fine-art images'.

This chapter also includes established 'artworks' that may well be familiar to you and your students from other areas within popular culture. In the first task, 7.1 Album covers, we look at classic album covers, from Nirvana's underwater baby for *Nevermind*, to Pink Floyd's rainbow prism for *Dark Side of the Moon*. A literary approach is followed in two tasks (7.3 and 7.4 Art poems) which compare poems which have been based on both classic and contemporary paintings, from Brueghel to Hopper.

Subversive or non-conventional art is presented in 7.5 In the gallery, in which the work of controversial figures in the art world, such as Damien Hirst and Banksy, is featured. Such images are not often found in international ELT materials, but have become ubiquitous in the media – another way to introduce the real world into the classroom. The same is true of graphic fiction, which is represented by Robert Crumb's brilliant 12-panel masterpiece in 7.7 Changing scenes. Once again, the intention is to bring students closer to the kind of powerful images that they might have encountered 'out there' in the wider world.

Elsewhere, there are a number of tasks in which the students are firmly at the centre of the activity (for example, 7.8 Tableaux vivants and 7.9 Art critics). In the former, the learners attempt to capture the spirit of a painting by acting it out, and in the latter, they try their hand at being art critics. Although specific artworks are featured here and many of these appear on the CD-ROM, some of the tasks don't require you to use these specific images. Where possible, I have suggested other options for artworks which would also work well in a particular task, and explained where to find them online.

7.1 Album covers

Outline	Developing cultural awareness of different music through album cover art.
Focus	Matching textual and visual clues. Developing strategies for finding images from the Internet.
Level	Intermediate–Advanced
Time	40 minutes
Materials and preparation	CD-ROM images 7.1A All four images similar to album covers; 7.1B–E Four photos which recall four well-known album covers: A zebra crossing, A triangle and prism, A baby swimming underwater, Jeans and US stars and stripes. You can access the original artworks for these album covers on Wikipedia. See task for specific links.

Procedure

1 Ask students to look at the four different images (CD-ROM 7.1A–E) and to describe them to each other.

© Rex Features / Ilpo Musto

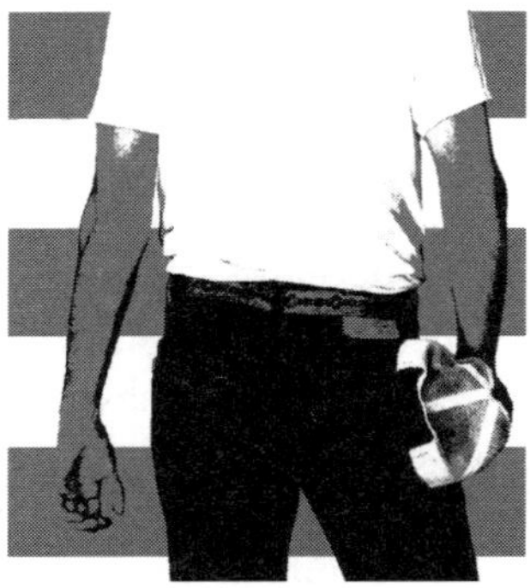

© Christian Yanchula

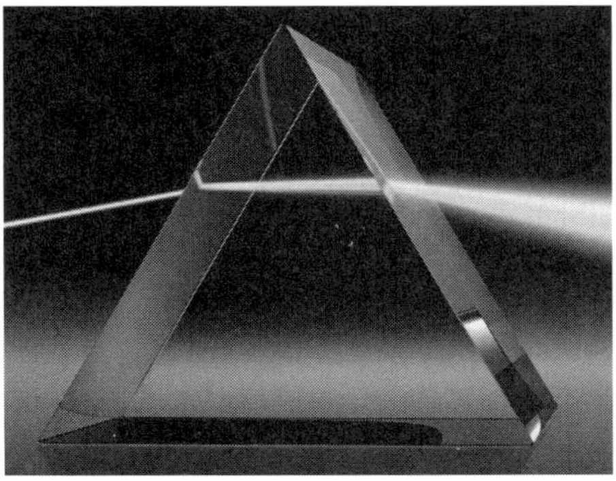

© Corbis / Matthias Kulka / Zefa

© Corbis / Zena Holloway / Zefa

2 Explain that the images are directly linked to well-known or iconic album covers. Ask in open class if anybody recognises the link between these images and famous recordings (but don't expect too much of a response).

The original album covers are:
1) The Beatles: *Abbey Road*
2) Bruce Springsteen: *Born in the USA*
3) Pink Floyd: *Dark Side of the Moon*
4) Nirvana: *Nevermind*.

Note

You might need to remind younger students that before CDs, 12" vinyl was very popular and the design of album covers was taken much more seriously than nowadays. Point out that some original covers were designed by artists and are considered as 'works of art' and not just examples of graphic design.

3 Write up on the board the following groups/artists and ask students the following questions orally:

Bruce Springsteen
The Beatles
Nirvana
Pink Floyd

- *Do you know the names of any of the people in these bands? Have you heard of Bruce Springsteen?*
- *Do you know any famous songs by these musicians?*
- *What kind of music did each of these groups/musicians play?*

- *In which decade were they famous?*
- *Which well-known musicians from the list had an untimely death?*

4 Students report back in open class, and then match the musicians with the images. Help them with the first one, if necessary.

Answers: 7.1B Zebra crossing: The Beatles, 7.1C Triangle and prism: Pink Floyd, 7.1D Baby: Nirvana, 7.1E Jeans and stars and stripes: Bruce Springsteen.

5 Students read the 'Texts about the album covers' and match them with each of the images and musicians.

Texts about the album covers

1) Apparently, late lead singer Kurt Cobain conceived the idea for this cover while watching a TV programme on water births. The fishhook and dollar bill were superimposed later. The juxtaposition of symbols of innocence and commerce still creates a powerful image today.

2) So famous is the image that the site in London has become a major tourist attraction. No text is needed. The four men are still instantly recognisable as symbols of that age, and this iconic and almost religious composition just reinforces that fame with its epic, painterly quality.

3) The refracted prism illustration is one of the most recognisable works of album art. It became a symbol for the band itself and has been reworked many times, especially for the re-released 20th- and 30th-anniversary editions. Again there is no text, adding to the image's iconic, universal quality.

4) The image of the baseball cap stuffed into the back pocket of a pair of jeans with the background of the 'stars and stripes' has become a much-copied popular icon for the USA. Some critics, however, called for a ban because they believed it showed lack of respect for the flag.

© Cambridge University Press 2008 PHOTOCOPIABLE

Answers: 1) Nirvana, 2) The Beatles, 3) Pink Floyd, 4) Bruce Springsteen.

6 Show the students the real album covers. You can print these out or project them from the following links, which also give more information about these classic albums:
The Beatles: http://en.wikipedia.org/wiki/Abbey_Road_%28album%29
Pink Floyd: http://en.wikipedia.org/wiki/The_Dark_Side_of_the_Moon
Nirvana: http://en.wikipedia.org/wiki/Nevermind
Bruce Springsteen: http://en.wikipedia.org/wiki/Born_in_the_U.S.A.

Follow-up

1 Students focus on one of the musicians and research other examples of album artwork that they have used. They could write texts on these covers as project work.
2 Students should bring in their favourite CD album covers to the next lesson. They should also write a short description of the album cover art to read out to the class.

7.2 Art fragments

Outline	Students reconstruct art images, both physically and verbally.
Focus	Fluency practice. Language of supposition and description. Asking questions.
Level	Elementary–Intermediate. (Good with large mixed-ability classes.)
Time	30 minutes
Materials and preparation	CD-ROM images 7.2A–D: Cut abstract images; 7.2E–H: Complete images. Four abstract compositions have each been cut up into four pieces, making 16 pieces in all. Print out these images (7.2A–D) and cut out as many of the pieces that you need for your class – up to a maximum of 16.

Procedure

1 Cut out the individual fragments from the four images (7.2A–D) so that you have up to 16 separate pieces. Distribute one piece at random to each student.
2 Students look at their pieces carefully and imagine the other parts of the image. Allow students ample time to prepare a description of their piece and any questions that might help them find the other pieces that match theirs. Put a series of prompts on the board if you feel it necessary:

__There are__ two lines of red and __I can see__ a patch of green in the corner.
__Are there any__ strong blue colours __in your fragment__?

3 Students stand up and circulate, trying to find pieces that combine with their own by asking and answering questions. Monitor carefully to check that students are not showing their pictures to other students or using gestures.

TIP

Tell students to focus on the colours, shapes, textures and any other visual clues to help them find their partners, as well as the edges and corners of their pieces, to give them clues to the pieces that they are missing.

4 Once they have found the other members of their group, students put the fragments together like a jigsaw puzzle. Once these are complete, groups show the other members of the class their complete composition.
5 Show the students the completed photographs (CD-ROM 7.2E–H). The students comment on these and discuss what they are.

Answers: The complete images are the same as those shown in 2.14J–M and represent the following: 7.2E football terracing, 7.2F green fence and white wall, 7.2G white lines on a football pitch, 7.2H surfboard.

Variation: Using figurative paintings

Use more figurative pictures for lower levels, to give them clearer visual clues to find their partners.

Note

The randomness of the activity means that weaker students have an equal role in the task. As such, it is ideal for mixed-ability groups.

Acknowledgement: *The original idea for using figurative-art jigsaws comes from 'Identikit', in* Drama Techniques, *by Maley, A. and Duff, A. (Cambridge University Press, 2005).*

7.3 Art poems 1

Outline	Establishing generic questions to ask of any poem based on an artwork.
Focus	Comparing visual content in a painting and written content in a poem. Reading comprehension.
Level	Intermediate–Advanced
Time	30 minutes
Materials and preparation	CD-ROM image 7.3 Painting by Edward Hopper – Early Sunday Morning. The work of popular artists like Hopper can be found in calendars and postcards, which are often better for showing in class. Aside from Hopper, you could choose any evocative images which you think will create an impact with your students.
Note	Edward Hopper's paintings are particularly appropriate for this kind of work because they often feature people in situations of alienation or in a contemplative mood. They therefore provoke a great deal of thought on the part of learners and it is relatively straightforward for students to think around the image and create a story/monologue.

Procedure

1 Show students the Edward Hopper painting (CD-ROM 7.3), but don't tell them its name. Set them the following questions:

1) Identify the main elements in the painting.
2) Identify the time of day. How do you know?
3) Which words spring to mind when looking at the painting?
4) Can you guess the title of the painting? Clue: it's quite literal. Will it refer to the scene, the atmosphere, the time of day?

Sample answers: 1. Suggestions: store entrances, awnings, windows with nobody looking out, a red and blue pole indicating a barber, a fire hydrant, the sun casting long shadows. 2. Early morning, long shadows. 3. Suggestions: *emptiness, closed, quiet, silent, bright*. 4. The painting is called *Early Sunday Morning*.

2 Students report back their impressions of the painting. Do their ideas coincide? Do they like it or do they find it boring? Tell them the title of the painting. Can they imagine a poem being written about this painting?

3 Present the students with John Stone's poem based on the same painting and the questions below which they can discuss in groups or pairs:

Questions on poem *Early Sunday Morning* by John Stone:

1) Is the poem simply an objective description of the work? Or does it attempt to get 'beneath the surface', at the deeper significance of the image? Or both?
2) How much of the poem is description and how much interpretation?
3) Is the poem about the artwork itself, or about how it was painted, or even the process of looking at it?
4) In what way is the painting just a springboard for the poet's own personal interests and reflections?
5) Are certain aspects highlighted while others are ignored by the poet? Why?
6) Does the poem stand alone? That is, does it need the image to be fully understood?
7) Do you agree with the poet's interpretation of the artwork? How else would you interpret it? What would you add to or subtract from the poem, if anything?

© Cambridge University Press 2008 PHOTOCOPIABLE

***Early Sunday Morning* by John Stone**

Somewhere in the next block
someone may be practicing the flute
but not here

where the entrances
to four stores are dark
the awnings rolled in

nothing open for business
Across the second story
ten faceless windows

In the foreground
a barber pole, a fire hydrant
as if there could ever again
be hair to cut
fire to burn
And far off, still low

in the imagined East
the sun that is again
right on time

adding to the Chinese red
of the building
despite which color

I do not believe
the day
is going to be hot

It was I think
on just such a day
it is on just such a morning

that every Edward Hopper
finishes, puts down his brush
as if to say

As important
as what is
happening

is what is not.

© Reproduced by permission of Louisiana State University Press

From *Working with Images* © Cambridge University Press 2008 PHOTOCOPIABLE

Note

These questions are generic and can therefore be about any poem based on an artwork.

4 Students report back their answers in open class.
5 Conduct a class discussion and bring out some of the points in the suggested answers.

Sample answers:

1/2 Parts of the poem are purely descriptive, but it opens with an image which is not present in the artwork (that of someone playing the flute). Here, the poet moves outside the frame to describe what *cannot* be seen. In this way, he attempts to get beneath the surface of the painting. The poet is suggesting that for Hopper what is *not* happening is as important as what is. That is its deeper message.

3 All of these things. The final stanzas discuss how the painting may have been painted. Here, the poet looks at this quiet scene and places the painter into it. In this way, it examines how he believed the painting was executed and how we look at it now, suggesting that the work is really about how Hopper worked and what he thought of the world.

4 The first part of the poem does not deal with the poet's own interests or reflections until the stanza beginning *I do not believe the day is going to be hot*. It is from here that he puts himself into Hopper's shoes, imagining the artist working in just such a scene. This is his way of looking beyond the frame. The image of Hopper *putting down his brush* runs parallel with the poet's work – he too seems to run out of words, images and metaphor as he puts down his pen to end the poem *(As important as what is happening is what is not)*.

5 Virtually all the painting's details are described by the poet. In the first part of the poem, he emphasises the fact that everything is closed for business and he refers to specific features of the painting – the doors, the awnings, the fire hydrant, etc. He doesn't refer to the lack of people in the scene (apart from in the first lines), but rather concentrates on the shadows and colours and the time of day, the *Chinese red* which may suggest heat.

6 The poem can stand alone perfectly because its central idea is very strong: what Hopper chooses not to show is the important thing. But, of course, looking at the painting as you read enhances the poem's effect. It captures the stillness and silence of the artwork very well.

7 Following the theme of 'what is missing' from the scene: another way to interpret the painting could be to imagine the people who work(ed) in the empty stores or live(d) above them. The poet could have talked more about the scene as that of an *abandoned town*, where nobody lives any more, and the memories that the place still can conjure up as you look at the painting.

Painting by Edward Hopper – *Early Sunday Morning*, © Corbis / Francis Mayer

Variation 2: Performing dialogues

Choose a number of different Hopper paintings. See if you can get hold of an old calendar of his works or access them online through Smithsonian American Art Museum at: http://nmaa-ryder.si.edu/collections/exhibits/hopper Ask students to select the one they prefer and write a monologue for a person in the painting. This could work well with a number of paintings of people alone (such as *New York Office*). This idea could be extended to writing dialogues and 'screenplays', where there is more than one person in the picture. These could then be rehearsed and performed in class.

See 1.5 Who am I? for another task in which students imagine themselves within a painting.

See 7.8 Tableaux vivants for one in which students also 'act out' a painting.

7.4 Art poems 2

Outline Memorising visual content in a painting. Identifying differences between a pictorial representation and a textual one.

Focus Language of description (*on the left*, etc.). Analysing different aspects of a poem.

Level Upper-intermediate +

Time 45 minutes – 1 hour

Materials and preparation CD-ROM image 7.4 Painting by Pieter Brueghel – Hunters in the Snow. A number of different poems and their corresponding paintings. A good source of poetry inspired by art can be found at: http://www.english.emory.edu/classes/paintings&poems/titlepage.html

Procedure

1 Ask students to close their eyes and think of the word *winter*. Which images come into their mind? After half a minute or so, ask them to open their eyes and write down a few key images.

2 Students report back their images. Which ones recurred most? (*snow, ice, cold*, etc.)

3 Show the students *Hunters in the Snow* by Pieter Brueghel the Elder (CD-ROM 7.4). Ask them to look at the painting silently for about three minutes and to remember as many details as possible.

4 Hide the image and in pairs or small groups, the students recall the details. Write up the following prompts on the board: *hunters, dogs, birds, skaters / skating rink, tree silhouettes, footsteps, church, bonfire.* Ask them, in pairs, to remember the whereabouts of these elements in the painting and anything else they can recall about them.

Example: *The hunters are in the foreground with their dogs. They are coming home, so it must be dusk . . .*

5 Tell students that they are going to read a poem describing the painting, *The Hunter in the Snow* by William Carlos Williams. Ask them to choose three features they think the poet will include and to write short descriptions of those details. Introduce any key vocabulary at this point.

6 Students read the poem and see which of their elements have been included. Ask them which details they had not noticed and why they think the poet mentioned them.

The Hunter in the Snow by William Carlos Williams

The over-all picture is winter
icy mountains
in the background the return

from the hunt it is toward evening
from the left
sturdy hunters lead in

their pack the inn-sign
hanging from a
broken hinge is a stag a crucifix

between his antlers the cold
inn yard is
deserted but for a huge bonfire

that flares wind-driven tended by
women who cluster
about it to the right beyond

the hill is a pattern of skaters
Brueghel the painter
concerned with it all has chosen

a winter-struck bush for his
foreground to
complete the picture

© Reprinted by permission of New Directions
Publishing Corp and Carcanet Press Limited
From *Working with Images* © Cambridge University Press 2008 PHOTOCOPIABLE

Note

You will need to go through some of the lower-frequency vocabulary here (*hinge, cluster, flares*, etc.) but the visual stimuli will make it easier for students to grasp the meaning.

7 Focus students' attention on how William Carlos Williams structures his poem, building up a series of three-line stanzas and using a very simple, descriptive style which is both 1) colloquial (mentioning Brueghel by name, the use of the word *picture* at the beginning and at the end) and 2) very richly textured (*a winter-struck bush, flares wind-driven*). Explain also how the lack of punctuation gives the poem a

special flow, all details merging in the same way as your eye travels over the canvas, taking in new elements.

8 Ask students in pairs/groups to choose a detail that the poet has not included (e.g. the birds flying above the hunters' heads) and tell them to write an extra three-line stanza about that detail, to add to the poem. They should decide the best place to insert their stanza.

9 Ask students to read out the poem again, complete with their addition. Here you could elicit and/or point out what the overall message of the poem might be.

Note

A possible reason for Williams's omissions is that he is more concerned with Brueghel and how he went about painting his topic than the painting itself – in other words, he is looking outside the frame.

10 In the next class, show the image once again and then ask students to reconstruct the poem in a number of different ways. For example:
- Present the poem in prose form with punctuation and ask students to write it out as the original.
- Give students key nouns and adjectives and see if they can remember the combinations used in the poem (*sturdy – hunters, broken – hinge,* etc.). This will help them reconstruct the poem.
- Reorganise the stanzas and ask students to order them correctly.

Follow-up

Other poems based on paintings which work very well in class:

Intermediate:
Painting: Cézanne, *L'Estaque*
Poem: Allan Ginsberg, *Cézanne's Ports*

Upper-intermediate:
Painting: Sir George Beaumont, *Peele Castle in a Storm*
Poem: William Wordsworth, *Elegiac Stanzas*

Advanced/Proficiency:
Painting: Larry Rivers, *Washington Crossing the Delaware*
Poem: Frank O'Hara, *On seeing Larry Rivers' 'Washington Crossing the Delaware' at the Museum of Modern Art*

Painting: Leonardo Da Vinci, *La Gioconda / Mona Lisa*
Poem: Michael Field, *La Gioconda*

Painting by Pieter Brueghel – *Hunters in the Snow,* © Corbis / The Gallery Collection

Variation 1: Hunters in the Snow Part 2

Many of Brueghel's paintings have inspired poetic works. But this particular work has inspired at least two other well-known poets, apart from Williams. Look at the following examples (see below):

- John Berryman: *Winter Landscape*
- Walter de la Mare: *Brueghel's Winter*

For advanced levels, follow the above procedure until step 5 for these two poems. These poems can both be found at:
http://www.english.emory.edu/classes/paintings&poems/titlepage.html
Students can get into groups and each read one of the poems. They can compare their impressions about what details are included and excluded in each of the paintings and the different styles used.

Sample answers: Next to Williams's minimalist style, Berryman is much more expansive, including much more detail and dwelling on the hunters' role to a far greater extent. De la Mare's poem starts as a list of details and builds up to a dramatic, and rather symbolic, finale.

Variation 2: Landscape with the Fall of Icarus and Auden

You can follow the same procedure with another of Brueghel's celebrated works (*The Fall of Icarus*) and another of Williams's poems, written in the same minimalist style (*Landscape with the Fall of Icarus*). An interesting point here is that there are some clear discrepancies between the poetic description and what seems to be going on in the painting.

Williams's poem was, in fact, written in response to W.H. Auden's celebrated poem *Musée des Beaux Arts*. The first half of the Auden poem is based on Brueghel's *The Census in Bethlehem* and the second on the same painter's *The Fall of Icarus*. These poems can both be found at the above web address.

Here are four possible lessons with these texts/artworks:

1 Students study Williams's and Brueghel's *Icarus* in the same way as the *Hunters in the Snow* model.
2 Students compare Williams's and Auden's poetic descriptions of Brueghel, analysing the two poems and the two Breughel paintings.
3 Students analyse Auden's poem and how Williams was inspired by this work. Williams went on to write no fewer than 12 poems based on 12 different Brueghel paintings. Students could analyse one or two of these for homework or as part of a group project.
4 Students are given lines from different poems by Williams and have to match them with the painting they refer to.

Acknowledgement: *The idea of using Brueghel's paintings and poetic texts by Auden and Williams came from Ceri Jones. Many of her original ideas are expressed in Variation 2.*

7.5 In the gallery

Outline	Students role play conversations in an art gallery. They practise explaining a painting and convincing others to buy it.
Focus	Language of persuasion and exaggeration. Revision of question forms.
Level	Pre-intermediate–Advanced
Time	45 minutes
Materials and preparation	Art postcards or digital images showing different genres (i.e. portraits, sculpture, etc.). A great resource for this task is the Saatchi collection website: http://www.saatchi-gallery.co.uk/, which is a truly interactive online art gallery and allows thousands of both amateur and professional artists to exhibit their work every day. It also gives great examples of street art. You will also need photos of a selection of artworks that have recently been sold at auction houses, e.g. Sotheby's.

Procedure

1 As a warmer, ask students how often they go to art galleries. If not, why not? If yes, ask these other questions:
- *What kinds of galleries do you go to?*
- *How long do you spend, on average, in an exhibition?*
- *Do you look at all of the artworks?*
- *How long might you spend in front of an exhibit?*
- *Do you, or does anyone you know, ever go to private galleries to buy art?*
- *What reasons are there for buying art?*

Alternatively, encourage students, working in pairs or small groups, to quiz one another about their art viewing and/or buying experiences.

2 Show students a selection of paintings or other works of art that belong to different genres (i.e. portraits, landscapes, sculpture, etc.) and come from different eras, if possible.

Ask the following questions:
- *If these artworks were exhibited in a gallery, which would you buy? Why?*
- *Which are you least inclined to buy? Why?*
- *Imagine you were working in an art gallery. How would you try and sell one of the artworks?*

3 Group students in pairs. Assign each student an artwork – or let them choose one. The aim is for each student to try to sell their artwork to their partner.

4 Give students time to prepare some background information about the artwork and the artist. They can invent this and should make it as attractive as possible. They should also prepare some questions that they can ask the other students about the artwork that he/she wants to sell.

5 Write some key expressions on the board for the role play:

Persuasion
It's an excellent investment/price.
It's a bargain.
You won't regret it.
Aren't you tempted by . . .?
Can't you imagine this in your living room?

Exaggeration:
X is the greatest artist of his/her generation.
This is one of the finest (landscapes) ever painted.

<u>*Doubt/refusal:*</u>
I don't really like the colours.
I find it a bit depressing / disturbing / too colourful.
It's a bit too abstract/realistic, for my taste.
It's not really my kind of thing.
It's a bit expensive.

6 In pairs, students take turns to sell their artworks, as persuasively as possible. The students who are being offered the artworks should be suitably reluctant. Alternatively, if the class is not too big, the role play can be conducted as a mingling activity.
7 Monitor carefully, correcting where necessary. Identify a couple of entertaining dialogues and ask students to perform them in front of the whole class.

Variation 1: Art auction

Divide the class up into 'art buyers' and 'art dealers' and group the class in pairs – one 'art buyer' with one 'art dealer'. Select famous artworks which have recently been sold at auction. Choose between six and ten different works of art. You can find out this information by going to the websites of famous auction houses (Sotheby's and Christie's) and clicking on 'past auction results'.

The 'art buyers' interview the 'art dealers' about each work in order to choose one to buy at auction or in the gallery. Tell students to imagine that all the paintings cost the same (say $10,000), so that the buyers are not simply opting for the cheapest. The art dealers can invent any details they like about the paintings in order to make them sound attractive purchases. The art buyers have to choose the artwork they think will be the best investment.

Once each 'art buyer' has selected a painting, the class comes together and discusses the selected painting and decides on the most popular. The teacher uses the information from the website to tell students which painting is the most valuable.

Variation 2: Arguing your case

Set up the situation in which the purchasing committee of an art gallery or museum is deciding on just *one* painting (or sculpture, etc.) from a selection. (Alternatively, it might be the members of the local town council who have to choose one artwork, such as a sculpture, for public display.) Divide the class into groups of five or six (or, if the class is small, the whole class can perform the simulation together). Distribute photos of the candidates' artworks, and assign one item to each member of the group. They must argue the case for their item. (As preparation, you might want to let pairs who have the same artwork work together in advance of the actual discussion.) Each group must then decide which artwork they'd like to purchase. Finally, get each group to feed back their decision to the class.

7.6 Art with a message

Outline	Students look at controversial artworks and photos and attempt to identify the statement they are trying to make.
Focus	Fluency practice. Giving opinions.
Level	Upper intermediate–Advanced
Time	45 minutes
Materials and preparation	CD-ROM image 7.6 Artwork by Marcel Duchamp - Fountain. Iconic artworks by Andy Warhol. See weblinks at end of task for sources of other artworks.

Procedure

1 As a lead-in, ask students to consider why one image/object can be considered a work of art and not another. What does an image/object require to be considered 'art'?

Put students in pairs and ask them to rank these qualities in order of importance for them, and then compare with other pairs:

A work of art should be . . .
expressive / beautiful / realistic / well-crafted / imaginative / original / intriguing / meaningful / controversial.

Alternatively, take a dictionary definition of *art* or *artistic* and ask students to improve on it, e.g. *art: things that are considered to be expressive or beautiful.*

2 Ask students if they know anything about Andy Warhol and the images that made him famous. Show the students any iconic Andy Warhol images – soup can, portrait of Marilyn, cow wallpaper, etc. These are quite easily available in pop-art postcards and in calendars. Ask students what makes these images 'different' from conventional art.

Sample answer: These images come from popular media and highlight the banality/emptiness of commercial culture. They are mass-produced, and not unique and elitist, which was how 'high art' was traditionally seen.

3 Show students Duchamp's *Fountain* (CD-ROM 7.6) and five other artworks (see weblinks at end of task): Damien Hirst, *The Physical Impossibility of Death in the Mind of Someone Living*, 1991; Tracey Emin, *My Bed*, 1998; Banksy, *One nation under CCTV*; Picasso (any of the Dadaist collages with newspaper clippings); Jackson Pollock (any of the large abstract expressionist 'drip' paintings).

Get students to discuss the artistic message for each artwork.

Sample answers: Marcel Duchamp's *Fountain* (1917). Here, the artist made 'art' from an existing object – a urinal! The way that this is angled towards the viewer and its signature give it its 'artistic quality'. The idea of doing this is more important than the impact of the visual image itself.

4 Students read the quotations (A–F) by the artists who did the pieces and match the artwork with the quotation. What clues can they find in the visual image that help them do this?

A 'What I really like is minimum effort for maximum effect.' HIRST
B 'It doesn't matter how the paint is put on, as long as something is said.' POLLOCK
C 'Two weeks before the show, Jay came to my flat and all I could show him was this crap, smelly old ancient things like my old passport or bits of fabric from my sofa when I was three years old. There was nothing that looked like an exhibition.' EMIN
D 'Bus stops are far more interesting and useful places to have art than in museums.' BANKSY
E 'I am interested in ideas, not merely in visual products.' DUCHAMP
F 'The artist is a receptacle for emotions that come from all over the place; from the sky, from the earth, from a scrap of paper, from a passing shape, from a spider's web.' PICASSO

© Cambridge University Press 2008 PHOTOCOPIABLE

5 Students, in pairs or small groups, discuss which of these artworks they believe to be the most original or powerful. Ask them to give reasons. Refer them to the points made in step 1. Get students to feed back in open class.

6 Put students into pairs. Student A selects one of the artworks and takes on the role of the artist who produced it. Student B is an art collector / gallery owner.

   Tell Student A that they have to convince the collector that his/her work of art is worth buying and that it is great 'art', explaining his/her message to the collector.

   Tell Student B that they should be very sceptical and not want to buy it, suggesting that the work is not 'art' at all and that anybody could have done it.

7 Monitor the students' dialogues and ask one or two of the most entertaining pairs to act out the role play before the whole class.

Artwork weblinks:
Hirst: http://en.wikipedia.org/wiki/The_Physical_Impossibility_of_Death_in_the_Mind_of_Someone_Living
Emin: http://en.wikipedia.org/wiki/My_Bed
Banksy: http://en.wikipedia.org/wiki/Image:Bansky_one_nation_under_cctv.jpg
Picasso (example of Dadaist collage): http://en.wikipedia.org/wiki/Image:Compotier_avec_fruits%2C_violon_et_verre.jpg
Pollock (example of drip painting): http://en.wikipedia.org/wiki/Image:No._5%2C_1948.jpg

Note

In December 2004, Duchamp's *Fountain* was voted the most influential artwork of the twentieth century by 500 selected British art-world professionals.

Follow-up: Controversial photos

Contemporary press photos, of course, also carry important messages about the world. Some images have entered public consciousness, such as the portrait of the nine-year-old child in the Vietnam war, running naked down the street after being burned by a napalm attack.

Likewise, two images taken by photographers Kevin Carter and Javier Bauluz have become celebrated for their portrayal of human suffering and bring into question the role of the photographer. The former, an image of a floundering tiny Sudanese toddler being watched over by a predatory vulture became the photo that 'made the world weep' in the 1990s. The second, an image of a couple sitting on the beach next to a dead refugee, whose body has just been washed ashore, raises similar questions: at what point do you put the camera down and help? At what point does your humanity become more important than your journalism? Similar questions are asked today about the role of the paparazzi.

Ask students to choose an iconic and controversial image and read up about its history and the consequences of its release.

For more information about Kevin Carter and his photo:
http://www.time.com/time/magazine/article/0,9171,981431,00.html

Information about Javier Bauluz can be found at his blog:
http://javierbauluz.blogspot.com/ (this blog is in Spanish).

7.7 Changing scenes

Outline	Students practise describing changes to a place by looking at an example from graphic fiction. Students describe the image twice, reformulating their descriptions using collocations.
Focus	Fluency practice. Present perfect tense. Listening for specific information (Variation). Collocations (step 9).
Level	Intermediate–Advanced
Time	45 minutes
Materials and preparation	CD-ROM image 7.7 Shanghai photos. Robert Crumb's A Short History of America (see pages 232–33); Robert Crumb's Epilogue (see page 234). You will also need a historical photo of a city and a contemporary one of the same place and Internet access.

Procedure

1 Find an historical image of a city and compare it with a contemporary photo of the same place. Ask students to identify the differences between them.

2 Initiate a dialogue about how these changes have taken place – because of man's intervention, natural ageing, influence of technology, etc. Show students two images of Shanghai from the CD-ROM (7.7). Ask *In what way are these images symptomatic of global changes?*

3 Discuss with students how their city has changed in recent years. Have these changes been fast or gradual? Have the changes been positive or negative?

Sample answer: There are more hotels and supermarkets, and more cars on the roads.

You may wish to reformulate some student statements into the present perfect (e.g. active or passive), and to highlight these examples on the board:

Some of the old shops have disappeared.

4 Find out if there is a consensus in the class on this.
5 Show students the first image from Crumb's 12-image set, *A Short History of America*, or type into a search engine 'Robert Crumb, A Short History of America' to find a larger version of the image. Elicit a description of the scene, e.g.

There is a field, a meadow and some trees in the background. A flock of birds is flying above.

6 Show the complete storyboard to the students, image by image from a website. Ask the class to look at each picture very carefully, identifying the changes that are taking place. Some of the changes are quite subtle (e.g. the tree disappearing from picture 8 to 9 and, in general, the slope of the land). When students are describing, ask them to try and make connections between one change and the next.

Example: *In the second image, the forest has been cut down to make way for a railway line.*

7 Allow students to work in groups. Ask them to make notes for each image, but not to write down a complete description.
8 Give students a copy of the nouns and verbs that can be used to describe the changes. Ask them to match the nouns and verbs to form collocations.

Nouns:	Verbs:
horse and cart / tram / train / railway track / highway / tramline / road / power lines / telegraph poles / lamppost / gas station / junkyard / liquor store / signpost / fence / billboard / neon / line of trees / vegetation / field / plot of land / tractor / saloon car / traffic / pollution	*to appear / to disappear / to be built / to be erected / to be put up / to widen / to enlarge / to make bigger / to arrive / to go / to cut down / to get rid of / to remove / to get bigger / to get smaller / to grow / to shrink / to get worse / to turn into / to become*

© Cambridge University Press 2008 PHOTOCOPIABLE

Example: *road → widen → to widen a road*

Encourage students to construct longer sentences and link them together.

Example: *They have put up more power lines. The tree has gone. The sky has become orange.*

9 Show the class once more Crumb's complete cartoon. Ask the students to take it in turns to describe the changes that take place from one panel to the next. Encourage them to use as many of the collocations as possible.

10 Open up the topic for class debate. Ask students the following questions:

The artwork is called A Short History of America. *Do you agree with this pessimistic vision of recent times? How could you create a more positive image of changes that have taken place in the last 150 years? Does this 'history' apply to all countries in the world? And what will come next?*

Follow-up

1 Copy and distribute this text:

> One of Robert Crumb's most celebrated images, *A Short History of America*, shows how bucolic heaven can turn into an urban hell in 12 panels. It first appeared in a black and white version in the late 1970s in *Snoid Comics* and was rearranged and coloured by Peter Poplaski in 1981, which helped turn it into a best-selling poster. Crumb went on to add three panels to answer the 'What next?' question posed in his original 12th illustration. In this 15-panel version, Crumb depicts three possible futures:
> Top panel: *Worst case scenario: ecological disaster*
> Centre panel: *The fun future: Techno fix on the march!*
> Bottom panel: *The Ecotopian solution.*
>
> © Cambridge University Press 2008 PHOTOCOPIABLE

Show students Crumb's final three panels (the Epilogue) on page 234 or type 'Robert Crumb, A Short History of America, Epilogue' into a search engine and project the images from a website. *Which of the three images do you think is the most realistic vision of the future? Why? What is wrong with the others?*

2 Ask students to find old postcards/photos of their own town and bring them to class the next day. They can compare these with contemporary images and describe the changes, whether positive or negative.

A Short History of America, Copyright © Robert Crumb, 2008. Used with permission from the author, as represented by Agence Littéraire Lora Fountain & Associates, Paris, France

Epilogue, Copyright © Robert Crumb, 2008. Used with permission from the author, as represented by Agence Littéraire Lora Fountain & Associates, Paris, France

Conduct a debate in which two groups in the class argue in favour of or against the changes that have taken place in their town/city in recent times.

See 2.8 What's changed? and 2.9 Sequencing for related tasks.

7.8 Tableaux vivants

Outline	Students look at a work of art in detail and give formal instructions to the rest of the class to get into the correct positions to imitate it.
Focus	Listening and speaking practice (giving orders to others, using imperatives). Verbs of position and movement.
Level	Intermediate–Advanced
Time	45 minutes
Materials and preparation	Any artwork in which there are quite a lot of people and there is some action. Advise students to bring cameras or mobile phones to class to take photos of the formations.
Note	William Hogarth's six paintings in the series *Marriage à-la-mode* include many scenes which would be ideal for the task and are also good fun. They are suitable for big or small groups, with only four people needed in *The Tête-à-Tête*, but up to 11 in *The Toilette*. See: http://en.wikipedia.org/wiki/Marriage_a-la-mode

Procedure

1 Select three students to be 'directors'. Give them a copy of a painting or a photo in which there is considerable action and a number of different people doing different things. Tell them not to show this image to any other members of the class.

2 The 'directors' instruct the right number of other students, telling them to imitate – as closely as possible – the formation and posture of the characters in the image. To do this, they should give verbal instructions only, avoiding mime or the use of gesture. As such, they will need to use a large number of verbs of movement and prepositions.

Note

If one or two props are required, you can provide substitutes, and arrange the furniture in an appropriate way.

3 The other students have to follow the instructions, adopting and maintaining the positions dictated by the directors.

4 The students watching then have to decide what is going on in the scene and who each character is.
5 Reveal the original image by projecting it so that all the students can see. Explain or elicit what actions are taking place in the original and its overall context.
6 If students have cameras, they can then take photos of the formation and compare it with the original. They can evaluate it in terms of how closely it matches the original – or how it improves on it.

Follow-up

Once students have established what is going on in the scene, they can begin to imagine what the characters might be saying, and what the scene's outcome will be. The same students in the formation can then develop a theatrical dramatisation of the scene, either spontaneously or by drawing up a rough script. The directors can make suggestions as to how to improve it dramatically. This could be rehearsed and then performed in front of the rest of the class.

Variation: Researching the scene

Using paintings such as Hogarth's *Marriage à-la-mode* series, choose the students who will be giving instructions (i.e. the 'directors') in the class beforehand. Ask them to study the painting and research it on the Internet. Once they have given the instructions to the other students and the formation has been made, invite the rest of the class to ask them questions about the painting and the people featured in it.

See 7.10 Conversations, for developing fully dramatised scenes from a painting.

7.9 Art critics

Outline	The teacher and students transform the classroom into an art gallery and give their opinions about the artworks.
Focus	Modifiers and intensifiers, adjectives to describe artworks. Summarising opinions into a single text.
Level	Pre-intermediate–Advanced
Time	30 minutes
Materials and preparation	CD-ROM image 7.9 Painting by Raoul Dufy – Interior with open windows, or ask your students to bring their own images to class. A selection of different artworks in a variety of styles.

Procedure

1 Select a number of different artworks in a variety of styles, or you could forewarn the students and ask them to bring in artworks of their choice. Art postcards will do, but the bigger the image, the better.

2 Post these artworks around the room. Make sure you put up more artworks than there are students. For a class of 15, 20 different artworks would work well. Next to each artwork, place a blank sheet of paper. Show the Dufy painting (CD-ROM 7.9) and the comments as an example.

Comments on *Interior with open windows* by Raoul Dufy

'I love this view. It makes me want to go there.'

'I don't like the colours much. They're too bright.'

'This is very cheerful. I love the blue colours.'

'I don't like seeing the view *and* the inside of the room. I don't understand why he did that.'

'There are too many colours, there's too much happening. It gives me a headache.'

'Can I go to that beach?'

'I quite like the blue: the blue table is the same colour as the sea.'

© Cambridge University Press 2008 PHOTOCOPIABLE

3 Ask students to walk around the classroom and pretend it is an art gallery. Ask them to write a one-sentence comment about each work, either approving or disapproving. Tell them to keep their comments anonymous and that they should not be influenced by any previous comments on the list. Encourage students to use modifiers such as *quite, a lot, not much*, according to the level, and emphasise how frequently these are used in English.

4 When there are enough comments on each piece of paper, take down all the artworks and the comments and redistribute them, handing out one artwork and its corresponding comments to each student, pair or small group of students (depending on your class size).

5 Students (either individually or in pairs / small groups) look at the comments for the artwork they were given and select those that they

consider the most interesting. Ask them to incorporate these into a text which summarises the different opinions of the students in the class.

6 Give the class plenty of time to write up their summaries and monitor carefully. Students then read out their summaries. The class listens and has to decide which is the most and least popular artwork from those exhibited.

Variation: Guessing the artwork

Rather than writing out the summary from the students' opinions, the students read them aloud and the rest of the class has to guess which painting the opinions refer to.

Acknowledgement: *From an original idea in* Personalizing Language Learning, *by Griffiths, G. and Keohane, K., (Cambridge University Press, 2000).*

7.10 Conversations

Outline	Transforming a background description into a dialogue.
Focus	Descriptive language.
Level	Intermediate–Advanced
Time	45 minutes
Materials and preparation	CD-ROM image 7.10 Painting by Edouard Vuillard – Two Schoolboys. Or ask your students to bring their own images to class. You could also use photos, cartoons or other images for this task. All that is required is an image with two people who find themselves in an interesting situation and could possibly be in conversation.

1 Show the whole class an artwork image of two people engaged in some kind of activity or posing for the painter. The image should be engaging and allow students to put themselves in the role of the characters present.

2 Students in pairs have to make the following decisions about the work:
- *Background detail about the two characters and their personalities.*
- *What is their conversation about?*
- *How are they feeling?*
- *Where are they?*
- *The outcome of this conversation.*

3 Students prepare the background story to the artwork. Encourage them to use sufficient adjectives and the present continuous tense here, to make their descriptions sufficiently dynamic. For example, this text is about the Vuillard painting (CD-ROM 7.10) of two boys whispering to each other:

Example background based on *Two Schoolboys* by Vuillard

They are two friends, George and Anthony, who are also neighbours. They are about nine years old. George is shy and Anthony much more extrovert and daring. Anthony is always getting his friend into trouble. They're talking about the women they can see in front of them. One of them is George's mother, and they are trying to avoid her because they shouldn't be out in the park at this time alone. In fact, they are lost. They want to hide behind the trees, but the trees are very narrow and the boys think that they can be seen easily. They are talking about somewhere to hide. They decide to run in the opposite direction and make for home, hoping that George's mother doesn't see them.

4 Go around monitoring the students' work. Each pair will have created a different context, which is the fun aspect of this task.
5 The same pairs of students now create a dialogue between the two characters and write up a first draft. Monitor carefully and correct where necessary. The dialogue should be no longer than a few lines, but should give hints to the background story they have already created. See below for an example dialogue based on the Vuillard painting.
6 Select some pairs to read out their dialogues. The class have to listen carefully and piece together the background. They can ask the pair of students to repeat the dialogue as many times as necessary.

Example dialogue based on *Two Schoolboys* by Vuillard

George: That's her!
Anthony: Now we're really in trouble!
George: Oh, no! And I don't even know where we are. I don't have a clue.
Anthony: Oh, don't be silly. We'll be OK. We've got to get out of here before she sees us, that's all.
George: It's your fault. I shouldn't have listened to you in the first place. I don't even know how we ended up here. We're miles from home.
Anthony: We can hide behind this tree.
George: She'll see us.
Anthony: Look! She's just turned her back. Let's run for it!
George: What?
Anthony: Don't be scared! Come on!

7 The students who performed the role play answer questions until the rest of the class have a clear idea of their story. Other students report the differences between this version and their own.
8 Another pair read out their dialogue and repeat the same procedure. The stories will probably be very different.

Variation 1: Change the genre

Suitable for advanced learners. Ask selected students to re-enact their dialogues from different perspectives or genres. For example, they have to alter the context to imagine that they are in a melodrama, a thriller or a soap opera. You could even suggest that this is an advert and that the two people are selling something or they are part of a news story.

Get students to role play their new contexts to the class. Other students have to guess the contexts.

Variation 2: A third presence

Alternatively, students can insert an invented third character into the painting and their dialogue. This could be presented in any way – it does not matter if the visual image clashes with the original image of the two people. Pose the following questions to students: *Who will this character be? And what effect will he/she have on the others? How will the outcome of the story change as a result of this other person?*

See 1.4 Points of view and 1.7 Speech bubbles for other tasks in which students create stories around artworks and photographs.

Further reading

1000 *Signs* (2004) Köln: Taschen/Colors Magazine.

Abdullah, R. and Hübner, R. (2006) *Pictograms, Icons and Signs*. London: Thames and Hudson.

Ambrose, G. and Harris, P. (2005) *Image*. Lausanne: Ava Publishing.

Arnold, J., Puchta, H. and Rinvolucri, M. (2007) *Imagine That! Mental Imagery in the EFL classroom*. Helbling Languages.

Berger, J. (1972) *Ways of Seeing*. London: Penguin.

Callow, J. (2005) Literacy and the Visual: Broadening our Vision in *English Teaching: Practice and Critique*, University of Waikato, NZ. Downloadable at: http://education.waikato.ac.nz/research/files/etpc/files/2005v4n1art1.pdf

Crow, D. (2006) *Left to Right: The Cultural Shift from Words to Pictures*. Lausanne: Ava Publishing.

Fletcher, A. (2001) *The Art of Looking Sideways*. London: Phaidon Press.

Frosh, P. (2003) *The Image Factory*. Oxford / New York: Berg.

Goddard, A. (1998) *The Language of Advertising*. London: Routledge.

Graddol, D., Goodman, S. and Lillis, T. (eds.) (2007) *Redesigning English*. London: Routledge.

Kress, G. and van Leeuwen, T. (1996) *Reading Images. The Grammar of Visual Design*.

Levin, G. (ed.) (1995) *The Poetry of Solitude: A Tribute to Edward Hopper*. New York: Universe Publishing.

Lionni, P. (2001) *Facts of Life*. London: Laurence King Publishing.

Long, A. (2006) *Fotolog Book. A global snapshot for the digital age*. London: Thames and Hudson.

Maley, A., Duff, A. and Grellet, F. (1980) *The Mind's Eye. Using pictures creatively in language learning*. Cambridge: Cambridge University Press.

Mitchell, W.J.T. (2005) *What Do Pictures Want?* Chicago: Chicago University Press.

Sherman, J. (2003) *Using Authentic Video in the Language Classroom*. Cambridge: Cambridge University Press.

Stevick, E. (1986) *Images and Options in the Language Classroom*. Cambridge: Cambridge University Press.

Thomas, P. (2005) *Black and White*. Barcelona: Studio laVista.

The Art Book (1994) London: Phaidon Press.

The Photography Book (2000) London: Phaidon Press.
Wigan, M. (2006) *Thinking Visually*. Lausanne: Ava Publishing.
Wright, A. (1989) *Pictures for Language Learning*. Cambridge: Cambridge University Press.